# Blades Business Crew

## THE SHOCKING DIARY OF A SOCCER HOOLIGAN TOP BOY

# Blades Business Crew

*This is my life, and this is how it reads.*
*For every chapter, a thousand memories.*

Paul Heaton, 1991

TO MY WIFE, DEBBIE.

BLADES BUSINESS CREW

THE SHOCKING DIARY OF A
SOCCER HOOLIGAN TOP BOY

By Steve Cowens
First published in April 2001 by Milo Books
Reprinted three times in 2001
Reprinted 2003

Copyright © Steve Cowens

ISBN 0 9530847 8 7

Typography and layout by
Barron Hatchett Design, Manchester

Printed and bound in Great Britain by
Cox & Wyman Ltd, Reading, Berkshire

MILO BOOKS
P.O.Box 153
Bury
Lancs BL0 9FX
info@milobooks.com

# ACKNOWLEDGEMENTS

To my great friend Dave, without whose help and enthusiasm this book would not have been possible. Thanks to my long-term mate Gary. Cheers to Andy, a 'boss boy'. And last but not least, a massive thanks to Mr Heaton (you are my sunshine, my only sunshine). Ta, fella.

To all the boys: thanks for the memories.

Kav, Glen, Pete, Bolly, Jay, Housey, The Howard Bros, Nobby, Norm, Roy Zide (R.I.P), Rowley, Paul, Terry, Phil G, Phil D, Drip (R.I.P), Drid, The Smedley Bros, Scuffles, John G, Matt, The Loz Bros, Frank, Dwaine, Peck, Renk, Groves, Trev, Lester, Leslie, Billy, Foxy, Dodge, Scotty, Pie Eye (R.I.P), Lincoln, Bon, Patch, Tash, Bert, Budge, Bullet, Herman, The Fabbits, Adam, Ian, Blakey, 2 Mitches, Shotgun, Simon, Dave P, Dave S, Ronnie, Colin, The Sellars Bros, Mash, Wizz, Nicky, Lance, Sully, Irish, Jammy, Derek, The Milner Bros, Daz, Joe, Mick, Ricky, Sammy, Jamie (R.I.P), The Sampson Bros, Claus, Spender, Gary, Pat, Andy, Kev, Danny, The Oliver Bros, Mr Sertees, The Rodgers Bros, Tufty, Baz, Festa, Ronco, Brian, Wayne, Whit, Kenny, Vinny, Puddin, Kev M, Sainey, Maggot, Mark, The Mowitt Bros, Sharpy, The Webb Bros, Bagga Ragga Muffin, all the B.D.S, Paul, The Race Bros, Big Trev, Barry, Jason, Benny, Eight-fingered Ray, Palmer, Carl, Wraggy, Greg, Craig, Dave R, Vincent, The Bowlin Bros, Dave O, Gilly, Gaz,

Shaun, Vaz, Mad Dog, Booshy, Stubby, Spinner, Talbot, Steve Chapman (R.I.P), Cats, Damien, Stocker, Mick, Binzo, Russ, Glynn, Stuart, Scott, John, Waz, Pez, Doyley, Cockney, Malc, Pash, Bob F, Nige C, Duggie, Pete G, Jonnie, Perkin Bros, Lee, Norman, Woz, The Steves, P, B, M, G, Mosborough boys, Handsworth boys, The Suicide Squad, Slasher Dearden, Pricey, Tallis, Darnall Blades, Hackenthorpe Blades, China, Rotherham Blades, Simon, Sharpy, Dinky, Frog, Kivo Blades, Manor Blades, The BBC2, Ian, Colly, 2 Cogs, Chalks, H, Deano, Les, Heato, Woz, Miff, Ricards, Lee, Willey, Stocksy, Bullimore, Millwall, Tank, Ozz, Dayi, Cosack, Tony, Wayne, Neil, Esso, Darren (R.I.P). The Toffee's Bruce, Boz, Bernie, Oldham Keith, Ian, Shaun, Russell, John W, Kenty, Barry, Dummy, Waffer, Shaggy, John C, Mark R, Mustaffa, Scotty, Lloyd, Paddy, Chris, Paul, Scott, Kelly, Bri, Tim, Casper, Bunny, Slater, Brandon, Horsehead, Bullet Price, Tigger, Alan, Matthew, Bob Moore, Iron Bar Jack, Micky and Nicky (R.I.P.).

*Light of my life, bring back those memories*
*When we were kids on the corner of Shoreham Street*
*We were rough and ready guys*
*But boy how we could harmonise.*

# GLOSSARY

**AFTER-BIRD** *After-hours drinking*

**BARMY ARMY** *Shoreham Barmy Army 1970-82*

**BBC** *Blades Business Crew*

**BDS** *Blades Drug Squad*

**BERTIES** *Wednesday term for United fans*

**BILLY, SPEED, WHIZZ** *Amphetamines*

**BIZZIES, OLD BILL, FUZZ, PLOD, DIBBLE** *Police*

**BLADE** *United follower or hooligan*

**BLAGGED** *Lied or conned*

**BOSS** *Great*

**BOYS** *Hooligans*

**CASUALS** *Well-dressed hooligans*

**CHABS, CHABBIES** *Sheffield term for youngster*

**CHARLIE, COKE** *Cocaine*

**CHOCKER, SNIDED** *Full*

**CLOCK, DIAL, MINCER, MUSH** *Face*

**DEXY BOYS** *Runners*

**DIVS, DIVVIES** *Clueless lads*

**DO ONE** *Run off or move away*

**FRONT, FRONTED** *Confront/confrontation*

**GAME AS FUCK** *Fearless and willing to fight*

**GARGLE, SHERBETS** *Drink*

**GIVIN' IT THE BIG 'UN** *Posing or showing off*

**KHAZI** *Toilet*

**KICKED OFF** *Fight starts*

**KIDDY MUGS** *Young clueless hooligans*

**LAIRY** *Show off or acting clever*

**LEO SAYER** *All day drinking (as in 'all-dayer')*

**MUSHY, WEDGEHEAD** *Trendy 1980s haircut*

**OCS** *Owls Crime Squad*

**OFF, BEANO, RUCK** *Fight between two gangs*
**ON ONE** *Lose control*
**ON THEIR TOES** *Run away*
**PIGS, GRUNTERS, SNORT BEASTS** *United terms for Wednesday fans*
**PIGSTY** *Hillsborough football ground*
**PINKIE** *Charge sheet*
**POPPERS** *Amyl nitrate*
**RAGGED, RAG-DOLLED** *To suffer a beating*
**ROB, PILFER** *Steal*
**SCALLIES, TRENDIES** *Young well-dressed hooligans*
**SEAT SMASHERS** *Leeds fans (circa 1970s-80s)*
**SHIRTERS** *Replica kit-wearing football fans*
**SHITESVILLE** *Nothing*
**SHITFACED, KETTLED, BOLLOXED** *Drunk*
**SNIDE** *Fake*
**SPLIFF, REEFER** *Cannabis joint*
**SRA** *Shoreham Republican Army*
**STANLEY FAMILY** *Craft/carpet knife carriers*
**STEAM IN** *Run in to fight*
**STONEY** *Stone Island designer clothing*
**STRIPED** *Slashed*
**SWEENEY** *Alone*
**TOE-TO-TOE** *Fighting at close quarters*
**TOGS, CLOBBER** *Clothes*
**TOOLED UP** *Carrying weapons*
**TOY TOWN** *Rotherham*
**WOOLLYBACKS** *Poorly dressed youths*
**WORLDER** *Brilliant*

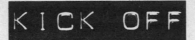

# BY PAUL HEATON

BEING SHEFFIELD United hasn't always been the easiest thing to explain. Outside of Sheffield, the announcement that you support United is usually greeted with the sidesplitting comment that 'someone has to'. But that glib response perhaps holds the answer to why many others and I not only follow our team so passionately but also took part in hooligan activities at the club's matches.

As our team lurched downwards to the Third and Fourth Divisions, the good time supporters disappeared. Those that were left supporting the Blades, especially away from home, were the most vocal, the heavier drinkers and, within them, those most likely to defend the club's good name. As United's name was being dragged through the mud by the club itself, this so-called 'mindless minority' were simply doing their best to ensure that our club were good at one thing – fighting. As the club rose again and the business suits and private boxes appeared, so did the police. This new class of football supporter not only demanded a larger space in which to view the game but also needed guarantees that 'their' match-day wouldn't be spoilt by the 'yob element'. As football's televisual golden era dawned, even more pressure was put on the police force to ensure that this minority was heard but not seen. Television celebrities and pop stars alike were rolled out in front of the cameras to convince the unsuspecting public that here was a family sport, a family day out. But to look at Sheffield United through Sky-tinted spectacles is to miss out on a sizeable chunk of our history.

My first match at Bramall Lane was on November 22 in the 1969-70 season, against Aston Villa in the old Second Division. Only my dad, now deceased, will ever know why I demanded to go, but one thing he did recall was the fact that I wouldn't take no for an answer. My father had already taken my two elder brothers and I along to Hillsborough a few times. My brothers had settled into their new-found Wednesday allegiance by buying scarves, hats and match day programmes. I don't really remember much of what I thought at the time, only that I didn't like the stupid owl on the programme and that I didn't feel at home. So after much persuasion I was off to the Lane.

At the turnstiles of the John Street Stand, my dad asked, 'How much for one adult and one child?'

'Fifteen shilling for you and the nipper can sit on your knee,' came the reply. I immediately felt a warm glow. I was in the ground and they hadn't charged me a penny. This, I thought, was a special club where nippers like me sat on dad's knees. So, sensing the fact that my dad had got off lightly, I demanded that he bought me a rattle. After all, I was a seven year old and slight of voice and I had to make some noise for my team.

Sheffield United won the game 5-0 that day but it was the next match that really cemented my feelings of being a Blade. On the March 28 in the same season, the Blades were at home to Bolton. Naively, I had built United up to be the greatest team in the world to my mates, and my dad had agreed to ferry a car full of us to the match. 'You wait,' I said excitedly, 'they're brilliant.'

The silence in the car on the way home was deafening. 'I thought you said they were good,' said my brother, smirking.

'They are, they were, I think they were missing a few players, weren't they dad?' I replied. Dad said they were and I took comfort in his words. 'I don't care, we're still better than Wednesday.' That was the first time I had said it. United had lost 1-0 at home to Bolton and embarrassed me in front of my mates and brother, but they were still 'better than Wednesday'. I was now a Blade and I had better get used to it! I spent the rest of the Seventies lying, exaggerating and defending them to the hilt.

Lydgate Lane junior school was in a predominantly Wednesday area of the city but if United ever enjoyed a period of success – and in the early Seventies we did – the lunch break United v Wednesday kick about would be pretty even-sided. Any slip in form, combined with a purple patch for Wednesday, would invariably result in myself and a few other misfits defending our end against 20 or so of them. With the Wednesday mob marauding towards us, we would resort to a tactic that not only wasted time but also guaranteed alienating any floating supporter against United: we'd throw the ball over Jonathon Wilkinson's dad's wall. This, of course, was unfair; it was blatant cheating. It also led to too many 0-0 draws. But we were different, we were Blades.

'Watch it, he's got a massive dog,' we would say, as incensed Wednesday fans climbed the wall to retrieve the ball.

During this period, Mark, my eldest brother, would return from Hillsborough every second Saturday with different stories of violence and mayhem. 'Man United took the kop and trouble erupted everywhere' – 'Birmingham fans threw snooker balls at Wednesday fans outside the ground' – 'Wednesday fans threw some Forest fans in the River Don.' Soon the stories changed to ones of the North Stand, Chelsea, the Docklands, Millwall, and the Clock End at Arsenal, as my dad had taken a job down south and we were to move to Surrey. North Park School in Banstead was a similar school to our secondary one in Sheffield, King Edwards. It was situated in a middle class area but still had that special mixture of ruffians, oddballs, and the briefcase freaks that Seventies comprehensives seemed to throw together. My stories of Shoreham bootboys and our Adrian's tales of Wednesday's Eastbank Army were dwarfed by 'Babsy the one armed bandit' (Chelsea) taking West Ham, Tufty Ellis (Crystal Palace) taking Man Utd and Ginger Brixtan and Tiny (Millwall) taking everybody. Both Adrian and I wildly exaggerated our stories, spicing them up with tales of notorious Sheffield gangs roaming the city centre with iron bars. It really was a case of 'someone has to'.

Meanwhile I attended matches with schoolmates. Millwall v Chelsea, Chelsea v Cardiff, any game where there might be trouble. In between these games I would travel to any fixtures United had in London with my classroom mate Joe Sweetinburgh. Joe was a Norwich City fan but was soon to become a Blade. Being black had already presented Joe with enough barriers with certain Millwall and Chelsea fans at school, let alone the ones at their matches, and he seemed to be much more at ease at United games, where after a few away excursions we were accepted and referred to as 'Cockney Blades'. This was a term that I didn't like; after all, I was a northerner in exile, but for Joe it represented a considerable leap from the 'sambo' and 'nig-nog' attitudes that he was receiving at school. At United matches, Joe was a Blade and was referred to by his accent and not by the colour of his skin.

It wasn't long before we experienced our first taste of football violence. This time it was Joe and I who had the stories that gripped the schoolyard. Neither of us were violent people but we soon divorced the fighting at football from the cowardly attacks we had witnessed at school. The 1976-77 football season saw us in skirmishes at Luton (standing our ground against 15 or so near the main shopping centre), Orient (again just the two of us fighting with six West Ham at the train station) and Fulham (a five-minute punch-up on the tube station platform).

But it was Bristol Rovers away that was to provide us with our first big taste of violence at football. It was the last game of the season and Joe and myself were walking under a flyover towards the ground. We bumped into around 50 United lads who were ready to jump a large group of Bristol fans walking 100 yards behind us. "These two are Blades,' someone shouted and we were quickly whisked out of sight behind the massive concrete pillars. Neither of us was wearing any club colours and neither of us really knew any of our new-found friends but we were soon taking part in a brutal ambush as though every one of them was a close pal. Joe and myself were already a team but now we were suddenly part of the 'the big team'. Unnecessary attacks like these were the 'norm' for this period in time and became more of a focal point than the actual matches themselves. As our football team became more meaningless, these stories of violence and unruliness seemed to gain a meaning.

Call it mindless, childish or whatever you want but our club had the chance to harness this passionate support. Time and time again they turned their back on it. I have been accused by the club before of going to the matches with the 'boys' but all I'm doing is going to the games with friendships I forged away at Brighton, away at Darlington and at Arsenal. Yes there was violence at all these games but it was a hell of a lot more than the club had to offer at the time.

Football hooliganism is a disease but at one stage it was nothing more than a rash until badly-run clubs along with moronic chairmen decided to inject their veins with sky-high ticket prices, senseless transfers and a deliberate us-and-them policy. Football hooligans eventually tone down their misdemeanours, then disappear from the scene. The people who supposedly run the game never do. In the Seventies and Eighties, much was made of the cost of damage that hooligans caused, but this pales into insignificance at the millions wasted by uncaring chairmen up and down the country. The trouble that followed football was hardly worth a mention. Over the years, football violence has moved on from the days when smashing city centres up and attacking anyone who supported a rival team was the norm. The violence that happens now is two sets of willing participants engaging in combat: it is blown out of proportion considering the shortfalls our country seems to conveniently sweep under the carpet. I've been out of it for years now; the buzz of it all went a long time ago.

Here's Steve's story, putting these crimes in perspective and lending them a humour and honesty the boardroom quite simply will never have.

# INTRODUCTION: STILL CRAZY

'CELL THREE, Cowens. Take your shoes off.'

With a shove in the back, the sour-faced custody officer propelled me into a bare cell and slammed the heavy metal door. His key clunked in the lock. I was alone. I looked around: four bare walls, a worn wooden bench, misspelled graffiti on the peeling paint work, the smell of stupidity and wasted lives. My thoughts crowded in to fill the silence, and they were not happy ones. My old ways had returned. I had been dragged into something that I felt I had to confront head-on. Now I was paying the price. It was February 5, 2000. A new millennium but the same old shit.

It had been several years since my 'retirement' from football violence. After two decades of terrace warfare, I had begun to relax and unwind. Though I had kept in touch with 'the boys', and even shown my face at the odd big game, I stayed away from trouble. My new, peaceable demeanour was helped by the fact that the hooligan firm of our city rivals Sheffield Wednesday – with whom I had spent much of my adult life locked in combat – was a spent force.

I sat down on the scratched bench. So how had I ended up here? Ten months earlier, I had bumped into around 30 Wednesday boys in Hotshots Bar in the Attercliffe district of Sheffield. The main lads shook my hand and we talked. I felt calm. They knew me well and also knew that I wasn't running around town with United any more.

'He's the only Blade I wish was Wednesday,' one of them even said.

I took it as a compliment. But as I looked at their little firm, I felt sorry for them. Judged by the unforgiving standards of the soccer gangs, all they had left were four or five main faces and around 30 younger lads who would be in the starting blocks and off faster than Linford Christie at the sign of trouble.

Yet, six months later, our unstable peace was at an end. On the 11 September 1999, myself and two mates went to watch Everton play Wednesday at Hillsborough. I was friendly with some of Everton's hooligans and was with three of them before the game when we were attacked by a mob of 25 Wednesday fans. I suppose I could have ignored it but it's not in my nature. I was pissed off big time. They knew I was no longer involved in trouble yet had still taken liberties. A few people were going to get it.

Payback came five months later. Since the early Eighties, Wednesday had had a rivalry with Derby County's firm, the DLF (Derby Lunatic Fringe), and for months they had been planning a big turnout for the game at Pride Park in February 2000. They also put it around that on their return from Derby they were going to 'give it' to the Blades. United were at home to Tranmere Rovers that day. I knew United's boys would be more than willing to accept the challenge.

On February 5, Wednesday turned out a firm of between 250-300 lads, a huge show of numbers that they had never seemed to manage before. While they were in Derby, a few United boys kept in touch with them by mobile phone. It was agreed that United would wait in the Royal Standard, a pub about 800 metres from Sheffield railway station, and that Wednesday would head there on their return. The Royal Standard was an ideal place for it to 'go off'. Not only was it close to the train station but also there were no CCTV cameras in the vicinity.

After watching United beat Tranmere 3-1, up to 90 Blades hooligans headed for the Royal Standard. All were seasoned football thugs. From the mood they were in, it wouldn't have mattered if Wednesday had 500 out. They knew that, of the Wednesday firm, perhaps only 50 were boys (seasoned hooligans), and that left an awful lot of passengers who would not know what had hit them when a major off erupted. I had been in similar scenarios where United had a massive crew out but far too many lightweights with us. Doubt creeps in. I had learned that you were much better off with smaller numbers, people you can trust.

Wednesday were watched out of the station by one of our spotters, Sep. He reported that they were in fact heading into town, away from where we were. Feanie was straight on the mobile to one of Wednesday's main actors.

'Where the fuck are you going?'

'We're going into town to meet a few more lads.'

'What, is two hundred and fifty not enough? There's only eighty of us out, for fuck's sake.'

After half an hour, everyone started to get restless. It was up to us to go looking for them. As soon as we set off, the police were on our case. I hung back, knowing there was no way the bizzies would allow us to reach them. Wednesday's mob were in the Yorick pub on Division Street. As United headed up Trafalgar Street, which leads directly to Division Street, around 50 police blocked off the road. Still we approached the police line and, as the lads at the front reached it, the bizzies waded in, swinging their batons wildly. I stood on a corner 30 yards down the road. I could see a few of our lads had been knocked to the floor; one was completely out due to a truncheon to the skull.

Then a huge roar went up: 'Come on!'

Our lot had spotted their rivals at the end of the road. I watched as they steamed the police line to get through to the Wednesday. A wild fist-to-truncheon brawl developed. Police officers were being dragged to the floor and beaten with their own sticks. I had never seen anything like it.

Then someone shouted that Wednesday were heading around the block. Only ten of us ran to head them off, as most of our boys were at it with the bizzies. As we ran up, a couple of taxis went past with a few Wednesday in them. Zuey and a few others attacked them. We rounded another corner and saw the first few Wednesday coming down the road.

'Don't fuckin' shift. I'm goin' nowhere,' I screamed.

We were around 20 yards away when more bizzies screeched up and began to block off this road as well. It was at this point I spotted Jester, one of the Wednesday lads who had attacked us at Hillsborough. I was 'on one' and I had to have him, even though he was standing behind three police officers. I completely lost the plot and did something very stupid for a boy who has been around as long as I had. The red mist came down and I ran towards him. Jester looked shocked as I approached full steam. I threw a punch over a bizzy's shoulder and connected. Jester reeled back and I went to kick him but fell as the police jumped on me. They pushed me face down and sat on my back. More came and tried to handcuff me.

'They've got Steve,' someone shouted.

United's lads attacked the police to get me free. I was caught in the crossfire as officers held me whilst hitting out with truncheons. I was dragged 30 yards down the road. My trousers were ripped open, I tore the skin off my knees and my mobile phone was lost in the fracas. Despite the lads' bold efforts, I was arrested and bent over a parked car.

So it was that I found myself sitting in a cell at Bridge Street police station, rueing the error of my ways. When I was finally allowed to phone my wife, she was, as you can imagine, far from happy that I was in trouble again. I was meant to be meeting her later for a drink.

After six hours in custody, I was released. 'We are going to study CCTV and go through the evidence which may lead to a charge of violent disorder,' an officer told me. 'If we do not gain any further evidence, then you will be charged with threatening behaviour. You are bailed to appear at this police station on the twenty-sixth of February. Do you understand?'

I nodded and headed out into the darkness.

Over the next few days, the local press and TV made that night's events into headline news. Five police officers had been injured and one detained in hospital overnight. Fifteen people had been arrested in the city's worst outbreak of trouble for years. My bail was eventually moved to March 25, the day of Birmingham City's visit to Bramall Lane. The previous two years of my retirement had been shelved for this fixture, but not this time. Not only did I have the charge hanging over me but also I had agreed to work on the door of a pub close to Bramall Lane that day. I answered my bail to be told that I would be charged with threatening behaviour. The arresting officer explained that I could consider myself very lucky I was not facing a more serious charge. 'Football violence has increased around United matches and we are stamping down on it,' he said. 'You won't be as lucky as this next time. Last week, twelve Man City fans were charged with violent disorder at Barnsley.'

I attended Sheffield Magistrates court on April 5, 2000. The prosecutor read out the facts:

> *At about 7:40pm on Saturday, 5 February, 2000, PS Brooks and PC Cook were answering a call for urgent assistance to Trafalgar Street regarding large numbers of football fans*

*heading towards each other. As they approached they saw police with batons attempting to stop a large number of males coming down the road.*

*There was a large male with a shaven head standing behind the police and, as PS Brooks ran towards the officers, a male with a shaven head, the defendant Steven Cowens, ran from his right and threw a punch with his right fist at the large shaven-headed male standing behind a police officer. At this point PS Brooks caught up with Cowens and took hold of him. He struggled to get away and fell to the floor. PS Brooks took hold of his arm and was then aware that officers were surrounded by a large group of males who were shouting and swearing at them. They were intent on freeing Cowens and also intended to injure officers. PS Brooks had his jumper pulled and felt kicks to his legs.*

*At this point it was extremely frightening. The officers drew their batons and PS Brooks yelled, 'Get back,' a number of times and made a number of clearing strikes with his baton. The males continued to surround them and at one point they pulled the defendant from PS Brooks's grasp. PS Brooks regained his hold at which point a male removed his baton from his grasp. Other officers made 'power strikes' as they were in real danger of being seriously injured. Cowens again pulled away from PS Brooks and again he managed to take hold of him. Finally at this point they were joined by more officers and around 15 yards from where he had originally taken hold of Cowens, PS Brookes was able to restrain him long enough to handcuff him. Cowens was placed in the rear of a police vehicle and PS Brooks arrested him for threatening behaviour. After a caution, he made no reply.*

I pleaded guilty and was fined £100.

My mind went back to how, as a young hooligan, I used to laugh at Wednesday's firm, all 35-40 year-olds. 'I hope I'm not involved in all this shit when I'm their age,' I once remarked. Those words returned to haunt me as I left the courtroom.

The *Sheffield Star* reported on the case under the headline, 'BLADES FAN IN CITY CENTRE ATTACK'. A 170-word account began: 'A football supporter punched a man in Sheffield city centre and then struggled with police officers trying to arrest him. Sheffield United fan Steven Cowens, aged 35, struck out as he walked along Trafalgar Street, Sheffield Magistrates heard...'

The Wednesday propaganda machine was also in full swing. According to them, they had done the Blades, when in fact not one Snort Beast had thrown a punch in anger. Various legends came out of my arrest: I had been nicked for trying to kick Jester but fell on my arse; I'd hit Jester over the head with a bottle; the police had picked me off the floor after I had been beaten up by four Wednesday. Typical bollocks.

Those hours in the cells made me think about the previous 20 years of my life. I had gone full circle, from up-and-coming trendy to top boy to retirement – and now what? Enough was enough. I knew I needed to draw the line. I could afford no more backsliding. So I decided there and then that I would write down my experiences, offering an insight into the world of football violence and how I got so wrapped up in it that at times nothing else mattered. Through the years, I was slashed, coshed, bottled, hit with bats, planks and bricks, sprayed with CS gas, Mace and ammonia and shot at with distress flares. I have been 'grassed' up and attacked while playing Sunday morning football. I have been arrested ten times. All for what? My pride and passion for Sheffield United and the love of the buzz and adrenaline fix of the violence I encountered.

Why? Sociologists, anthropologists and other so-called academic 'experts' have had their say and largely they haven't a clue. For me, the answer has never been a simple one. Young men of my generation who went to football matches were almost certain to meet trouble. The choice was to take it or leave it. I took it and took it big time. And once accepted, it is hard to drop. Something takes a hold, be it the buzz, the adrenaline, the power, or the fear. Everybody wants to be somebody – and to belong, to be a part of something. Football is a shut-off valve from people's normal, mundane lives.

This is my story. I don't claim to be a great author or intellectual. I've presented this narrative as honestly as possible and as accurately as my memory allows and before anyone calls me a parasite on the game, let me assure them if the violence had stopped at any time, I'd have still been there cheering on my lifelong love, Sheffield United FC.

So, what is a hooligan? What is a Blade? And, is it possible to be both? In my case, I have been both, but first and foremost I am a Blade, that is to say a fan of Sheffield United Football Club. I love the club with a passion which to many may have been channelled in the wrong direction. However, in my eyes I've been fighting for the club's good name and reputation. The term Blade is taken from the club's nickname and is widely used to describe a fellow fan of Sheffield United. Through the years I have travelled the length and breadth of the country to watch the Red and White Wizards and visited 91 of the 92 League grounds. Only Swansea has eluded me. So I was a Blades supporter before I was a hooligan.

Our name is a misnomer. We don't use blades, though other gangs do.

I hate the word *hooligan*. It actually originates from a wild Irish family called the Hoolihans. After bank holiday riots in the 1890s the word became more commonly used to describe tearaways.

I often wonder why I have such a passion for a football club which has been so bad over the years. In 28 years of watching the Blades, I have seen them win just one trophy, the Fourth Division Championship: not much for a 110-year-old club steeped in tradition. The proverbial sleeping giant but one which cannot be woken.

Sheffield is the home of football yet neither of the City's two professional teams can get a side together to hold its own in the Premier League, never mind win anything. Rumours and actual talks of a merger between the two fierce Sheffield rivals are a complete non-starter. I had to smile when United's (thankfully) ex-chairman, Mike McDonald, revealed in the local press that 'talks of a merger were at the advanced stages.' It was on the same day (7 February 2000) that local press and TV were reporting that 500 rival Sheffield football fans clashed in the city centre streets: *back page; merger, front page; murder!* If the clubs did actually merge, Sheffield's ground would be the only one in history to have three segregated areas, one for away fans, one for old United fans and one for old Wednesday fans. It would take 30 years for fans to accept the idea, which is basically why it is a non-starter. Sheffield is a divided city, you are either 'red' or 'blue' and this fact has split families and friendships.

During the Eighties and early Nineties, Sheffield city centre had it's own Berlin Wall. Wednesday's hooligan element, known as the OCS (Owls Crime Squad), roamed around West Street; their nightclub was The Limit located on the same road. United's firm the BBC (Blades Business Crew) patrolled London Road with the Locarno/Music Factory as their club. The Berlin Wall was in the middle of town and on countless occasions both sides 'invaded' enemy territory. This in turn led to vicious brawls and hundreds of arrests over the years. Sheffield city centre only calmed down around 1994 due to the demise of Wednesday's hooligan group. It has all started up again recently as Wednesday try to get their act back together. I can't see an end to the trouble, which has been around for over 30 years.

So why write a book? And in what way is this book different from other books on football violence? Firstly I believe it is unique in the fact that it covers violence through all four divisions. Secondly it is a diarised account of a city, which in terms of football is completely divided. Thirdly it is a life story, my life story as a football fan and as a hooligan. The fun that goes with following a football team with the 'bad lads' has not been missed. The amount of violence I have been involved in has been frightening. This book has been immensely enjoyable to write, all the memories came flooding back, to be honest and frank they are fond memories, which I do not regret.

What's this book about? It's about a lad who left school with four O'levels and had hardly ever had a fight let alone been in trouble with the police. It is also about how a normal lad slowly but surely became a 'boy', whom almost everyone in the right/ wrong circles in Sheffield either knew or had heard of him. It's a story of reputation, challenge, gossip and ridicule. Football violence is a kind of drug, maybe a social drug but when it is attached to football rational thinking goes straight out of the window. Reading this book you will probably gather that apart from my misdemeanors at football I'm no hardened criminal. I have worked all my life and although this may sound hypocritical I have strong beliefs in rights and wrongs. All I have done is fight with like-minded people; no innocent football fan has ever suffered by my hand.

The recent slip into my old ways is hopefully just temporary. I owe it to my wife whom I have been with since I was 16 and also to the rest of my family to keep out of trouble. They are more important to me than running around with the boys. Once you're a 'boy' with a reputation it's hard to drop. You get people looking up to you, you get the phone calls, 'Steve were meeting at so and so, they're bringing a right firm". It's never ending and it's a buzz at first. Then the buzz goes and you look at life differently. My wife has been through a lot and it is time I repaid her loyalty. She knows me better than anyone really, sometimes better than I know myself. On the morning of my recent arrest, as I left the house she told me to 'be careful', she hasn't had any reason to say that for a few years, so maybe I had the glint of trouble in my eyes. I really find it hard to keep away from the violence and my recent arrest proved to me that I have to block out my past. At the end of the day it hasn't been worth getting into trouble fighting at football, especially against Wednesday. It is a never ending war that cannot be won.

# THE EARLY YEARS

RELEGATION

MAJOR OFF AT
BRADFORD

HARTLEPOOL

DARLINGTON

OLD LADIES IN PITCH
BATTLE

LINCOLN:
THE SURPRISE
PACKAGE

BARNSLEY:
NIGHT OF SHAME

WOPPED AT WIGAN

THE TURNING
POINT:
A CITY AT WAR

MILLWALL:
MAD OR MYTH?

CAUGHT COLD BY
CARDIFF

CURSE OF
THE CAR COAT

SITTING IN the South Stand at Bramall Lane in 1978 was a 13-year-old boy watching a cup tie between Sheffield United and Arsenal. Beside him sat his grandad, cursing Arsenal centre forward Malcolm McDonald. SuperMac may have been the most famous striker of his day, but the young boy paid scant attention. His eyes were focused on United's kop, the Shoreham End. Two rival groups of fans were engaged in a mass brawl. The fascination as the Arsenal contingent was beaten back by home fans and spilled onto the pitch to escape mesmerised the youngster.

'Got 'em off our kop, grandad,' said the boy, smiling up at the old man.

'Yeah, son. Idiots, the lot of them,' he grumbled.

That youngster was me. Although I had seen fights at games before, notably when Leeds and Man City had visited Bramall Lane, this was my first close-up experience. It made a lasting impression.

I don't know why this was. I came from a law-abiding household which had never know a visit from a policeman. I was born in Sheffield in June 1964. My dad, David, a Sheffield steelworker, and my mum, Kathleen, were loving parents. At school I was polite, quiet and never in any sort of trouble. But one thing I was imbued with, from the time as a seven-year-old when I first went to a game with my grandad, was a love of United. It ran in the family: my sister proudly bears the club crest tattooed at the top of one thigh. I became so wrapped up in the club and its fortunes that at times nothing else mattered.

My assimilation into the hooligan world was gradual, starting as an intrigued observer and gradually edging nearer and nearer to the action. I remember watching a now legendary BBC TV documentary about Millwall in 1977 and being fascinated. In the early to mid-Seventies, Millwall had built up a reputation for violence that was second to none. Harry the Dog and his head-the-ball mates in 'F Troop' caused mayhem at many a game and the documentary graphically captured their wild excesses. A trip to their intimidating home ground, the Den, was a kind of rite of passage for any would-be soccer lout.

My first of four visits to Cold Blow Lane came in 1980. I travelled by a supporters' club coach with two school pals: three 15-year-olds thinking we were well hard going down to Millwall. I had put on my Harrington jacket complete with SHOREHAM

ENDER printed on the back (oh dear). There was trouble before, during and after the game. What both shocked and pleased me was the willingness of Sheffield's travelling fans to mix it with Millwall. During the game, missiles rained back and forth over the fencing. These included a six-foot plank with nails protruding through it. Our coach returned home minus a few windows, which put paid to our adolescent bravado. I was terrified, basically. But I was also hooked.

And so began my life as a thug, and with it my diary.

# RELEGATION    2 MAY 1981

SHEFFIELD United needed a point from the final fixture of the 1980-81 season to save them from relegation to the Fourth Division. The club had sunk to a low that no one could have foreseen. Only seven years earlier the Blades had missed out on Europe by one point. That team included greats like Tony Currie, Alan Woodward, Len Badger and Eddie Colquhoun. In this vital last game we had to rely on superannuated hasbeens like Don Givens, John Matthews and Stewart Houston to keep us out of the basement of the Football League.

Nil-nil with five minutes to go, and a penalty is awarded to Walsall. They score. Division Four and the likes of Rochdale are calling us.

One minute to go, United are awarded a penalty. Euphoria sweeps the ground. Don Givens steps up, hands on hips, looking terrified. He runs and hits a tame shot straight at the keeper. The euphoria turns to despair and anger. The final whistle blows and we're down. Thousands of Blades invade the pitch, hundreds charge the away end and Walsall players are attacked. The police, knowing a full-scale riot is on the cards, relay messages that results elsewhere have gone our way and we have, in fact, stayed up. The jubilant scenes last a few seconds until fans with radios contradict the police porkies. I slump to my knees on the Bramall Lane turf, head in hands. Tears roll down my cheeks. Unashamedly, I cry. It's like the end of the world.

That night violence erupts in Sheffield city centre as thousands of Blades drown their sorrows in a sea of beer. Two police cars are turned over and numerous arrests made. Pubs are damaged in attacks of drunken vandalism. It is just too much for many to take. Sheffield United hooligans wait for Wednesday to return from Watford and attack them in Sheffield bus station.

Looking back, dropping to the depths of English football was probably the best thing to happen to the club. The following season, 1981-2, saw a new chairman, new money, and new players. It was without doubt the best and most enjoyable season I have witnessed. I never missed a game home or away and we won the Division Four championship. Just as importantly for a fledgling hooligan like myself, everywhere we went Uncle Tom Cobleigh and all turned out for a 'pop' at their big time opponents. From Carlisle to Crewe, Halifax to Hereford, our opponents turned out in numbers to take on Sheffield's vast travelling army. This season was the first time I started to travel with lads who loved a bit of friction with their equivalents, known as 'their boys'. It would end with over 11,000 Sheffielders making the trip to Darlington for our final-match celebration.

What follows is a chronicled diary of trouble the length and breadth of England. From 1981-2000, Sheffield United's hooligan element were involved in disorder that earned them a formidable reputation within hooligan circles. At the height of it all, from 1985 to 1998, I have no doubt that the Blades were amongst the top five hooligan firms in the country.

# MAJOR OFF AT BRADFORD
## 24 OCTOBER 1981.

When big clubs are relegated to lower divisions, it often sparks renewed outbreaks of violence among their supporters. The smaller clubs tend to have fewer police on duty, poor segregation and less experience of coping with big crowds. So it was that my first injuries with United's hooligan element came 15 games into the 1981-82 season.

The club's slip into Division Four had, ironically, produced a new optimism amongst its fans, based on their confidence in a new multi-millionaire chairman, a new young manager and half a million pounds spent on new players.

I travelled with an 80-strong contingent of hooligans, a mix of experienced old heads and young wannabes, and arrived in Bradford town centre 'early windows' (*i.e.* midday). After drinking in several pubs, we were sussed by Bradford spotters: these are the spies that gangs send out, alone or in twos, to surreptitiously find the opposition and assess their numbers. We knew it was now only a matter of time before Bradford's 'Ointment Crew' showed. Our firm contained a lot of 'scallies' (young hooligans), which can sometimes be a liability, but the older main boys seemed in good spirits, pleased that they had arrived undetected by police.

We settled in a pub just out of the centre on Manningham Lane. While most went into the back room to play pool and cards, ten scallies, myself included, were on guard at the entrance doors. We did not do a very good job, as most were preoccupied sniffing amyl nitrate 'poppers' and chatting.

Then Skinner, one of the older lads, glanced down the road: Bradford were upon us. It was too late to warn the rest. Around 100 of their lads attacked the doors. We picked up pub stools. Bradford were tooled up and Skinner copped a bat on the bonce. He was out of it in the doorway as bricks and bottles smashed around us. We managed to pull him in by the legs but, as the bricks fell, Luey and Griz also went down. The rest of our mob were oblivious to our plight until someone went to fetch them.

I was just thinking how relatively unscathed I was when an arm appeared round the door and threw a broken stool leg. I watched almost in slow motion as it span like a boomerang towards my face. As I ducked, it crashed into the top of my skull. I went flying and crawled to one side, just as our lot came cascading out through the pub. An older Blade picked me up, asked if I was all right, then said:

'Come on, into 'em.'

Fuckin' hell. There I am, a virgin in terms of football violence, caught up in a major off, concussed and intimidated, and he wants me to steam in. I somehow ended up being pushed out into the riot and had to fight like mad as Bradford attacked the front lads trying to get out. We managed to surge and get into them. Bradford didn't budge: it was toe-to-toe in the road. Then we had them moving. That was it, their bottle went and they were off, with us in pursuit. A huge fat lad couldn't get away as he wobbled after the fleeing Bradford crew. He copped a few punches before running up the steps of a church (or was it a mosque?) seeking sanctuary. He was given a bad beating.

We went at Bradford again after they had tried to regroup and counter attack. Skelly was walking down the road towards us and, on seeing us chasing Bradford, he mashed a few with a golf umbrella. Bradford had been seen off but not without cost. Several lads had blood dripping from head wounds.

It went off again at the ground and our group was split up. I ended up with eight fellow scallies and bumped into some Bradford at the back of their kop. By now I was into the swing of things. I steamed in and was promptly arrested. I tried to get away, as only one bizzy had me. Our youngsters, sensing they might get me free, ran over and started pulling and pushing. I managed to break free and ran with the bizzy after me. I got to the away end, where two more police took up the chase. The area outside the turnstiles was packed with Blades queuing to get in. I felt like Moses as the sea of human bodies parted and smuggled me to the front.

I had just got through the turnstiles when the bizzy grabbed at my 'mushie'. I pulled my head away leaving clumps of hair in his mitt, and ducked into the crowd again, mingling in among the bodies and swapping my leather coat for a green Pilot jacket with a Blade I knew. The bizzies looked for me but, with a quarter of the 5,000 travelling Blades already in the ground, it was easy to hide.

During the match, missiles rained back and forth over the 20-metre gap between our following and Bradford's boys. Pool balls, bricks, bottles and even darts were thrown. I have never seen so many people led away with head injuries. The highlight of the match was when the fat lad that had been battered on the church steps walked down the steep road to the ground. In full view of United's travelling army, he wobbled like a huge mummy, his head completely bandaged, one arm in a sling.

We gave him loads:

'You fat bastard! You fat bastard!'

That's the way it is with rival hoolies. We won the game 2-0.

I had had my first taste of a major football confrontation. I had a huge bump on my head, which needed three stitches and had nearly been nicked, but I had caught the bug. I wanted more of being part of an army fighting for my team and city. There was no looking back. The season ahead was an apprentice hooligan's dream: everywhere we went the natives were out in force wanting to put one over their big city rivals.

# HARTLEPOOL
# 6 MARCH 1982.

Hartlepool has a rough reputation: one of those one-horse towns where the locals would punch you as soon as look at you. Around 70 Blades hit their town centre early and, after drinking in a few pubs, settled down in a bar next to a shopping precinct. I noticed a few of the local lads drifting into the pub but no one in our party seemed concerned, so why should I be, a young scally?

Thirty minutes later, 50 Hartlepool had gathered at the far side of the pub. Still our lot didn't seem too bothered as they played cards. The Sheffield 'beer heads' couldn't see a riot unfolding right before them. My young eyes were trained on the local 50. I soon realised that they were stockpiling glasses and bottles behind their seats. I went over to tell some of the older Blades what was going on but before I could get my words out, the lot went. Hartlepool threw everything at us and we returned fire. A lot of lads received injuries from flying glass shards. I picked up a round table and used it as a shield.

Sheffield backed away when the ammo ran dry. A brawl broke out and spilled onto the streets. Police arrived but were powerless as Sheffield chased Hartlepool through the shopping precinct. A couple of local lads were caught and suffered beatings; one fell through a shop window. The police arrested a few Blades, including a deaf and dumb lad who went to all the United games. We pleaded with police, explaining his handicap, but they wouldn't release him.

During the walk to the ground, our numbers swelled to around 100 as Blades joined from other pubs. Hartlepool had also mobbed up and were trying to get at us. As we neared the ground, around 200 Hartlepool steamed up a side street. They had bricks and threw them at us but we were too far away. As the police moved towards them, they left us unattended and we charged in. With truncheons drawn the police beat each group back.

At the ground, 50 of us entered their stand. It was to be the most uncomfortable 90 minutes I have ever sat through. Their boys were in front and at the side of us. It kicked off endless times and numerous arrests were made. However the police didn't send enough bodies in, and each time they hauled out some arrested fans, it went off even more. It all came to a head when we went *en masse* to the toilets at half time – safety in numbers and all that. Fighting broke out in the refreshment area and we had literally to punch our way back to the seats.

There was even more trouble after the game. I don't know what they feed them on up there but Hartlepool is one rough-arsed town.

# DARLINGTON
## 15 MAY 1982.

One of the best days I've had at football came at the end of the 1981-82 season. Our visit to Darlington was nothing short of a carnival. We'd got promotion from the old Division Four and this, the final game, would see United clinch the championship. Everyone went in fancy dress including all United's boys. Minibuses ferried gorillas, referees, cowboys and penguins to the game as over 11,000 Sheffield travelled north. We drank in a town centre bar and the atmosphere was brilliant then someone shouted, 'They're here', which raised the question: who's fuckin' here, Darlington? The pub emptied. I half-heartedly went out not expecting to see much. Around 100 Middlesborough had turned out for us. It went 'off' as boys in Fila and Ellesse fought with chickens and pandas. We chased them down the road. I (a fluffy grey elephant) was at the front of the charge. As I ran after them the pink panther overtook me then two turtles and a cowboy firing a cap gun in the air screaming, 'Yee ha'.

I just cracked up laughing and stopped. Everyone was in fits then police arrested Welshy the cowboy, two burglars and a lollipop man. Boro came again outside the ground, with more this time. We ran into 'em but police were on hand and escorted Boro away from the ground. United won 2-0 and secured the championship. I couldn't stop laughing to myself as pictures flashed through my mind of Boro in full flight with half a zoo chasing them. Later, in a Sheffield nightclub, Marty got a blowjob from a girl whilst dressed as a huge yellow chicken: BIRD GOBBLES CHICKEN OFF IN CLUB. Priceless memories.

Now bigger teams with bigger firms lay in wait.

## OLD LADIES IN PITCHED BATTLE
### 11 SEPTEMBER 1982.

A new season and now in the Third Division. Our fixture away at Bournemouth had the lot: a great weekend piss up, a right laugh and a battle on the pitch for good measure. The 30 youngsters I hung around with had a few things in common, namely clothes, violence and a unified love of our football club. We had hired a minibus and were joined by a removal van full of boys. They set off straight from the Limit nightclub and travelled through the night. The Limit was THE club of the Eighties in Sheffield, home to a mix of football hooligans, students, music lovers and punks, all mingling peacefully.

When we arrived in Bournemouth in the morning it was chucking down with rain but everyone had the giddies on. Tim was acting daft, as usual. He was a good lad, game, and knew how to tell a tall story. We nicknamed him Chelsea Tim, as he was always going on about how he travelled down to London when the Stamford Bridge side had a big game, how they would fight 1,000-a-side battles and the main boys called him Chelsea Blade. He had actually been spotted shopping in Sheffield twice on the days in question. A proper bullshitter was Tim, but a good lad, nevertheless.

We were driving down a road in Bournemouth as two girls walked towards the van. Tim opened the side door and offered some verbal abuse of the sexual kind. I leaned back in the seat and booted him with the bottom of my foot: I was only trying to give him a fright but he went flying out of the van, which was doing 30 mph. I looked on in horror as he tumbled down the wet road and came to rest in a large puddle.

Tim slowly got to his feet, gazing down at his skinless knees. He went 'on one' and charged towards the van. Oh dear, I thought, I've got to fight one of my best mates over an accident.

I jumped out of the van and squared up. But as Tim approached, he cracked up laughing.

'You all right, mate?' I asked.

'Glad we weren't on the motorway,' he smiled, still mates.

We parked up and went on a drinking bender. After a gallon or two, we headed unsteadily to Dean Court, Bournemouth's ground. I noticed Tim was missing. I hated it when he was drunk, as he was so unpredictable. We waited a few minutes, then he appeared. The clown had gone into a jumble sale and rigged himself out in old woman's clothes. There he stood in a long purple coat complete with fur collar and cuffs, a big ruffle hat with a veil, a handbag and a chiffon scarf around his neck.

Following his lead, we all went into the sale and got dressed up, then 15 'old ladies' set off for the ground. Horsehead (so called because, you guessed it, he looks like a horse), couldn't get any of the gear to fit, so he bought a turban and a long orange shawl.

At the game, we were the centre of attention. United won 1-0 and at the final whistle a few Blades got on the pitch to congratulate the players. They were attacked by hordes of Bournemouth. That was it: hundreds of our fans ran across the pitch from the away end, including the 15 old ladies. I can only imagine what people watching from the stands must have thought as over a dozen old women slugged it out. Bournemouth's hooligans were certainly nonplussed: we ran them across the pitch and then headed back to the away end, to the cheers of the United contingent.

Outside, we drove our van across the car park to the removal van with our boys in. As the two vehicles edged their way out towards the road, a large group of lads, many of them skinheads, headed over. Our boys in the removal van in front were preparing to jump out, so I told our lot to get ready. The skins approached our van. Horsehead was sitting with his window open, the turban still on his nut.

'Paki bastard,' said one of the skinheads, and gobbed in his face.

Horsehead whipped off his turban. The van doors opened and we jumped out and steamed in. The removal van emptied and the chase was on as the Bournemouth baldies scattered to the winds. I couldn't stop laughing at Horsehead later. He wasn't bothered about being spat on, just bewildered at being called a Pakistani.

# LINCOLN: THE SURPRISE PACKAGE
## 29 SEPTEMBER 1982.

We got our biggest surprise as a football firm at Lincoln. Any boys who visited Sincel Bank in the early Eighties will testify that the Lincoln Transit Elite – so called because their preferred mode of transport was the transit van – were a tidy crew. When we first played them, in some nondescript pre-season cup game, we had never heard of them. Around 35 of us travelled on a coach, expecting just a booze-up with little local opposition. Nobody was prepared for what awaited us.

Before our throats had tasted a lager, we were on our toes. As we headed up a small shopping precinct, a group of 20 geezers headed our way. We spread out, knowing it was going to kick off. Then more Lincoln spilled out of a boozer. We ran at each other, then engaged in battle. Lincoln were so up for it that they soon had us backing off, then ran us. Mike and myself got chased down a subway and split up from the rest. Mike was perhaps United's top boy at the time and was well annoyed; all he had at his side was me, a 17-year-old Pringle-wearing 'wedge-head'.

In the early days I looked up to Mike. Not only was he game, he was also the best-dressed and most fashion-conscious boy in our crew. As the years went by, he always seemed to be one step ahead with the gear. He wore Stone Island years before it became the battledress for boys up and down the country. He once bought a beaut of a coat in Italy; it changed colour with conditions, yellow when cold and green as it warmed up. He was first with other names, Armani, Boss, three-star jumpers (only kidding Mike). Mike knew boys from all over the country, proper lads who knew the score, and also spent a lot of time abroad. These two reasons gave him a head start in fashion on the rest of our lot. I personally love my clothes, especially the styles generated through the terrace culture. Stone Island, Paul & Shark and C P Company may have replaced the styles of the early years such as Fila BJ, Lyle & Scott and Tacchini but the general gist of it all remains the same.

We eventually relocated our mob and fared a bit better as we met Lincoln again near the ground, managing to back them off before the bizzies interrupted. The game passed off without much trouble, although ten Blades who went in the home end were soon booted out. We discussed the forthcoming football season. One month later we had to travel to Lincoln again for a Division Three evening fixture; this time we'd be ready and bring our proper boys. They had taken a liberty and it was up to us to put them in their place.

On Wednesday, September 29, around 100 Blades headed via a service train to Lincoln. Most of our main boys were on and some of them, having missed the unfriendly friendly game, were sceptical about the merits of Lincoln's firm.

'Lincoln? Who the fuck are Lincoln?' said one of them.

'Wait and see, we'll have a good ruck today,' replied Kizzer.

The train pulled into Lincoln station. We alighted to be greeted by a few bizzies. Then, as we headed into the city streets, bang. Lincoln showed straight away. A pub called the Barbican, facing the station, was their meet. They poured across the road at us, with a few glasses and bottles thrown our way. Then everybody was into them in a flurry of fists and boots, neither side budging. The police were too few and helpless.

I got trapped between two cars with Kenny. A few Lincoln had us but Kenny was a tall, handy lad and I steamed in and backed him all the way. More police arrived and broke up the melee. We headed up towards town with the bizzies on our tail. Kenny came over to me.

'Nice one Stevie,' he said.

It wasn't much, but when the older lads sang your praises it made you feel like ten men. The cops took us away from town, so we settled in a pub at the top of a long road that led up towards the ground. Within an hour Lincoln came again, with glasses, bottles, and pool cues. We battled outside the pub. They had good numbers and quite a few of them got around the back of the pub and came through the beer gardens. Only ten of us sussed it and repelled the attack with a load of old slates stockpiled in the yard. After the match it briefly kicked off on a side street. We'd had a good day but it was nothing compared to what was to follow next season.

# BARNSLEY: A NIGHT OF SHAME 9 NOVEMBER 1982.

One of the most regrettable experiences I had at football came when Barnsley visited Bramall Lane for a night match in 1982. We had 50-60 boys waiting in the Penny Black pub in Pond Street, a regular meeting place in those days. Firms still head there now but take my advice, boys, it has been years since we used it. Word went out that Barnsley had arrived and were holed up in The Howard opposite Sheffield train station. We moved out and headed the short distance there. The Barnsley inside made their intentions clear by closing the curtains and locking the doors.

We decided to hide in wait on a spare car park that overlooked the pub. A couple of Barnsley's mob popped out for a look around and went back in. Then they all came out. Around 50 very nervous-looking boys found themselves with two choices: walk along Shoreham Street or along the back road where we hid. At first they went down Shoreham Street but then they doubled back towards us. The events that followed made me wish they had gone the other way.

We ran down the car park towards them. They jumped around shouting until a number of them lost their bottle, causing them all to run. A couple were dropped as they tried to escape. After the scuffling and the chase, one of my mates turned to me and under the street light I could see his Fila jumper had splashes of blood down it. We couldn't suss out what had happened. Then we realised a Barnsley lad had been slashed. He was screaming and his diamond Lyle & Scott jumper was hanging off his back. It did my head in. I was up for a brawl but not that.

Carrying and using a blade is out of order in my book. Two Barnsley fans were slashed in that incident. One needed 38 stitches in a wound that went from the nape of his neck down to his backside. The local paper showed a photo of him with his shirt pulled up. After the game I went home, my appetite for mayhem gone.

We don't carry knives. In all the years I have followed United, that is the only time I have seen a rival fan slashed. Maybe some firms accept it – especially Scousers, who think nothing of it at all – but not us. We can all take a battering – we've all had one – but we have always maintained a code of conduct. Knifing is out of order. If anyone is seen or heard to be 'carrying,' i.e. tooled up, they are ostracised. It's the way we are. Sheffield might be known as the Steel City and is a tough place with some very rough areas: it is 'fight or flight' but not knives.

Lately, more and more firms have increased their use of knives, so I am glad I'm out of it. Having been slashed at Hull, it is not something I would wish on anyone. I'll tell you this, if you are a hooligan, do you think you're a better boy than the guy who fronts you then turns to run on seeing you've pulled a blade? You are the mug, you are the one hiding behind a knife and you are the coward.

In fights with Sheffield Wednesday over the years, five Blades have been stabbed or slashed, whilst no Owls boys have been. One Wednesday lad known to us all has stabbed two United boys and always carries a knife. His victims have never grassed him up. I suppose it is his problem, as he's the coward hiding behind his Stocksbridge steel.

Two 15-year-old youths were arrested and convicted for slashing those Barnsley fans. Both got two years in a young offenders' institute.

# WOPPED AT WIGAN
## 4 DECEMBER 1982.

We knew Wigan had a decent crew. Our game at the beginning of the 1981-82 season saw a running battle on the streets near the ground. Fruit was emptied from a shop display so the crates could be used as weapons. But the flimsy crates weren't as lethal as the 12-inch cucumbers or rock hard pomegranates that flew at Wigan's boys. It went off around the ground and on the terraces during the game. Thirty-two boys were arrested by the overstretched police force.

So when we headed there a year later, by train, we knew what to expect and our numbers pushed 100. Our mob at the time had around 30 young lads, all clad in Lyle and Scott and Pringle jumpers. We headed for a pub on a street opposite the station and had hardly knocked the froth off our first pint when the shout went up:

'They're here.'

We ran out to be confronted by 60 boys. A lad with a snarling Doberman fronted their crew. Everyone went into them and they scattered like pigeons. An hour later, most of our older lads moved off into their town, leaving us 30 scallies in the pub. Wigan came again and this time they had numbers. As we left the pub to front them, a builder's van was stuck in traffic outside. We helped ourselves to brushes, shovels, and anything else that could be used. This time Wigan briefly stood before turning and running.

Our scallies met up with the rest of our older boys in town. We were well pleased with ourselves and relayed our account of the kick-off to the seasoned campaigners, who smiled at the perceived novelty of our story. As we were talking, Wigan came for a third time. This time, everyone went out and although Wigan had gained in numbers we ran them again. This was getting boring. One of the older boys, Munny, suggested that the natives were that weak we should send 20 or so out. 'That's the only way you'll get a ruck with them,' he said.

So we did just that. Ten older lads were joined by 15 scallies. I had to be in there, so I headed out into the shopping precinct. Wigan backed off at first, then charged. We stood solid and traded. I was at one side of our mob doing okay when some snide came from behind and banged me one on the temple. Goodnight. The next thing I remember is waking up on a pool table in the pub, with some 'helpful' chap pouring lager on my face.

'What the fuck happened?' I genuinely didn't know where I was. Everyone grinned. Dave told me that I had been thumped and when on the deck they nearly had me, but our lot had gone in and dragged my limp body back to the boozer. It took me ten minutes to come round and remember what match I had travelled to see. I can still see the older lads laughing now as I asked, 'What match are we going to?'

Despite the kayo, I was still up for it. I wanted revenge. At the ground, it went off again in the car park, and I steamed in. Naz copped a sneaky one that had his eyes double-glazed. After the match we steamed in again outside the ground. The brolly mob were bang at it. (In the early Eighties, there was a craze for carrying umbrellas to use as weapons, not because everyone expected sudden downpours. Police sussed the Mary Poppins brigade and their legally-carried weapon after a couple of years and football fans were stopped from taking them into games).

Black Greg was nicked after a geezer grassed him up to the bizzies. Smithy wasn't pleased and bent his golf umbrella over the grasser's head. Smithy was a proper lad but quite mad. Once at Boston in an FA Cup tie, we had a ruck with a load of local skinheads. The police arrested quite a few of our lot, despite our best efforts ot get them out of the riot van, and we all split up. I ended up with Crackerjack (Smithy). As we walked past Boots, he asked me, 'Steve, do you like punks?'

'No, not really.' I didn't quite catch what he was getting at.

'Good, come on.'

He then doubled back and pounded a Mohican geezer who stood with ten others of mixed sex. Jesus, two of us onto ten punks. Anyhow, we did all right.

Back at Wigan, our crew headed for the train station. Then the local firm came out of the end of a side street. A huge roar went up as they charged at us. Bricks filled the air and we had hands on our heads, as you couldn't see the oncoming rocks. A fierce battle went off. I got carried away and ended up mixed with their mob. I couldn't risk punching one, as they would have sussed me and beaten me to a pulp, so I danced about pretending to be a Wigan fan and fronted my own firm.

Our lot charged and, as Wigan backed away, I ran and dropped one from behind. I turned round and was just about to shout 'Come on!' when one of our lot cracked me. I don't know who it was but these things happen, it is easily done in a mad one. Police on horseback broke up the trouble. Later at the station, Eyes told me how he had been chased and nearly cut up by three Stanley family boys.

# THE TURNING POINT: A CITY AT WAR. 1982.

The followers of Sheffield's rival clubs hate each other with a passion that has led to the death of an innocent United fan, the near-death of a Wednesday 'boy', countless injuries and hundreds of arrests. At the height of the fighting, between 1985 and 1995, Sheffield city centre would resemble a war zone on Saturday evenings.

The struggle for supremacy went back to the late Seventies, when a Wednesday mob called the East Bank Republican Army held the upper hand. They had a big crew with some big, game lads and United's mob, the Shoreham Republican Army, later to become the Shoreham Barmy Army, usually finished runners up.

The turning point came on a winter's night in 1982. We had begun to get a good firm of young dressers together. A new casual breed had surfaced; the older lads (aged 20-25) were mainly thieves and petty criminals. The youngsters (16-19), including myself, had been involved in quite a few serious offs. These had gone United's way so we were a young cocksure bunch really.

Wednesday still ran the show at the top end of the city centre – but things took a dramatic change this winter's night. Around 25 of our young trendies were heading up town from the Penny Black pub in Pond Street. The rest of our firm had gone to the Blue Bell in the middle of town. Whilst walking up to meet the rest of our boys we bumped into around 40 Wednesday. We were edgy as Wednesday spat at us and tried to take the piss. I was looked up to by most of our younger lads and in an act of bravado I ran into Wednesday, our lot followed and the 'snort beasts' were well shocked. We had them on the go for a minute then they came back at us before police intervened. We were buzzing. I went into the Blue Bell and told the rest of our older boys what had happened. Everyone spilled out and headed for the Penny Black where we guessed Wednesday would be. The pub was totalled and a few Wednesday took a bad beating.

That in my eyes was the turning point and United's firm have been number one in Sheffield ever since.

# CAUGHT COLD BY CARDIFF
# 5 FEBRUARY 1983.

Cardiff City were pushing for promotion and attracting a big following to all their away games. We knew they would turn out in force, yet only around 20 of us had settled in the Blue Bell boozer in Sheffield city centre by 11.30am. One of our lads came in and told us that Cardiff were drinking in The Globe just up from Sheffield railway station. Without really thinking, our lads set off for war. As we came down past the Registry Office, Cardiff spotted us and within seconds had 150 boys going demented as they surged from the pub. We decided to pick up whatever we could, make a stand and wait for the leek-eaters to cross the perimeter fence which separated both sides of the dual carriageway.

Cardiff looked good as they closed in, the colours of their casual clothes still vivid in my mind, although quite a few had shitty Patrick 'cags' on. Battle commenced. We did well for a time. Then Cardiff spread and it was hard to keep their numbers at bay. I had a two-foot piece of wood that I had scavenged from some bushes and could keep the marauding masses off from where I was. Further down the road, Cardiff had got across and were involved in hand-to-hand combat with some of our lads. Inevitably we were overpowered and did one. I had just managed to get away up a grass bank when I heard a shout of 'Get him down' in that shitty Welsh accent that goes through me. They had got my mate Waz, who was still trying to fight as 15 Cardiff laid into him. A game little sod was Waz. I went to his aid with my lump of wood; he was my best mate at the time and I knew he would have been there for me.

'Come on!'

I cracked one round the head while he had his back to me. Waz managed to scramble to his feet and we both fended off a barrage of punches. I grabbed Waz's collar and tried to run, dragging him with me. I think he would still be there now having a pop if I hadn't.

Just as I thought we were clear, one of them grabbed my arm and held on despite a flurry of punches from my free hand. The rest closed in. In panic, I managed to yank myself free: a loud 'rrrrrip' meant I was away, although I had lost one arm of my jacket. Once we got back into town, Waz and I stopped to get our breath back. We looked at each other and both cracked up laughing with relief. We had got out of jail.

Down on London Road, we got our firm together. Cardiff were on the move and we went to head them off. It went off near St Mary's Gate roundabout. Cardiff, to be fair were a game crew. We managed to back the Taff's away but they didn't run. Police broke up the trouble, rounded up Cardiff and escorted them to the ground. After the match Cardiff received another police escort back to Sheffield station, so the fun and games were over for the day. We had learned another lesson about being caught on the hop.

# MILLWALL: MAD OR MYTH?
# 12 MARCH 1983.

In March 1983, I travelled in one of three cars containing United's top boys. The plan was to meet up with more of our lads who had travelled in two vans. I was now going to games with the main actors. I'll show Millwall an 18-year-old on a mission, or so I thought. The planned meeting never came to fruition, as one of the cars broke down. We crammed everyone into two vehicles, with seven people in each. Then we got lost in London and didn't reach the ground until after kick-off. As we drove under the railway bridge that led to a waste ground car park outside the ground, I was half gutted that we had not got our crew together and half relieved that we wouldn't bump into Millwall with such poor numbers. My relief lasted 30 seconds. As we pulled onto the top of the car park, 40 Millwall boys arrived, heading for the game. The Fila and Tacchini tracksuit mob spotted us and turned.

'Get out,' Spacey yelled.

As Millwall headed at us, we spread. I bounced around on the balls of my feet, my hands hidden in the cuffs of my Cerruti tracky. It was obvious from the off that it was well on top. Steve drove his yellow Ford Cortina straight at them, causing them to scatter temporarily. He span round wildly. It was all right for him showing off. He had metal round him, not fine cotton like the rest of us. As Millwall closed in, I noticed a smiling, Greek-looking geezer. The flash of steel in his outstretched hand was enough for me and we all backed away. We got ran and after a quick 50-yard dash, we turned to see Spacey had stood on his Sweeney. Spacey was one of our main boys at the time and was fearless. To our surprise, Millwall's boys shook his hand and didn't lay a finger on him. In the ground we met up with the rest of our boys. They had had a ruck outside a pub and had, apparently, held their own.

United were winning 2-1 with minutes to go when the ball came into the away end. We decided to waste some time with a spot of head tennis. As police moved in to retrieve the ball, Spacey headed it back with his first touch. The Met fuzz promptly threw him out of the ground. The next time I saw Spacey he was properly done in. Like a fool, he had gone for a walk around the ground – as you do at Millwall – and had bumped into the handshakers he met before the game. Instead of heading back to the away end, he walked up to them large as life. They promptly battered him. Minus his Adidas Trim-Trab trainers, and with his nose looking like he had borrowed it from Joe Bugner, he was a sorry sight. In stocking feet and covered in blood, he moaned about his Trim-Trab. The Trabbies weren't available in England at the time – Lilywhites sports store in Piccadilly, London, was the first to stock them. Most of our lot had them, as a few of our light-fingered brigade used to go to Germany. The German shops displayed them in pairs, so our thieves bagged them up and made a nice earner.

United's manager at the time was Ian Porterfield, more famous for his 1973 FA Cup winning goal for Sunderland against Leeds than anything he did in management. Spacey went to United's team coach before it left the ground, in the hope he could scrounge some trainers. Porterfield gave him some boots to wear. Later, we all met up in Leicester Square, but Spacey wanted home, not surprising considering he was clumping around in football boots and with his nose end nearer to his ear than his top lip. To make matters worse, the following season Spacey's Trim-Trab reappeared on United's away end, as you'll read in a bit.

## CURSE OF THE CAR COAT

I had bought a black car coat for the winter. A lot of our boys wore them at the time. Faded jeans and 'Jesus boots' sand creeper suede hide were the accompaniments. The car coat curse started in 1981 at Colchester. United took a large following, as they did everywhere that season. The game was on *Match of the Day* and I was clearly visible running on the pitch at the end in a red Lyle and Scott jumper and white 'strapos'. I had gone in my car coat but in a brawl at half time, Paul had been arrested wearing it. I lent it to him for a bit as he was freezing in his Slazenger polo neck. We had a tug of war with the bizzies trying to get Paul free, but I let go when I heard my coat rip.

Car coat 1, me 0.

Two months later at Halifax, we were in a pub when a joint Halifax/Leeds mob arrived. Punches were traded and then the chase was on. We legged them to the ground. The police saw Dean punching a local. We ran into a shop and I gave him my car coat to wear as a disguise. No such luck. He was promptly arrested. I think his blond wedgie gave him away. The game saw fighting on the home terraces as we went on their end 20-strong and had a beano. But I was coatless again.

Car coat 2, me 0.

My close mates joked about the coat being possessed. I though it was just hard luck until the next season. United had drawn non-league Boston away in the FA Cup second round. We had a good day, a nice battle with the locals. The scallies had a fine day on the rob and I acquired a Fila BJ shirt for a tenner courtesy of one of our sticky-fingered crew. I rammed it in the pocket of my car coat, as I already had a Lacoste shirt and jumper on.

On the train on the way home, one of our lot had robbed the buffet car till and the police got on. Ten of us were playing cards in a compartment. I had around £90 on me in ten-pound notes. The officers sealed off our carriage but I thought nothing of it until one of them searched me, took my wallet and then said, 'Got him. Come with me.'

He arrested me for the theft of £200 from the train buffet. I protested but was placed in the cells in Sheffield station. I was searched again. Like an idiot, I had forgotten about the 'bandit fiddler' concealed in the inside pocket of my car coat. A few of us used to screw fruit machines with them: a simple nylon mower strimmer, bent over at one end, would be fed into the coin slot to click up as many credits as you could without getting sussed.

'What's this?' said the copper.

'Dunno. I just picked it up on the train.'

'So how have you got all this money?'

'Well, I go to work, clock in and sort of earn it.'

'What do you know of the money being stolen from the train?'

'Fuck all. Look, you know that that money will have been mostly in pound notes, not crisp tenners.'

It didn't need a rocket scientist to work it out. I continued, 'Look I'm into fashion, so I take money to get clobber you can't get in Sheffield. I've bought this today.'

I produced the BJ shirt from my pocket.

'How much was that?'

'Thirty quid.'

'Thirty pounds for that. You're joking. I could get four nice shirts for that.'

They knew I was innocent but kept me for over an hour.

'Off you go son. We've checked and most of the money was in pound notes. Sorry for keeping you.'

'Yeah.'

The car coat was history after this. I went to work in it. The curse had got to me. The next week I went to Manchester and bought a Tacchini coat and had a bit of trouble with that as well, but that's another story.

# COMING OF AGE

## LINCOLN AGAIN: COMING OF AGE

## THE LIONS' DEN

## TO HULL AND BACK

## PITCH BATTLE AT OXFORD

## THE FOUR MS STAND AT BURNLEY

## BATTLE OF THE TRAMWAY

## MILLWALL AT HOME

## BRENTFORD: BATTERED BY FISHERMEN

## BEANO AT BOLTON

## PROMOTION

# LINCOLN AGAIN: COMING OF AGE
## 3 SEPTEMBER 1983.

The train was used again to ferry our motley football crew of mugs, pugs, thugs, nitwits, half-wits, shitkickers, ass lickers, flaggers, blaggers, boolis, hoolis, pallys, skallies and Methodists to Lincoln. Approximately 100 top boys on board, no one on the missing list. Adding to the numbers were 20 up-and-coming trendies. Everyone was looking forward to it, as Lincoln had proved they had a good firm. We were determined to put them in their place. My own reputation was growing a lot quicker than the hair on my top lip and I was ready to enhance it even further.

I had been more than accepted by our top lads and never had the trouble other rising youngsters had. A couple of the older lads used to 'tax' the chabs (a Sheffield term for youngsters). Taxing means taking money or items of clothing – basically, mugging. I used to hate it when a lad of my age would ask me to retrieve an item they had been relieved of by older Blades who were supposedly their mates in battle. I was only a fresh-faced youngster myself but they saw me as having gone a stage further. I managed to get Frankie's Kappa top back and another kid's sovereign ring. Two or three of the lads who taxed the chabs later stopped this habit.

I nearly had a fight with one after he had robbed one young 'un. I fronted him up, saying, 'These are our future boys. We won't have any lads coming through if you keep nicking off them.'

My remarks were not taken kindly and I was told in no uncertain terms to 'fuck off'. But I fronted it, as much as I thought I was going to get battered. It never came to blows and I had made my point. My reputation grew even more.

At Lincoln station, it again kicked off as soon as we hit the streets. The bizzies didn't have sufficient numbers to cope. We backed the Lincoln firm down the road. It is weird how the police used to let you move on after it had kicked off. They broke up the trouble and left us walking into Lincoln town centre. It did not take Albert Einstein to suss we were out for trouble, not some mass shopping expedition, but that's how it used to be: once it had gone off and everything had settled down, the Law left you, so it could go off again.

We settled down in a pub at the end of a shopping precinct and, as the beer flowed, the scallies went out on the rob. A sports shop was the target and the Fila BJ rail was getting hammered. Titch, Lee, Rags and Jakes all helped themselves to full tracksuits. I was going to get one myself but I have never been one for shoplifting – I had loads of bottle for fighting but none for stealing. As the 15 or so urchins raided the shop, I noticed around ten big fellers heading our way.

'Come on, they're here,' I shouted. Everyone headed outside, along with two hockey sticks. Lincoln came at us. I fronted up a huge bloke that stood in a boxing pose. I ran into him football style. They were soon off as our youngsters went to work. Mr Boxer left it late, then ran between two parked cars and straight into the path of an oncoming vehicle. Thud. He went down and rolled around on the floor. Three, two, one, scoundrel's gone. We went back to meet the rest of our lot, who were supping up, and all moved on.

Now what's the worst scenario possible on your wedding day? The best man forgets the ring? Someone shouts up when the vicar asks if anyone present objects? Wedding car breaks down? No. It's having 120 hooligans walking into the pub where you are holding the reception. God knows why the pub wasn't closed for the private party. We filed down the steep stairs into a room complete with guests and a top buffet. They looked on in sheer horror as everyone tucked into the grub. Scully shouted up, chicken leg in hand:

'Pint o' beer, luv, when ya get a minute.'

Luckily for the unhappy couple, Lincoln came. We tried to get up the stairs and out to fight but it was impossible. Kinny copped a display sign in the mush and the lads at the front took a beating as we surged from the back to try and get at Lincoln. Eventually we got out and chased the 30 or so Lincoln off. They must have split up after our first lot of shenanigans.

Next stop was a pub on the way to the ground. The bizzies again left us to our own devices. As I basked in the warm September sun, my thoughts trained on the certain battle we would have today. Sure enough, up went the shout: 'They're here.' Lincoln came from nowhere. I was in the khazi and had to head outside mid-piss. A few Blades backed into the pub as bricks rained down.

'Get out, you wankers,' I screamed and pushed a retreating Blade. I was out and into the street, breathing heavily. This is it. Our lot and Lincoln battled it out over a three-foot fence. It was quite strange: an easily-jumped obstacle was not breached by either side. I decided to show who was the gamest boy around by running and hurdling the fence, nearly falling in my frenzy. The domino effect kicked in, everyone followed me over and, after a few seconds, Lincoln turned and ran. Two poor guys were dragged down. I always feel for the lads who cop for this kind of beating, as they were usually the good lads who were the last to run. The vultures picked over their prey with a few kicks as the rest of us chased Lincoln towards some allotments. They kept turning and throwing stuff but as soon as we closed in they were off again. There was no way they would turn our lot over now.

United won the game 2-0, thanks to Mike Trusson and that ever-reliable goal machine Keith Edwards. After the match, we headed for the back of their main stand. As 200 of us eased our way through the crowds, Lincoln were seen mobbed up in the car park. A unique event then followed. It would have been easy for both sets of lads to steam each other but between us were innocent men, women and children. Football thugs are supposed to be mindless but everyone was shouting, 'Not here, on the grass.' There was a large playing field to the right of us, so we all scaled the five-foot high fence onto the grass. Lincoln, on seeing this did the same. Everyone who was on that field wanted a pop and was fair game.

Both groups gathered all their troops and the 30-yard gap was breached. Four hundred boys headed into each other. Griff ran in first and I followed. Police looked on as a 200-a-side brawl, spread over 40 yards, ensued right under their noses. I bet they loved watching it from the safety of the car park.

'Come on,' went that roar that came from the bottom of your Adidas Gazelle trainers. We had them backing away at one side but the fight was spread. I dropped one with an absolute peach. The roar went up again and this time Lincoln's bottle went. It was a great sight for a Blade to see watch heads bobbing up and down as they ran *en masse*, arms spread out, trying to avoid a fall and a certain beating. Job done, get the cigars out, feet up, mine's a lager, mate.

Police on horseback came and shepherded us away. It was murder all the way back to the train station as Lincoln attacked from every side street. I was on one, my yellow Sergio Tacchini jumper hanging off my shoulder thanks to some local overgrown and out-of-date Sham 69er pulling at me. Every Lincoln attack was repelled by our now fully confident mob. I steamed in so many times that I lost count. This was my hooligan coming of age: no longer an up-and-comer but now a recognised boy, soon to be a top face.

It went off again in the train station. Lincoln ran down the tracks throwing everything at us. We alighted the train but the police got heavy; they had had enough for one day. Faz, one of our younger boys my age, was nicked. An overweight, Terry Wogan-lookalike plod slung him in a room opposite the carriage in which we sat. Two or three minutes later the door was opened and Faz was slung out. He looked like he had done ten rounds with Muhammad Ali and did not have a clue where he was. Blood poured from his nose as we pulled him onto the train. The cops had given him a hiding but at the end of the day it was better than having a 'pinkie' charge slip in your pocket.

# THE LIONS' DEN
## 1 OCTOBER 1983.

United were off to a flyer in the new season, undefeated in the first nine games and top of the division, and consequently 2,000 Sheffielders make the trip south to Millwall. We borrowed a van but it turned up with no seats in the back and was filthy. No one would travel in it and ruin their togs, so Tez had the idea of looting a local foam shop. We ran in and helped ourselves to a pile of ready-made cushions while four of the lads grabbed a huge, foot-thick foam sheet from the window display. The two shop owners were going ballistic as we drove off, giggling.

As with our previous trip to Cold Blow Lane, the journey was a nightmare. The van would only do 50mph, tops. Fumes made their way into the back, causing a few of our lot to feel proper bad. We coughed and spluttered our way to London. I did a bit of driving to get some fresh air to my fume-filled lungs. All our crew had travelled and the plan was to meet up at Swiss Cottage in north London, then travel to Millwall on the underground. As usual we missed the meet. In our van was a tall, mixed-race lad called Dickie. He was a cockney and had been one of Arsenal's top boys before settling in Sheffield and adopting United as his team; the red and white, I suppose. His snakeskin shoes, sockless feet, faded frayed jeans and expensive leather jackets made him a bit of a cool dude in his own cockney kind of way. He didn't know south London though, as he had us all over the place. Once more we missed the kick-off despite setting off at the crack of dawn.

Another 2-1 win had us in good spirits. We were at the verbals with Millwall during the game and had a tidy crew out. The trouble was that everyone was parked all over the place, so after the game it was every man for himself. Our vanload had a quick punch-up with a few Millwall and the bizzies got us and gave the van the once over. Under the seat was a sack with items that could be used if it came on top, but couldn't be classed as weapons: car-jacks, spanners and other tools. They let us go.

Around 45 minutes after we had set off home, and miles from the ground, it came on top. As we headed across a bridge over the Thames at Borough, Millwall came from nowhere. Our driver Neil put his foot down but we got stuck in traffic. As 50 or so Bushwhackers converged on the van, we had two options: get out and have a pop or do a runner. The sack was emptied and we piled out, tools in hand. We had to do it or we would be walking home. As Millwall closed in, Neil lost his bottle and drove the van across to the other side of the road and through oncoming traffic. A few of our lot had jumped back in, leaving eight of us standing in the road. Millwall were only 20 yards away. We looked at each other and legged it after the van. A few heated arguments took place back inside. We had managed to get away unscathed but I was annoyed: twice in two visits I had ended up on my toes.

On the way home we stopped at Watford Gap for a bite to eat. As we headed out of the service station we pulled over to pick up a hitchhiker who had a sign for Leicester. His face was a picture when he went around the back of the van and opened the door. Fifteen football thugs sat barely visible in the darkness.

'Oh, cheers lads, but I'll wait for another lift,' he stammered.

Luey told him not to be so rude. The poor guy got in and sat in the middle with his rucksack on his lap. It must have been the worst two-hour journey of his life. All the way home he was bombed with clumps of ripped up foam. We went straight past Leicester and dropped him in Sheffield town centre. I felt for the guy, but it was funny, honest!

# TO HULL AND BACK
## 8 OCTOBER 1983.

Hull away always produced a good turnout. Our boys had once been very friendly with their mob, a relationship that dated from the Northern Soul all-nighters of the Seventies. People would travel from all over the country to these events and they were generally peaceful. Lads would swap football stories, dance and listen to the soul music. Then for some reason the friendship turned sour. Four United lads had their car attacked by their so-called Hull mates prior to a game at Boothferry Park in 1981. Revenge followed almost immediately when the same Hull lads were beaten unconscious at Samanthas all-nighter in Sheffield.

For this fixture, 80 travelled by train. Hull had a tidy crew, known variously as the Silver Cod Squad or the Hull City Psychos. The casual movement was in full swing, although we called ourselves trendies at the time. Fila, Tacchini, Ellesse and Kappa were all the rage. Our faded jeans or cords had slits cut up the side so they fitted over Adidas Barrington's or Diadora Borg Elite trainers. We frayed the bottom of our jeans for added effect.

After walking through Hull's town centre without challenge, we went in a pub called The Manchester. It was like a cave inside with a corridor leading to it. After a couple of drinks, Maz and I went to a burger bar across the road. As we stood there munching, I glanced up the road and saw Hull's boys heading our way. They had a large mob, all dressed in the gear. I screamed at Maz to go and get our lot, quick, and he legged across to the pub.

Hull's boys had clocked us and started running with the usual roar going up. I picked up a weighted traffic cone and bounced into the middle of the road. I glanced at the pub to see what was taking so long, only to realise that the doors had been locked by the bouncers and our lot couldn't get out. I could hear the muffled shouts as they tried to kick the doors out.

By now the Hull boys were nearly on me. I could have run but I had earned myself a lot of respect at the time. I stood in an act of ultimate gameness. Stupid, really. As they approached me, I knew I was done. Still, I lashed out: 'Come on, divvies.'

It seemed ages but was probably only seconds before they steamed me. Punches and kicks rained down. I dropped and did the old curled-up hedgehog in the middle of the road as shouts of 'Carve him, carve him' were screamed. Hospital here I come.

Our lot managed to open the pub doors and a huge roar went up. It kicked off all around my prostrate body. As I stumbled to my feet, dazed and beaten, Hull backed off, then ran. Maz and a few others checked if I was okay.

'I've been slashed,' I stammered.

Two long cuts ran down my Munsingwear jumper and through my Cerruti 1881 shirt. Luckily I had only a small nick on my back. I think the tosser that did it was trying to cut my clothes, not me. We ran up behind our boys who were chasing Hull, who in turn kept turning briefly then running again. A few Hull got boshed, with one ending up laid out in a women's shoe shop entrance after the lads had stiletto-heeled him.

The police arrived and quite a few Blades were arrested. One was Rowls, a good mate of mine who had gone too far in his revenge for my beating. After police had gained control, we all walked up the long road that led from town to the ground. Our lot were trying to shake off the bizzies as Hull walked up the other side of the road. I wasn't in the mood really as I trudged up looking like Robinson Crusoe, my clobber hanging from my back. Scuffling broke out in the car park as the two factions infiltrated each other. Forty of us went in the main stand and I bumped into my grandad and uncle, who looked at me complete with black eye and bedraggled clothes. I sheepishly smiled at them. I might have looked the worse for wear but I knew I had been very lucky that day.

# PITCH BATTLE AT OXFORD
# 5 NOVEMBER 1983.

I drove my car to Oxford with my best mates at the time, Maz, Pez and Doyley. We nearly always got into scrapes somehow but always stuck together. We called ourselves the Four M's – the Mad Marina Mafia Mob – due to my car being a Morris Marina (a bit embarrassing, really). We got to Oxford early and after a few drinks in town, headed up to the ground. Our boys were holed up in a pub in the centre but, knowing we would not get a fight with such numbers, we moved off. After parking, we went for a walk around their dump of a ground. As we went up the main road leading to the Oxford end, seven black lads came round the corner and walked towards us. I knew something was going to happen, so I quickened my pace to be first to meet them. Stares were exchanged as we walked past each other, then one barged into me.

'Northern wankers.'

I turned towards them and we squared up. As I tried to detach the hood from my Tacchini coat, one booted me in the groin. We ran into them. Maz in particular was as game as fuck: while small and not particularly handy, he was up for it and that's all that matters in football confrontations. We were doing all right and one of them ended up on his arse after a haymaker from me. We stuck together and they couldn't budge us.

Then it all went pear-shaped.

Unbeknown to us, a bus from the town centre had pulled up behind us. Quite a few Oxford got off and the black lads shouted to them. I thought they were bullshitting: I've done it before at football, been in a ruck then glanced over a rival's shoulder shouting, 'Coppers.' As they stop fighting you steam in and take them by surprise. I soon found out this was no wind-up, as a punch from behind hit me in the temple. It came right on top.

As we fled, Maz was nearly caught, his little legs were going like the clappers. Around six United shirters (normal fans) stood by and watched. I know they were just football fans but Blades usually help each other out no matter what. I've helped shirters no end of times. When we got clear, we realised Doyley wasn't with us. I looked back up the road; 15 people were kicking him.

We ragged a wooden fence for weapons and ran back to help. I shouted to the on-looking United fans, 'Call yourselves Blades?' We attacked the Oxford lads. Then the coppers came, thankfully. Doyley was in a right tangle: his jaw looked broken and one of his eyes was closed.

I was fizzing at the match. United were leading 2-0 in a vital promotion clash. Oxford pulled a goal back, then equalised with the last kick of the game to get a 2-2 draw. The final whistle saw hundreds of Oxford fans invade the pitch. After the players had disappeared up the tunnel, they came over to the away end. In response loads of Blades climbed the seven-foot high fence, including myself. I saw a couple of the black guys we'd had the bollocks with earlier. My head went and I jumped down onto the pitch. This led to around 200 Blades spilling over the fence.

Battle commenced and after a short time Oxford ran, with us in pursuit. We chased them the length of the pitch. Quite a few got battered as they tried to reach their kop. I saw one of the blacks and made a beeline for him. He was just about to get over the fence when I grabbed him and punched him to the ground. I wanted revenge for Doyley. Then I got punched. There was fighting everywhere. A few Blades got onto their kop and a major battle erupted as the police struggled to control the situation. When the police restored order, we walked across the pitch towards the away end. Reg Brealey, United's chairman at the time, came onto the grass to appeal for calm. I put my arm around him.

'They were taking the piss, Reg, so we give it 'em,' I explained.

'That's all well and good but let's have you off the pitch now,' he said.

The 3,000 United fans clapped us as we returned to the away end, which showed that 'normal' Blades had a certain amount of pride in their hooligan element. Their Monday morning workplace conversations would centre on United's boys chasing Oxford off the pitch.

Doyley was a mess. On the way home I stopped at a chippy. In the queue a few older Blades asked what had happened to Doyley. 'You've got some good mates pal,' commented one smartarse, looking at Doyley's battered face.

'Fuck off,' I replied, adding that I didn't see him on the pitch doing it for the Blades. I was fuming and had to be dragged away.

Back in Sheffield, Doyley was indeed found to have a broken jaw, which had to be wired up. Soup through a straw for a month, poor bastard. I suppose you could say Bonfire Night went with a bang.

# THE FOUR M'S STAND
## AT BURNLEY
### 8 NOVEMBER 1983.

An evening game at Burnley produced a good Blade turnout of around 80. Burnley had some boys but just how good, or bad, they were was still to be discovered. We headed straight for the seats opposite the away end. Everyone was outside the turnstiles umming and ahhing about going in. If we had hung around any longer the bizzies would have spotted us, so I got my close mates and told them we were going in. I was first through the turnstile, followed by a few others.

We were sussed straight away, so I ran at a couple of Burnley 'dressers', who promptly bolted up the steps of the stand. Unbeknown to me and the eight lads who followed me in, the rest of the boys were turned away by the police. As we got to the top of the gangway, I looked down. The two Burnley I'd chased had obviously told their boys and around 40 were stood looking up at us. I bounced down the steps followed by our little mob, still thinking the rest of our lads were filing through the turnstiles.

'Come on boys, were here,' I announced, as we clambered over the seats.

To my surprise, Burnley spilled over the barrier onto the pitch and went into the stand behind the goal. We took their seats. I stood up looking for our lads but no more came in and after a couple of minutes we knew we were on our own. The Burnley lads, who now numbered around 60, sat staring at us, running their fingers across their throats. We were only 30 yards away. I stood up doing a 'runners' action. I knew it would come on top after but enjoyed myself while I could.

The final whistle went and we got ourselves together. Perry, Dill and a couple of others were 'kacking' it and wanted to walk around the pitch to our end. I was having none of it. I loved situations like these, the ultimate challenge in gameness, nothing to lose. If you got some fist, so be it: if you had a right go and stood, despite such bad numbers, Sheffield United's hooligan rep could only be enhanced.

As we hit the dark, crowded streets, I saw their boys waiting across the road. I clapped my hands and spread them out as I headed towards them. Maz pulled me back. He wasn't as headstrong as me.

'Steve, walk up the road a bit, there's coppers at the end, we can have a pop and not get battered.'

This made sense. Bizzies usually were the last thing you want to see in a ruck but we were outnumbered big time and I knew a few of our lot were already in their starting blocks. We headed up the road. Glancing back, I could see around 40 Burnley jogging up behind us. There was no way we'd get another ten yards and I was ready.

'Steam! Steam! Steam!' the Burnley lads shouted.

I span around and waded in. Pez, Maz, Doyley and Gaz flew in too. The rest bottled out. We traded toe-to-toe and an avalanche of punches came at me. In seconds the police arrived, just as we had hoped. Maz grabbed me as I pounded a Burnley lad repeatedly. Pez was oblivious and continued to fight. I shouted as a copper with a dog ran across to him. The dog sank its teeth into his arse and he let out a scream, like a tart. But no one was arrested and we were proud that we had not budged an inch. None of us had copped any bad punches or injuries, apart from Pez with the seat of his his faded jeans hanging down.

We met the rest of our boys and explained with glee what had happened. One of those boys who had run and left us came over. 'Fuck off to Hillsborough,' were my only words to him.

The next day at work, I told Whitey what had happened. He looked a little disbelieving. Whitey knew a few Burnley boys he had met on holiday abroad and thought they were the dog's bollocks. A few weeks later, Burnley visited Toy Town (Rotherham) for a game. Whitey met his Burnley mates and they talked about our encounter with them. He later came over to me at work and excitedly told me.

'The Burnley lads told me about a Sheffield lad who was game as fuck, faded jeans, Lacoste coat, wouldn't move an inch. I told them I worked with you and you'd already told me what happened. They said to tell you, you're a good fuckin' boy.'

I felt proud. No matter how much you hate your opposition in fights, respect is sometimes due. I have seen boys stand on their own as their firm scattered to the four winds. They're the proper boys.

# BATTLE OF THE TRAMWAY
# 7 JANUARY 1984.

One of the most vicious fights I have experienced was with Birmingham City's infamous Zulu Warriors at Bramall Lane in this third round FA Cup tie. We had turned a useful crew out to meet the Zulus, who had a fierce reputation among hooligan groups. We wanted to put one over on them. Wednesday were also drawn at home in the FA Cup that day. It was very rare for Sheffield's police to let both sides play at home at the same time.

After drinking in town centre bars, we headed towards London Road. We'd been frustrated at the no show of Birmingham and Wednesday. London Road is half a mile from Bramall Lane and the ten public houses that run along the road are popular with fans and boys alike. On entering the Pheasant, we were told by some of our boys that Birmingham were drinking in the Tramway, a pub only 80 yards away. While we had been in town searching, the Zulus were drinking on our doorstep. Nobody got a drink as we headed the short distance up London Road.

Birmingham had seen the activity and came pouring out to greet us. The two groups clashed. Running battles went on before we got on top and ran them back into the pub. The Tramway was totalled. Everything was going through, and coming out of, the now missing windows. Chairs, glasses, bottles, brass ornaments, even an ornamental sword flew in and out of the pub. It went on for five minutes with no police arriving. London Road was usually heavily policed, but for some reason not today.

As the fight continued, down London Road came 30 more Zulus who had been drinking in a pub further up. On the way down to help their colleagues, they had raided a DIY shop. The sight of some rather large black youths carrying shovels, pitchforks and hammers was enough for most of our lot, who backed away. Then Sherpy, an older Barmy Army Blade, ran into them. That was the signal for everyone to steam in. Outnumbered,

Birmingham threw the gardening equipment at us, turned and ran. We chased them almost to the ground, where we saw the first police since it had kicked off. At the game, fighting broke out in the seats of the John Street stand.

The local press had a field day. Pictures of the wrecked pub, under the headline 'Battle of the Tramway,' splashed the front pages. The landlady complained it was 12 minutes from when it kicked off, to the police arriving on the scene. The landlord, meanwhile, had been at Hillsborough preparing to watch Wednesday. Before the match kicked off there was a loudspeaker announcement for him to go back to his pub!

The day was one of the most violent of my young hooligan life. And, as the result was a draw, a midweek replay at St Andrews followed three days later. We took around 150 boys and had a good ruck before the game. Inside the ground, Birmingham's boys traded insults from a stand at the side of the away end. A big black geezer was in full swing.

'Yer gonna get it after the game, were gonna ...'

Interruption. Black Paul cuts him off in mid-sentence.

'Shut it, nigger.'

We collapsed laughing as the stunned black Brummie lost it. 'You're a fuckin' nigger,' he screamed, leaping to his feet.

After the game Birmingham attacked us but it was very much a brick-slinging affair as the bizzies had us under wraps.

# MILLWALL AT HOME
## 4 FEBRUARY 1984.

The game against Millwall at Bramall Lane was going to be a big one. Spacey's re-arranged face plus the fact that we had been attacked on our last two visits there added spice to an already explosive fixture. One of the country's top firms were coming to the Steel City and I wanted to see the backs of their heads. Sheffield bus workers decided to strike for the weekend on the Friday before the game. Nevertheless we managed to turn out 80-100 good lads. News came through that around 50 Millwall were in the train station waiting for the rest of their crew. We set straight off through town.

As our lot straggled down Paternoster Row, which overlooks Sheffield station, I was at the front with Smeg and Dwight, a six foot four inch black guy who is as game as they come. As we approached the station over the roundabout, Millwall saw us and came screaming out. I glanced around and as usual our lot were coming up in dribs and drabs. We had to hold them off until we got ourselves together. Punches were exchanged and we did all right. I hit and knocked out a Millwall lad with a beauty and we backed the Londoners towards the station before police arrived and chased us all over the place. An ambulance sped up and took one of their boys away. I think it was the one I punched. He'd had a knife in his hand, so it served him right.

That was it for the day as Sheffield bizzies had Millwall off to the ground under escort. The only thing to note was that a tall ginger nut, one of Millwall's main boys, had Spacey's Trim-Trab on – the ones he had been relieved of on an earlier trip to the Den (see page 20) – and was taking the piss from the away end. Spacey completely lost it, although later he saw the funny side.

# BRENTFORD:
## BATTERED BY FISHERMEN
## 25 FEBRUARY 1984.

Football violence can come from very unexpected quarters and you have to keep your wits about you all the time. An away fixture at Brentford engendered little enthusiasm from United's hooligan element, and taking a crew was deemed unnecessary. I went everywhere, no matter what. Following United was a must in my book and for games that produced little trouble I would regularly travel with non-hooligan Blades. The lads I went to Brentford with liked a laugh and a drink, fighting wasn't their top priority. Most of them would still have a go if the need arose. I made some good friends on trips like this. Even though they knew I was bang at it most Saturdays, they accepted that I was as keen a supporter of the club as anybody.

The lads in our van were a mixed bunch: four miners from Kiveton, four Manor Estate Blades, two Rotherham Blades, Whiskey, a harmonica-playing old Barmy Army boy and a couple of others. Only around four or five of them had ever been involved in any violence worth talking about. I enjoyed days like these, it made a change from charging round mobbed up looking for action.

Our 3-1 victory at Brentford had everyone in good spirits and drink flowed freely at various London hostelries. We ended up near St Pancras Station in a pub called the Eliza Dolittle. It was not only was full of 'fags' but was also a Republican bar, a fairly unlikely combination, with Irish flags behind the bar and anti-British slogans in the toilets, plus some mean-looking paddies scattered around. I drank up and was about to head outside when two of my miner mates started.

'This is England, shouldn't be allowed in pubs like this.'

It was getting heavy but we managed to get everyone out before the kneecappings started. It was around 11.30pm and we stood pissing up walls, getting ready for our long journey home. Then, wham, a large mob of boys came from nowhere and attacked us. I picked up a plank to fend a few off. Our van sped away as it came right on top. Only six of our lot managed to get in. The rest of us chased the van down Euston Road, still being pursued by the twats who had ambushed us. I managed to get in the van and stood on the back step trying to get the rest of our lot in.

'Slow down,' I yelled.

Chris, the driver, was trying to keep a good distance between the ensuing mob but our lot couldn't catch up. Chris slowed and we had just about got everyone in when he accelerated, leaving three Blades still chasing. I managed to grab Whiskey and tried to pull him in. His legs went from under him and I held on as he was dragged Wild West-style. His 'dealer' boots had metal segs in them and as his legs bounced around on the road, sparks flew everywhere. He managed to climb in with my help. At the bottom of St Pancras Station we again stopped and managed to get the last two in.

'Go, go,' we yelled, as our tormentors closed in on the van.

Chris accelerated like Nigel Mansell and I went flying straight out of the back, landing headfirst and scraping all the skin off my chin. This was the least of my worries, as I landed virtually at the feet of the mob. I was kicked and punched a few times but managed to escape. Kyle tried to have a pop but had his jumper ripped off his back. We legged it up the ramp heading for St Pancras. Our van drove right through the entrance and up onto one of the boarding platforms. Chris had driven as far as he could. Everyone got together and Chippy picked up a heavy railway sleeper. This was it. We stood together despite being outnumbered three to one. As the mob came at us up the platform, four Blades who were on the last train home must have seen our plight. They got off and had a right pop. We immediately recognised Smeg, a tall, long-haired Blade who usually ran coaches to away games for the beer belly element. He really surprised me; as we ran down to help there must have been 15 lads attacking him but he would not go down. He stood there lashing out, although he ended up looking like John Merrick's uglier brother for his trouble.

We ran at them and backed them off. Once we had them on the back foot, everyone steamed in together. One lad was caught and suffered a really bad beating. He was knocked unconscious and lay face up, one of his arms twitching with nerves. Miffy jumped up and landed on his arm with both feet. Then he looked down and his fingers were moving, so he stamped on them as well. This was excessive but we had just been ransacked and Miffy was on one. The poor victim on the floor was arrested. Later in court it was revealed his arm was broken.

The police arrived. Our van was a write-off. A large piece of timber was protruding from the smashed windscreen. I argued with a big, bearded bloke who informed me they were Grimsby, who had played Palace that day. Grimsby! I thought West Ham or someone else decent had jumped us, not Grimsby. As we argued, he chinned Chippy. The bizzies were all over the place.

'You dickhead, lets take a walk.' I gestured for him to follow me but one of his mates kicked me. I swung a punch. A ginger-haired copper saw me, ran over and grabbed me. It was pretty obvious that we were all going to be locked up for the night. We were all put into vans and taken to the Grimsby coach parked just down the road. I had a black eye and was covered in blood from my skinless chin. All our lot with injuries were made to get on the coach to identify our attackers. There was no way I was going to pick anybody out but I decided to have some fun with the bearded bloke. As we walked up the aisle, I spotted him near the back. I got level with him and he was staring out of the window. I asked a copper if I could look at his face. The copper made him stand up and look at me. I smiled at him. I put my fingers to his chin and yanked his beard.

'No, mate,' I said to the copper.

'Cheers, pal,' a Grimsby boy thanked me as we headed off the coach.

When arrested we all had the soles of our trainers checked because the lad with the broken arm had a trainer print on his forehead. I was glad I had my Adidas Gazelles on, as they didn't match. I'm not a vulture anyway. As far as I'm concerned once you're out you're out, if the geezer is down and unable to fight you should leave him alone.

The cells were full of eight Grimsby and 16 Sheffield. I sat on a desk and chatted to a copper as she typed our charge sheets out. Affray, it read. That was a serious charge. My injuries were photographed, we gave statements and then they fed us McDonalds, not bad eh? I gave nothing away, as usual.

'I ran for my life, I was terrified,' I said, adding that I had run up the train tracks and had not seen anything. An hour later we were all in a large room when the ginger-haired copper came in with two CID. He nodded at me and I was carted off. Now I didn't think I was so clever. Under pressure (let's just say that a telephone directory travelling repeatedly at a man's head can change one's mind) I amended my statement a little.

We had to attend court two days later and it nearly kicked off between us again. A young Grimsby lad fainted and fell straight through the courtroom door. In all, we had to go to court five times before all of our lot were told we had no case to answer. I had had five days off work, five train journeys, five piss-ups after and couldn't claim a penny back. That pissed me off, as I was on a poor wage and money was tight. I ended up getting on well with two of the Grimsby lads. The next season while following Grimsby's escort from the train station to Bramall Lane, I saw them. They came across the road and we shook hands. I couldn't believe it; they had Blades badges on.

'What's that all about then?' I enquired. They explained that United had become their second team (strange, if you ask me). One of them had just done nine months for the incident. I couldn't believe that out of a full coach the courts could see fit to jail one lad. Three Grimsby got community service (60 hours) and four were acquitted. Did the jailed lad do all the fighting on his own, then?

At Grimsby the following season their boys were chased along Cleethorpes seafront by our lot. Two lads ran on the promenade and were thrown off the end and into the sea. It was ironic really, given the name of Grimsby's firm – the Cleethorpes Beach Patrol.

# BEANO AT BOLTON
## 7 MAY 1984.

Bolton, it is said, is a tough place full of tough people. Well, I'm not of that opinion. My first excursion to Blundell Park was in May 1984. The game was the penultimate one of the season and crucial for United, who were pushing for promotion from the then Third Division. The game would be followed by Newport at home and four points from these two fixtures would see us automatically promoted. Sheffield took a large following of around 4,500 fans. Waz and I had arranged to travel on one of two buses setting off from Sheffield station. Marty Carty was running ours.

'Seven pounds, lads,' Marty said as we boarded.

'Seven quid to Bolton? Do you get a ticket with that?'

It was expensive but I just put it down to old bagga-raggamuffin making a few quid to pay for his huge skunk habit. Call us naïve but when a woman in her early 40s got on with a man friend, the penny still didn't drop. It turned out she was a stripper, and an ugly one at that. Newspapers were taped to the windows and off we set. She walked up and down the coach until she had undressed entirely. I had trouble keeping my previous-night's ten pints and chicken Madras where it belonged. She was a grot bag.

She pulled Mike's trolleys down and began to suck his cock. Midge came up behind and thrust his black pud into her. When he had finished, some of our lot brought her down the coach. I was bricking it as she stood opposite me in the aisle. I would have sooner tackled ten Millwall. Fortunately she was pointed to Keron, who sat opposite, a tall, game black lad. She leaned over and undid his jeans.

'Christ.' She stood back.

Keron would have put a donkey to shame. No wonder he was game, carrying his own personal bat round in his kegs. Everyone had enough of the slapper and she was promptly thrown off the bus ten miles from Bolton. Her man friend was chinned when he complained.

A Blade unknown to me was completely off his trolley. One of our lot gave him a large cider bottle that everyone had pissed in and he drank quite a bit, then threw up all over the place. He missed the game and was still asleep in his spew as we returned afterwards.

Prior to the game our hooligan element, numbering around 150, drank in pubs near to the town centre. There was no trouble. Bolton either weren't around or weren't showing face. It went off though as we marched to the ground. A large boozer close to the ground emptied as we approached. We ran at them and they retreated sharpish without a punch being thrown. Another attempt in the club car park by Bolton to get into us was equally futile. Our lot just steamed in and Bolton scattered or got pounded.

In the ground I was surprised that we had been given seats bang behind Bolton's side terrace, where their mixed up mob of skins, bikers, Def Leppard types and a sprinkling of dressers all gathered.

Goal to Bolton. One-nil. They turn around, making insulting hand gestures. Without further ado, our lot steamed in and the next thing I knew I was on the terrace, punching. Anyone stupid enough to stand was steamrollered by our cashmere-clad boys and the game was held up as Bolton's so-called mob jumped onto the pitch. My beige Lacoste coat, bought recently from Hurley's in Manchester, was ripped as one of our boys pulled me back up into the seats.

The game was lost 3-1. United's centre forward Keith Edwards nearly had his head taken off scoring our goal (his 41st of the season). It was a brave header that lost him a few teeth but would clinch us promotion. As soon as the final whistle sounded, the charge was on again; this time it was down onto their terrace then a chase across the pitch. Slim and Kenny pummelled one lad to his knees only to look shamefaced as he screamed through bloodied teeth, 'I'm a Blade,' pulling up his tee-shirt to reveal a tattooed United badge on his arm. All the Blades fans, including the shirters, went mental as our dream of promotion had seemingly slipped from our grasp. Outside, a car showroom window was smashed and Blades fought with police and chased Bolton's beleaguered fans all over the place. We hit the media headlines as mindless morons, which was probably true that day. Thirty-three Sheffielders were arrested.

# PROMOTION
## 15 MAY 1984.

Burnley v Hull City at Turf Moor. This game had a bearing on United's plight for the following season. Hull needed to win by more than two goals to pip us for promotion. The Wednesday night fixture saw over 400 Blades make the trip to Lancashire, including 100 boys. Sheffield Police clocked us boarding coaches outside Sheffield station and tipped off their Lancashire colleagues about the impending invasion. When we arrived, the plod put us in a special car park near to the ground. They had made all the necessary arrangements for the coaches, but had overlooked one thing: where in the ground would we go?

As the game had kicked off, quite a few of us ran to the ground and to the nearest turnstiles. I had just paid when a roar went up; Hull had scored after only six minutes. We'd gone on the Burnley end behind the goal. After all we would be cheering them on. Around 15 of us had gone through the turnstile and up onto the terrace from one side. The rest of our lot came through in dribs and drabs. As the 15 of us stood on our side of the terrace, it kicked off in the middle. Burnley had attacked our lot as they came up the gangway. We ran over as our boys struggled to get up onto the terrace. As Burnley held them back we steamed in from the side and made enough of a gap for the rest of the lads to wade in.

Some twat grabbed my hair from over the gangway wall and yanked me up and down. It hurt like mad and clumps of my hair came out – he'd have a job trying that sketch now. An old-fashioned terrace ruck developed. More Blades joined the melee and we chased the Burnley across the terrace until the police restored order.

The match itself was the most tense 90 minutes of my football-watching life. Brian Marwood scored again for Hull leaving them 45 minutes to get the extra goal that would gain promotion for them and keep us in the Third Division. In the second half, 400 Blades cheered on the resolute Burnley defence. The full-time whistle went: 2-0 to Hull but we were up. The feeling was indescribable. The tension had got to most of us more than a few tears rolled down ecstatic faces. The Burnley players came and clapped us and I will never forget their number five, who was saluting us with a clenched fist. He'd had a stormer of a game. The Burnley fans invaded the pitch and came running over to us. This time there was no brawling as we clapped them and they did likewise. The rivals shook hands and hugged. United were up and my sore head didn't matter any more.

Now Division Two beckoned and with it visits to Cardiff, Man City, Birmingham, Portsmouth, Leeds, Middlesbrough and Wolves, not to mention Barnsley and Huddersfield. These teams had some of the most respected firms in the country. It was time to take things to another level.

# THE CASUAL YEARS

## CARDIFF: BOVRIL AND BENT STEWARDS

## LEEDS, LEEDS, LEEDS AWAY

## BLINDED AT BLACKBURN

## THE COOL CATS

## THE SEAT SMASHERS ARRIVE: LEEDS AT HOME

## VIOLENT WEEKEND AT BRIGHTON

# CARDIFF: BOVRIL AND BENT STEWARDS
# 1 SEPTEMBER 1984.

After the shock of Cardiff's visit two seasons earlier, we were ready this time. Around 100 lads waited for them in town. This time they didn't show in our city centre prior to game but news filtered through that around 40 lads had left the train station and headed towards Bramall Lane. I was gutted, we had a good crew out and I wanted revenge for our show-up last time and my sleeveless Lacoste coat.

On London Road, a few of our lot set off to scout the ground. Ten came back and said they had been fighting with Cardiff at the back of the South Stand. 'They're shit, only ten of us, forty of them and we still had to go into them,' Morgan informed me.

I took statements like this with a pinch of salt, as a lot of hooligans embellished these little 'offs' to sound like Custer's Last Stand. I once bumped into 15 Aston Villa in Holland on the way to France 98. We had a beer with them and I recognised three from the papers; they had been all over the national tabloids: 'CATEGORY 'C' HOOLIGANS DEPORTED.' We talked about rival mobs.

'Don't Wednesday have a mob?' one asked.

'Well, sort of,' was the best I could come up with. 'Do you kick off with Birmingham, then?'

'Blues are shit, think they're the bollocks though. They're taking a mob to Friday's game (Colombia) and they said they're going to show off. Full of niggers their mob. We don't have niggers with us. You got any niggers?'

I was a bit taken aback with the racism. I thought those days had gone.

'We've got around twenty to twenty-five blacks and they're sound. We've never had a race thing with our mob and our blacks are game as fuck, so that's all that counts really.'

'Can't trust them chimps I'll tell you,' said another Villa lad. 'Blues blathered you at yours this season, didn't they?'

'Blathered?' I queried.

'Yeah. Done you, like.'

'If you call getting run right down London Road a result, well, yeah, blathered us.'

The Villa lads laughed and one said, 'Go on, tell us what happened. Blues said it was the best off they've ever had.'

'Well they slashed two Blades, a young one across the face and one in the arm. They came out of the ground before the game finished and got to a pub on London Road. It went off and Brum attacked around twenty Blades outside the pub, more United came and it was a proper mad one. A Brum boy was badly beaten as our lot chased them down the road.'

'Fuckin' Blues. Never run? They're full of shit.' The Villa lads took the piss out of Birmingham for typical exaggeration.

Anyway, back in Sheffield Maz and Pez and myself went in the Bramall Lane seats for the Cardiff game. Our lot went in the John Street stand. Ten minutes into the game, I noticed our lot pointing to the other end of the stand that we were in. It was pretty obvious Cardiff were sat in the same stand as us. At half time we went down to the refreshment area, I leaned on a wall and prepared to devour my pie and Bovril. Around 25 boys came down the stairs. I clocked them and vice versa. A few walked over.

'Where's all your boys been?' one asked.

'In town waiting for you,' I replied.

One started to take the piss out of my Armani jumper. 'What the fuck's that?' he said, pointing to the eagle on my arm. I just laughed at him.

'We've been in town, your shit Sheffield.' A pissed up Taff stuck his head right up to my face. He was trouble with a capital T, so I gave him my hot Bovril right in the mush. He screamed and we fended off blows as the other Cardiff boys attacked us. I copped a few punches but put up a good show. The police came rushing over as I threw a wild one. They arrested me but I continued to mouth off at Cardiff. A steward who I knew vaguely came rushing over.

'It's not him, I saw it, that lot started on him.'

The coppers let me go. I thanked the steward, who laughed and said, 'You owe me one.'

More police came and took Cardiff to their seats. Our lot knew it had gone off and saluted us with as we arrived back.

With a couple of minutes to go, a few heads appeared up the two gangways on either side of Cardiff's posse. Our boys had come round from the other stand and bounced over the seats. Cardiff went at them in a sea of punches. I had just got to the action when dozens of plod arrived. A couple of our lads were nicked. Another scuffle outside brought a close to the day's events. One Blade that was arrested but not charged had three scuff burns on his face, caused by the leather gloves on a policeman's hands making repeated contact with his face.

# LEEDS, LEEDS, LEEDS AWAY    6 OCTOBER 1984.

An eagerly-awaited fixture. Next to the Pigs, Leeds are hated most by Blades. The 9.30am meet in town saw over 200 United boys board four coaches. We decided at the last minute to stop at Wakefield, where we could get together and arrive *en masse* via a route the police would not expect. Once in Wakefield, our numbers swelled to more than 300, although the extra consisted more of beer heads than boys. A couple of pints later and we were restless. I sat on the coach, eager, and after a lot of faffing we set off, four coaches in all. Our coach was in front; it contained United's core hooligans. The driver was a top man, he knew what we were after and said he knew where it would be perfect to drop us off. We arrived undetected.

'Sheffield, Sheffield,' echoed around the city centre streets. In response, Leeds poured out of a pub. Heavily outnumbered and straight on the back foot, they were shocked. We steamed them, everyone going crackers. More arrived and a couple of game lads stood and took a beating.

I was running round, having not landed a punch. Then this gigged-up geezer with a Seventies perm came at me, going berserk. I hit him with a peach of a shot, grabbed his collar then booted him. The police arrived to curtail our fun and we were escorted towards Elland Road. Leeds must have been fizzing. They soon mobbed up and came down at us from the town centre. Looking up the road towards the Scarborough Arms, they looked impressive. Just as they came under the bridge, a few of our lot realised the police didn't have sufficient numbers to hold us, as they had sent quite a few men to meet the Leeds Service Crew. The roar went up.

'Come on!'

We flew past the startled police and headed at the Leeds boys. As the two running groups got near each other, Leeds slowed. Punches were exchanged. I fell over as a copper went for me. Leeds backed off a good 20 yards. Then the 'barking bollock biters' moved in along with more pissed-off police. Luey, one of our main boys, got nicked and a couple of others were also shoved into a van. The escort took us past some wasteland. Leeds came again throwing bricks. We tried the same sketch again but the police had us sussed this time.

In the ground, the Leeds fans seated in the South Stand looked a mighty impressive mob. All stood up in a brilliant display of casual colour. Our boys gathered at the bottom of the terrace, only three skims (with a nicely shaped pebble) away from their hordes. To a man, Leeds stood up and chanted:

'Sieg heil. Sieg heil.'

Their arms pistoned like fiddlers' elbows. The Leeds Service Crew and their hangers-on were the most racist in the country; Chelsea were the only ones to come near them.

Our response was to get our black lads high up on their colleagues' shoulders. They mockingly sieg-heiled back at the Leeds masses. I admired their guts. Then, in a show of respect to our black Blades, all 300 or so boys packed together in the 4,000-strong following sang a tribute to each one of them, to the tune of the 1978 pop hit Black Betty.

'Woh-oh, Black Paul, bam ber lam.'

'Woh-oh Black Terry, bam ber lam.'

I don't know who started the song but we pogo-ed around until every black Blade's name had been sung. Class. One of our blacks did a hangman's noose impression as two bananas landed on the pitch in front of us. A Leeds lad had hung himself in Armley nick a few weeks earlier and although I didn't agree with the response, I wasn't the subject of the hatred levelled at our non-whites.

'What's it like to run at home?' echoed from the away end.

The match itself had become secondary and the 1-1 draw passed quickly. No further trouble followed. On our way home and in the pubs that night everyone was buzzing. We had gone to Leeds, showed in their town and got a result. We knew however that, like a two-legged semi final cup-tie, it was only half time.

Leeds' visit to Bramall Lane in March was surely going to see the Service Crew turn up in numbers seeking revenge.

# BLINDED AT BLACKBURN
# 8 DECEMBER 1984.

I must be one of a very small select group of people who have had a kicking at Blackburn, an away fixture that doesn't exactly send shivers down the spine of your average hooligan. A small group of our boys including myself travelled to Blackburn by train, our crew numbering about 15. The rest of our boys had travelled by cars, coaches and a mini-bus. We did not feel the need to travel together, as Blackburn had little or no reputation. Before the game we drank in various pubs on our way to the ground. After taking our positions in the stand, we watched a fight kick off on their kop. Several Blades were escorted to the away end.

The match finished nil-nil. Outside, we mobbed up about 60-70 lads and headed for their end. As we walked down the road we bumped into their firm. They offered little resistance as we chased them down the main drag towards town. Our boys doubled back and got on the coaches, leaving ten of us to walk to the train station. The obvious then happened: we bumped into about 50 Blackburn, the same ones we had just run. They sussed us; not hard really, as they were the biggest set of tramps I had ever seen, a right bunch of woollybacks (a Scouse term to describe poorly-dressed youths).

In the early Eighties we used to chant a song at such scruffy rivals:

*There's a woolly over there, (over there)*
*And he's wearing brown Air-wear (brown Air-wear)*
*With his three-star jumper halfway up his back*
*He's a fuckin' woolly back.*

As the tramps came at us, I shouted, 'No fucker run.'

I fronted the situation and bounced in the middle of the road, arms outstretched. A couple of my mates joined me but the rest lost it. Punches rained in from all angles as I tried to fight back. Then, Wham! Something hit me like never before, my senses departed, everything went black and my head span. In a daze I grabbed something to stay on my feet; it was a small tree and I just clung on. They continued punching and kicking me until Maz and a couple of others came to my rescue.

By the time the bizzies arrived, I was in a terrible state. One eye was shut tight, I had a broken tooth and my nose was pouring with blood. I was told after that someone had smashed a brick into my face from the side. At the train station I sat on the steps, spewing blood. The draw for the FA Cup third round came on the radio. Watford away, yip, yip, yip! A nothing draw if ever there was one.

We got back to Sheffield and Maz took me home in a taxi. My mam cracked up when she saw the state of me. I slept on and off for 24 hours. It was two weeks before my eye began to open again and when it did, it was obvious to me that I had damaged it badly. I kept going dizzy and at times was totally disorientated. I went to the hospital and subsequently had to return for loads of tests. Lights of different colours were shone into my eye. My head was put in a dome with my good eye taped over. I had to press a button when I saw a light; it was like staring into the night sky looking at the stars. Then I had to have needles in my eye. That really freaked me out.

Eventually I stopped going for treatment and to this day the vision in my right eye is poor. I suppose that's the gamble a football hooligan takes. What I didn't expect was that, about two months later, one of the lads told me that Cozzy had been saying I had lost my bottle a bit since Blackburn. This was a bit rich as he was one of those who had left me to cop it at Blackburn. The way I saw it, I had done more for our reputation in a weekend than he had done all his life. I was going to give it him but everyone knew the score, so I just pulled him in front of everyone. I reminded him of the fact that I was the 'boy' who had respect, that I was the 'boy' who got stuck in for the cause and that I was the 'boy' who never had a thought of taking a backward step, unlike him. I also reminded him that if he came out with any more comments like the one that I had heard, I would show him who was a boss 'boy' in one, maybe two punches.

People have asked me if you lose your appetite for the violence when you have been badly injured or seen someone badly hurt. The answer is quite simply no. I've seen a lad lose the sight of one eye, terrible glassing injuries, broken bones and a four-inch gash in the back of a friend's head caused by a machete. I've had countless injuries and witnessed merciless beatings. But you don't give your health a thought when it goes off. It is the survival of the fittest. Adrenaline takes over from the fear. Maybe I am unusual but I can honestly say I don't carry any fear when it kicks off at football. Fear to me is will my kids get on in life? Will the mortgage be paid or will I lose my job?

# THE COOL CATS
## 17 NOVEMBER 1984.

Manchester City had a good firm in the early to mid-Eighties. Their mob, the Cool Cats/Mayne Line Service Crew, had built up a tidy reputation in the hooligan underworld. Once in 1982, after travelling by train to Wigan, we had to change at Manchester from Victoria station to Piccadilly. Around 40 Sheff Utd boys had travelled that day and at Victoria we had our first encounter with City. They were into us as soon as we got off the train and although we managed to chase a few out of the station, we still had to get to the other side of the city centre. The bizzies gave us an escort through the back streets. I can't remember who City had played that day but they had a massive mob out. Three times they launched an attack on our escort. It was times like these when you took a liking to the boys in blue uniform. We were relieved to make the Sheffield-bound train still in one piece.

Two years later, we played City at home. Our firm was stronger now, our young casuals had a few years experience and our numbers had grown. Around 80 of us met in the Penny Black pub at midday. Stories were told of the Cool Cats' escapades. I never liked talking about the mob you were about to face. Too much talk leads to doubt. City didn't show in town, so at 2.15pm we headed for the ground and London Road. Some jumped on buses or took taxis, while I walked with about 50 others.

As we got nearer the ground we bumped straight into the City firm. About 70 Mayne Line boys were on the other side of the dual carriageway that led to St Mary's roundabout at the bottom of Bramall Lane. We ran across and leapt over the barrier and City ran at us. A top brawl kicked off. Usually in these fights one side can say they got on top but with this one no one budged. I remember seeing Sep, a young Blade, and thinking he was as game as they come, as he flew into them time and again.

The bizzies came and three United lads were arrested. I used to hate the fact that our bizzies always seemed to go for us and not the visiting fans. When we travelled away the local law were always on our case, not the home teams. I think the South Yorkshire force saw us as a complete pain in the arse and let visiting fans get away with a lot.

With 20 minutes to kick off, City were escorted the few hundred yards to the ground. We shadowed the escort, our numbers swelled as more lads joined us from London Road. City were shepherded into the queue for the away end on the corner of John Street and Bramall Lane. Our crew, now touching 150, walked by. Then, in a scene that wasn't to be repeated for years, everyone attacked the City crowd as they queued. City looked shocked that we had run into them despite a large police presence.

A well-built bald geezer chinned Toddy from behind, so I zapped him on the jaw. It was chaos: people were fighting in the packed streets with the bizzies not knowing which way to turn. Then, in a highly embarrassing scene, my dad grabbed me. He had clocked me performing and wasn't too pleased.

'Steven, what do you think you're playing at?' he said, whilst pulling me away from the trouble. 'Get in the ground before you get arrested.'

Right, dad.

It went off again, I lost my father in the crowds and ran back in. The police cordoned off John Street as a near-war had gone off. As we stood looking up John Street at the City boys, around 30 more City came up behind us. They were mainly blacks and it went off again. These boys were the bollocks. I've read Mickey Francis's book *Guvnors*, in which he says the Cool Cats, a mainly black and mixed-race gang, disbanded around 1983. Well Mickey, I think you're a year out, mate; these lads were no pussies (pardon the pun). Although the 30 City were well outnumbered they put on a good show.

We overpowered them and split them into two groups. Then this tall black guy with a big afro pulled a long cleaver out of his coat. He came at a few of us. His eyes were the devil's own, I swear. Swinging out wildly, he was nicked by three extremely nervous coppers.

During the match it went off in the John Street seats as around 30 City showed off. They didn't last long though as the John Street Stand contained 500 to 600 boys at big games. After the match it went off again, this time we had City on their toes. Later, at the train station, around 200 City tried to attack us as we walked by. Police on horseback and dog handlers kept the two sides apart. Afterwards in the boozer I thought about the return game at Maine Road and how we'd have to have a good firm out. This game could be murder.

Three coaches ferried over 150 boys to Maine Road on April 20. The plan was to get into Manchester City centre early, but as usual we didn't set off on time so we had a drink in Stockport. When we finally arrived in Manchester, we alighted not too far from the ground and walked the rest of the way. We passed a pub with a few boys outside. They looked shocked as we marched a small army past.

'Where's your firm?' a few of our lot shouted.

No answer was forthcoming. Around the corner the police spotted us, but we jogged up to the back of City's main stand. It was ten minutes to kick-off and City lads were everywhere. We charged at them and, outnumbered and not mobbed up, City backed off. Police on horseback charged us back and escorted us to the away end. Although it wasn't classed as a result, as we hadn't hit their mob head on, we were pleased to have bounced around and punched a few.

A couple of years later, City's firm became the Guvnors/Young Guvnors but never managed to carry off the reputation the Cool Cats/Mayne Line had created from 1978-85.

# THE SEAT SMASHERS ARRIVE: LEEDS AT HOME
## 23 MARCH 1985.

On the Friday night before the game against our Yorkshire rivals, Leeds United, I went out with 12 lads from Aston and Swallownest, two areas on the outskirts of Sheffield. We had a drink around

Sheffield city centre. Rumours did the rounds that the Service Crew would be about the night before the big derby game. Pockets of Sheffield United patrolled town and a large crew drank on London Road. Leeds didn't show and to be honest I did not expect them to. Late on we went into the Blue Ball on Campo Lane. Everything seemed fine until Matt came over and said, 'I think it's going to go off.'

I looked over his shoulder and it seemed that everyone in the place was staring at us. Then it registered: they thought we were Leeds. It must have been our casual clothes, the fact that four of us had Blades badges on had been missed by the 'townies'. As we drank up and headed outside even the bouncers eyeballed us.

'Outside if you want a pop,' shouted John as we left the boozer.

In the street, we spread out. Locals and bouncers started to surge out of the pub doors towards us. I punched someone with a beaut to the temple and he went down. Darren was going mental and even started making out we were Leeds fans: 'Come on, Sheffield.'

He ran into the doors as we backed our fellow city dwellers inside. A huge bouncer grabbed Darren and held him in a headlock. John and a couple of others had wrecked a fence for weapons and we ran in to rescue Darren. The bouncers got pounded with planks and Darren got away. We could hear the sound of police approaching fast, so we started a hasty retreat, then Darren ran back in again. He was 'on one' big time. The police screeched up and he was nicked. We were pointed out by bouncers but disappeared into the darkness of the back streets. Our bit of a 'to do' was a nice warm up for the expected battle next day.

The Leeds Service Crew – their name taken from the service trains they took to games in preference to the more heavily-policed 'special' trains – had built up a reputation as one of the country's most feared firms. The riot at their match with Chelsea in 1984 confirmed to hooligans that Leeds could mix it with the best. In Sheffield, however, they were seen in a different light. The common term for them was Seat Smashers or Football Vandals. Our boys argued that Leeds preferred to damage property and stadiums than to fight. I agreed with this up to a point. To me, it was obvious that Leeds had a decent crew but often let themselves down with wanton acts of vandalism, which proved nothing. A game at Odsal Stadium in 1986 summed it up. The tragic Bradford fire of the year before, which forced Bradford to play home games at Odsal, couldn't have meant much to the Leeds cavemen. They set fire to a chip van during the match. Television cameras caught the incident. Leeds had hit the headlines with nothing more than a Swan Vesta.

Blades distributed homemade leaflets around Sheffield, urging their fellows to have a welcome committee waiting. Leeds had not visited Bramall Lane since 1978 and this only added to the tension, as did our intrusion on Leeds city centre some five months earlier. Our firm had done something that not many other firms had managed, gone into Leeds and got a result.

On the morning of the game some 600 Blades gathered in two pubs on the High Street. I was praying Leeds would show. Then news filtered through that the Service Crew had just left Sheffield railway station. In the stampede that ensued, I managed to get in front of our hordes, stood on a van roof and took a photo of our mob. It would have made a fantastic cover for this book: unfortunately I burnt it along with my scrapbooks some years ago on Bonfire Night, for reasons I will explain later.

The rumour that Leeds had arrived proved to be just that. Police on foot and on horseback drove our reception committee back into the city centre. Most headed for London Road in the hope that Leeds might be near the ground. No such luck. After a few more beers, frustrated at Leeds no-show, we headed for the ground. It then kicked off outside the Bramall Lane End turnstiles. Around 80-100 Blades attacked hundreds of Leeds. At last we had found their boys and loads of them steamed in. Police broke up the fracas. Two Blades and a few Leeds were arrested.

In the ground we had three mobs, most in the John Street Stand and terrace. I sat in the South Stand, where we had around 200 boys. Another group stood on the Shoreham End. Leeds brought 8,000 fans; they were in the Bramall Lane seats and the terrace below. Around 200 Leeds were in the stand I was in, in the top left-hand corner surrounded by police. In a surge across the seats towards them, Daz, a 17-year-old Blade, fired a nautical distress flare. He should have known better as he was the one who was nicked the night before in our shenanigans with the townies. It hit the side of the stand and bounced back into the middle of the cheering Leeds lads. Police ran towards where the plume of smoke had emanated. The flare gun was thrown and landed right at my feet; as the police closed in I kicked it away. An old bloke grassed Daz up and he was later jailed for three months for his boatless SOS.

The ugly atmosphere sent tensions around Bramall Lane never seen before. When Leeds went 1-0 down, their fans lived up to image we had of them. Seats were thrown onto the pitch from the stand. Underneath, in the Bramall Lane terrace, loads of Leeds began scaling the fences. The 400 Blades on the John Street terrace, only 30 yards from the away end, did likewise. Police tried to keep both sets of fans at bay by hitting their hands with truncheons. One officer was carried away after being struck by a missile thrown by Blades in the terrace.

After half time both sets of fans settled down and stopped showing off. The game finished 2-1 to the Blades. Usually away fans are kept in the ground for around ten minutes but for some reason Leeds were allowed straight out. Both sets of fans fought battles all over the place. Our main group was split and I ended up with 30 of our boys. We bumped into around the same number of Leeds on Hill Street and a brawl developed. One Leeds lad was hit with a distress flare bullet fired by Perry. Police intervened. Then, as we grouped up at the bottom of London Road and headed towards town, it went off big time. Around 150 Leeds had broken away from the overworked police and reached the bottom of The Moor, a shopping precinct leading up to town. As around 100 of us, spread over 100 yards, headed into town a huge roar went up. Leeds poured around the corner outside the Moorfoot Tavern.

I was 20 yards from our front boys who were trying to repel the attack. I ran up and traded. The Moor was being repaired at the time, which meant Leeds were able to pick up ready-made weapons, such as the steel spikes that road workers stick in the ground to tape off an area. Buz, a mixed race Blade, was captured as Leeds backed us off. A few of us went to his aid and three distress flares were fired. This stopped our retreat and everyone steamed in. Leeds went for it again. Police came just in time as it was 'on top' for us. They chased both groups away. But for police intervention, we would have struggled. It went off again near

Sheffield station. The bizzies ran Leeds into the train station and us towards town.

An hour and a half after the final whistle, the battle was over. In various pubs we discussed the day's events. Sheffield United's hooligan element had turned a crew out in numbers never to be seen again (except at Wembley 1993, read later). Although we missed Leeds before the game, they had regained some face in the battle on the Moor. They wanted to know and gained some credit from our lads. The police had earned their money that day and I wondered what they told their wives as they put their feet up for a cup of tea and a ginger nut.

Yet events had not finished by a long way. Fifty Blades later attacked Wednesday in a town centre pub. Four lads needed the services of hospital casualty for wounds sustained by flying glass. Trouble between the two groups went on until midnight. A violent day if ever there was one. I reckon over the two games between Leeds and ourselves that season, our firm just about edged it, albeit in extra time.

# VIOLENT WEEKEND
# AT BRIGHTON
## 11 MAY 1985.

Most Blades looked for one thing when the fixture list was printed pre-season: a trip to the coast at the beginning or the end of the campaign. Over the years we have had some great nights out in places like Yarmouth (when playing Ipswich or Norwich), Bournemouth (Pompey), Blackpool and Weston-super-Mare (Bristol). This year the fixtures were again kind to us: our last away game was Brighton. A weekend trip was planned.

Thirty-five of our boys travelled by van and a few cars. We set off on Friday morning. Plenty more would travel down the following day but we wanted two nights on the beer. After we had sorted out our digs, we headed to a pub near the train station to meet some older Barmy Army Blades. Around 15 of them sat playing cards and smoking huge joints. They looked pleased to see us and we had a good crack with them. I reckon some of them saw us as hotheads, much in the same way as we saw them as beer heads that had slipped into semi-retirement from trouble.

After a few beers, we parted company and headed into town. The 30 or so we had out were a close-knit bunch, all from Sheffield and around 14 had all been to the same school in the United stronghold of Abbeydale. In truth, they were the core of United's hooligan element at the time. We all knew and trusted each other and were game to the core.

After frequenting a few bars, we ended up in a place with five stern-looking bouncers on the door. Our lot settled down at some tables and got the cards out (just for a change). It did my head in playing cards with the lads, they were all cheating bastards and the money they gambled and lost was stupid amongst mates. Five pounds blind, a tenner seen, on three card brag. I've seen more fall-outs over cards than anything else. Sam and I played the fruit machine, then I went to get some drinks. As I returned from the bar, I felt a sharp kick in my calf.

'Wanker.'

I turned round and six big ugly blokes were staring at me. The one who had kicked me stood a yard in front of his mates. I looked him up and down. He had a Lionel Ritchie perm, a pencil 'tash and a blue leather box jacket. I didn't know whether to punch him or dance with him. I have no idea why he kicked me but I wasn't going to discuss it with this Jackson Five reject. I placed the drinks back on the bar and steamed him. His mates took the unsurprising option of trying to kick me into the middle of next week.

Our lot were slow to respond, as I was out of sight, but Sam's shouting thankfully brought the cavalry to the rescue. The surly bouncers now waded in with the locals and a table, chair, glass and bottle brawl went off.

I went mental. These pricks had picked on the wrong geezers this time. We steamed them into the back of the pub, then beat a retreat before the bizzies arrived. Out on the street I realised my Armani jumper, which had been tied around my waist, had gone. I ran back into the bouncers who defended the doors. Vince launched a blackboard sign through the plate glass window and everyone ran in. Sam got my jumper back and we cleared off, job done.

Later, after doing all the usual blags like bandit fiddling and some tricky bar techniques, which involved getting back more change than you had actually paid, we headed toward the coastal bars. I have said before that United never carry weapons but quite a few took a liking around this time to nautical distress flares. They were a novelty and you could guarantee that, out of a mob of 50, around seven or eight would have flare guns. In some 'offs' it was like Bonfire Night, with the fiery red flares flying everywhere. The first time I saw one was when Birmingham's mob attacked the Blue Bell in Sheffield. We were all stunned. Soon our lot were into the novelty.

As we headed down a dark alleyway to the seafront we bumped into around 20 boys.

'Come 'ead, dickheads.' The accent was unmistakable. Scousers.

They attacked us. A flash of steel in the dimly lit street told me to keep a distance: I didn't fancy a 'scouse smile' for the rest of my life. Then, bang! bang! bang! Three distress flares dissected them, one hit a pub door and others flew over their heads. We ran in and they lost their bottle, turned and fled. One was caught and beaten to the ground. Mark tried shooting him at point blank range but thankfully the distress bullet was a dud. We found out they were Everton on return from a thieving session in Europe after their European Cup Winners' Cup Final.

By the end of the night we had split up and ten of us went in a pub that we had been told did after-bird. The locals didn't take a shine to us and I thought it would go off once again, but instead the locals had a tiff with each other and as it spilled into the street we went out to watch. The bizzies arrived and jumped on us. One of the lads had a distress flare in his hand and the cops got hold of it.

'What's this?'

'Dunno. I've just picked it up in there.'

The copper stood clicking it.

'It's some sort of gun, this.'

'Nah, it's just a pen or summat.'

A few of our lot were discretely dispersing their flares down their underpants in a panic.

'I'm keeping this and if I find out it's any kind of weapon you're in trouble.'

We departed. Two brawls in one night was enough and no arrests was a bonus.

The next day more Blades arrived, some having travelled through the night. Around 100 gathered in the bars around the train station. Older Blades told tales to younger lads of running battles with Arsenal and how it kicked off in a graveyard at Stoke. I liked to listen to stories from the older lads, there were some great characters amongst them: Irish, Sully, Herman, Frog, Dinky, Jasper, Martin, Wafer, Ronnie and Eight-Fingered Ray, all lads who were up for a laugh as well as a brawl. Pye-Eye sat reeling off a story with an eager group around him. I liked Pye-Eye, a good lad, game but mad as a hatter. I once saw him hit a Man City boy with a dog chain in Sheffield. Sadly Pye-Eye died years ago but I have fond memories of that sunken-jawed expression.

Kick-off time approached and the younger ones headed for the Goldstone Ground. We had not seen one opposing boy, so we didn't expect much trouble. Forty of us walked to the ground and went into seats opposite the away end. I sat down and bumped into a customer who came in the DIY merchants where I worked. We sat together discussing the rights and wrongs (mostly wrongs) of United, a club we both felt passionately about. Over 3,000 Sheffield had travelled, swelling the gate to 13,184, to watch a team which was basically useless. We deserved a better team than the one that finished the season in 18th place.

The casual fashion movement had by the end of the season gone into scruffy mode. I think it was the Mancs that started it off. It was more a music trend, with the indie scene beginning to stir. The football and music fashions interacted with each other: flared cords or jeans frayed at the bottom, old tweed jackets, checked Burberry or Aquascutum shirts, complete with the oldest pair of Adidas Gazelle graced many northern terraces. A few of our lot had a pattern embroidered on the bottom of their jeans, all very hip. It was a trampy look and didn't last long. The football hooligan looked more passive than ever; after all, who goes brawling in a tweed jacket?

The match was dire, 1-0 to them. Two Tottenham boys who sat with us during the game were punched and kicked by two dickhead Blades who had tagged along with us. This was considered out of order and we put them in their place. It is a tradition for United's fans to invade the pitch at the last home and away fixture in order to get the players' shirts. So as hundreds of Brighton fans invaded their pitch at the final whistle, the 40 of us ran on from the stand to try to grab a shirt from one of our useless 'heroes'. With Brighton fans all over, it was only a matter of time before the balloon went up. We stuck close together as it went off. We stood, then steamed into numbers which were five times ours and held our own. Bodies were falling to the floor as wild punches were traded. Everyone slugged it out, then they got around the back of us and we couldn't cope with the numbers. We backed up towards United's end. A flare was fired out of the travelling Blades, who were by now trying to scale the perimeter fences to help us out. We were cornered, with nowhere to go as the fence was too high to climb. So we stood, shoulder to shoulder, 40 lads against 232 Brighton (I know the exact number because a Blade took a brilliant photo from the away end and I counted them, sad really but there you go). What was interesting about the photo was the lack of police; only two were visible.

Nudge pulled the corner flag out and held it in front of him, a hooligan Sir Galahad. The flag was solid wood, not the bendy plastic ones used today. Brighton swarmed at us and more punches were exchanged. I grabbed the flag from Nudge: it was time to move these muppets along.

'Come on.'

I ran into them, slashing the flag furiously. They backed off and the shout went up. Everyone ran in. A great cheer rang out from our fellow Blades as we chased Brighton across the pitch. I was on one and continued past the halfway line. It was then I came to my senses. What the hell was I doing? I had a ground full of people watching me. As casually as possible in such a situation, I strolled over to a steward and handed him the flag.

'There you go, mate.'

The bizzies still hadn't got their act together at all and Brighton came back. I wished I still had the flag as it came on top again. The police eventually restored order and opened the gate to the away end. I was the hero of the hour.

'Fuckin' sound, Steve.'

All in a days work for a Blade. It went off again outside, and Blades vented their frustration at not being part of the action inside the ground by chasing Brighton all over the place. Our numbers swelled to around 150 as we walked back to Brighton station, showing off all the way. The bizzies got a bit heavy and let their dogs chew on our cords.

Later everyone met in a long seafront bar. The place was packed with 300 Blades. I went for a sports paper to check out the results. As I walked past an electrical store, I saw a TV relaying the news of a fire at Valley Parade, Bradford's ground. I went numb as it showed the stand ablaze. It really hit me when I thought of the women, children and old folk who wouldn't have stood a chance in all that. The copper who ran to put out the fire on an old man deserved a medal as big as a dustbin lid, as far as I'm concerned.

I relayed the news back at the pub. It was a sad day for football. No matter what people say about football hooligans, they still feel compassion, and for innocent people to die in such tragic circumstances is incomprehensible. Bradford, Heysel and Hillsborough all affected me in some way. The night was pretty sombre after that, until the police came into the pub in numbers. Why they did that I'll never know, there had been no suggestion of trouble. The atmosphere turned, everyone was hissing at the police and a few drinks were thrown at them. The night finished with around a dozen Blades clashing with Chelsea on the seafront. We ended up with 12 back at our room, the scroungers. I had paid for a room and ended up with Spenny's feet stuck in my face. I couldn't sleep with all the snoring and farting, so I found myself a bench on the sea front. I couldn't get the pictures of the Bradford fire out of my head.

Back in Sheffield on Monday evening, our local paper had a brilliant front page photo of us on the pitch at Brighton, bang at it, with the headline, 'BLADES IN RUNNING BATTLES'. I got a mention for my corner flag antics. Later, tee-shirts were printed with the picture from the Brighton game and cuttings from newspapers of the season's trouble. All the lads bought them.

Around a week after Brighton, the customer I had been sitting next to in the ground came to see me at work. 'God I couldn't believe it, I didn't think you were into all that,' he said excitedly. 'One minute you're sat in the stand with me, the next you're chasing everyone around the pitch.' He relayed the tale to a few of my work colleagues, which merely confirmed what they already thought, that I was radio rental.

# WELCOME TO THE BBC

SAD WEDNESDAY

SWFC V CHELSEA

HUNTED THEN
FRONTED

SHAME AT FRIENDLY
GAME

WEST BROM
ON THE RUN

RETURN TO
VIOLENCE:
THE ZULUS

NAMING OF THE BBC

HAMMERS IN THE CUP

WEDNESDAY BOTTLE
COCKNEY
CONFRONTATION

DONCASTER TOWN
CENTRE

POMPEY

VILLA PARK

MIDDLESBROUGH: THE
FRONTLINE

# SAD WEDNESDAY 1986

One of Sheffield Wednesday's top boys in the mid to late Eighties was a kid I'll refer to as Slimey. You'll see in what follows why he has copped for this name. Slimey was a stocky, well-built lad who was always causing bollocks. He was the type who would chin a Blade out with his girlfriend. I had several run-ins with him and once fronted him up on West Street when eight of us bumped into Wednesday.

About a week later, Kav and I were on one of our regular shopping trips. We were checking out a new clothes shop on Chapel Walk, a narrow shopping alleyway in Sheffield town centre. As we walked past a fruit shop where one of Wednesday's boys worked, we looked in. He saw us and looked away. After looking at clothes, we were walking back when we saw Slimey was outside the fruit shop talking to the aforementioned Wednesday boy. They didn't see us. We heard the Wednesday lad say to Slimey, 'He's just gone down there, Steve Cowens.'

'Yes I have,' I replied.

They both looked round, shocked. Kav stepped in front of me, walked right up to Slimey and said, 'Is your name Slimey?'

He bottled it and stammered, 'No.' Kav just looked at me and we both laughed as we walked away.

I expected some sort of reprisal for his loss of face and in February 1987 it was my Sunday football team that was targeted. It was a cold and wet morning. We had a crucial game away at Highcliffe. We needed to win to remain top of the table, while Highcliffe were in third place. I got changed and went to the pitch to warm up. Four of our team came out with me, including Holder and Batesy, two good mates who were also United hooligans. The rest stayed in the changing rooms until the last minute, as it was freezing. Our team was a mixture of mainly Blades, sprinkled with a few Pigs and a Leeds fan. We were all mates and football rivalries didn't come into it.

As I ran about trying to keep warm, I noticed five people walking briskly up towards the pitch. One was Slimey. The rest had scarves around their faces and hoods pulled over their heads. This didn't look good. I knew the score and shouted to my mates, 'I'll have Slimey, watch the rest.'

I headed straight for him. 'Come on then, dickhead.' I bounced over, arms outstretched. He fumbled in his black Crombie coat and pulled out a steel machete.

'You fuckin' divvy,' I screamed. 'One on one.'

The rest of them were closing in and I noticed a couple had bats and one a bottle. I ran at Slimey, who swung at me wildly with his weapon. One tried to do me from the side. I moved away and he slipped on the wet surface. I booted him. It was on top big time. No one came to my assistance, which shocked me. I was bouncing around, putting on a show, but they all came at me and I had to do one. At the side of the pitch was a cricket square, which was fenced off for the winter. I ran the 20 yards, pulled a four-foot rustic post out of the ground and turned on the five as they chased me. As I went towards them I could see them wavering.

'Come on, we're all tooled up now. Who wants it first?'

They stopped in their tracks and I went at them swinging the post. They backed off and then one threw a large Tizer bottle at me, which smashed on my knee. I went at them and they turned and ran. The lads with me now ran down and we chased them across the field. I nearly caught Slimey and swung the post. It would have taken his head off if I had connected. Some more of my team were now walking up and, on seeing what was happening, attacked the fleeing Pigs. My leg went numb and I slowed down. Blood ran down my shin from a two-inch gash just above the knee. The muscle had frayed and was protruding from my leg.

My dad had gone to fetch a ball from a farmer's field and had missed it all. As the lads stood around me, he came running over.

'What the hell's happened?'

'Nowt dad, I'm all right,' I replied, gazing down at my bloodsoaked leg. My dad knew that I was a bit of a thug and although he didn't approve of my activities he never really lectured me about it. Sometimes when he'd had a few too many gargles he'd talk as if he was quite proud of the fact that his son took no shit off anyone. He often retold a story of me dropping a huge centre half that had been bullying Griffy in a Sunday league game, so I suppose he was neither proud nor disgusted at the way I was.

I knew I had got to go to hospital and told the lads to get the points. At casualty I sat, still in my football kit, freezing. I could not stop thinking what a divvy, dirty stunt they had pulled. We meet them on the street and they run off, then they resort to these tactics. Feuds and problems stemming from football should be left on the streets, not brought to people's homes, work places or leisure pursuits. I never did the 'dirty' back, not even when I found out who threw the bottle. I got to know where he worked, lived and the way he walked home but left my arguments for the streets. Time was on my side. I knew I would catch up with him one day, and I did.

I vowed to find out the names of the faces behind the Burberry scarves. As I sat in hospital, all of the team came in. I was disappointed that some of my best mates had left me to it with five tooled-up lads. Holder, one of the gamest kids going, looked at me. Sorry, his expression said. He knew I would have been there for him. He explained later that he had just frozen and didn't know why. It was a one-off for him, as he continued to be the Holder I knew, first in and game as a pebble.

I eventually found out the names of all the Wednesday boys who attacked me. Tizer man killed himself a few years ago because of drug problems. Another was a lad I had been out drinking with before. I couldn't understand it. When I caught up with him, he told me that Slimey had promised him it would be a one-on-one. He regretted the incident but I chinned him anyway.

As for Slimey, six months later 40 BBC were out in town. Kav and I were walking ahead of the boys towards London Road. As we approached the top of The Moor, we saw a familiar figure approaching. It was Slimey, all suited and booted. I offered to fight him one-on-one. He didn't want to know, making some sorry excuse about being out with his workmates. It was a different story when I was trying to play football and he came across the field brandishing a machete like Attila the Hun.

As we were arguing, the rest of the lads arrived. Slimey looked at me and said, 'I'm going to get it, aren't I?'

'No, it's me and you.'

There was no love lost, as all our lot knew and disliked him. One of our boys tried to punch him. I, like a fool, tried to hold them off. I should have let them all fill him in, and joined in, but I hated situations like this. The BBC would have been classed as bullies and I didn't want that.

Tricky wanted Slimey bad, so I knew my fight with Slimey had to be put on hold as Tricky steamed in. I shouted to our lot

'One on one.'

Tricky rolled around on the floor and got the better of Slimey, who called out that he'd had enough. We intervened and pulled Tricky away. Slimey disappeared into the night, kicking a shop window in as he sulked off. I would have considered myself extremely lucky to escape so lightly, but then again I didn't want to drag us down to Wednesday's level.

I saw a few Wednesday weeks later and they told me Slimey couldn't believe that I ended up helping him out. Yet the next time I saw him, he tried to take my head off with a brick as Blades and Wednesday clashed. That's gratitude for you.

# SWFC V CHELSEA

Despite my dislike for all things blue and white, one of the best games of football I have seen was at Hillsborough. Chelsea were the visitors for a League Cup tie in 1986 and I had somehow got hold of two tickets. Now usually I wouldn't set foot in the sty, except to see the Blades. But Kav and I decided to go along to see Chelsea's firm – probably the biggest in England at that time – firsthand. The cold, drizzly evening, plus the fact that our tickets were for the North Stand, a place that left you to the mercy of the elements, saw me take along my red, white and black United golfing umbrella complete with club crest.

The North Stand was next to the Leppings Lane end that contained away supporters. Wednesday's mob used to situate themselves in this area. I thought we might get a bit of nonsense, as I was bang at it with Wednesday at the time. Kav and I knew each other inside out and neither of us would budge from each other's side if it came on top. As we took our seats near the front, Wednesday's mob filled the seats behind us. Around ten minutes before the match was due to start, we stood talking to Titch, a Blades hooligan, and his best mate Tinny, a Wednesday boy. I knew Tinny well and had a lot of time for him. I had stuck my neck out for him when he travelled with the Blades to Man City a few years previously: some Rotherham Blades wanted to shovel him in for his Wednesday allegiance. Tinny often travelled with United's core hooligans to games, as he explained that he was more likely to get a ruck and a rob with our lot than Wednesday. However, he remained fiercely Wednesday, this fact backed up by the daft parrot tattooed on his arm. Tinny in turn, saved me from a bad one at Barnsley once. We had gone on the Barnsley end and, as the 30 of us worked our way through the crowd, Tinny was about five lads back from me. Our human snake of hooligans tried to get to the back of their mob. The plan was to get everyone together then steam them but some idiot shouted 'Sheffield' before we had got through the crowd. A large gap opened up and I ran into them, fists flashing. It was like jumping into a human Venus flytrap as they closed around me and I suffered a bit of a ragging. Tinny came to my aid and battled at my side, so we developed a friendship despite the red-blue divide.

As we chatted just before the match kicked off, a red distress flare was fired into the air from behind Wednesday's mob. Chelsea had got into the seats 80-strong and that was their signal to steam in. As the Headhunters came across the seats at them, Wednesday boys fell over themselves in the panic to get out of the way and onto the pitch perimeter.

Me, Kav, Titch and Tinny headed towards Chelsea. We fronted them with a handful more Wednesday boys. Chelsea just stood there like the cat that got the cream. They had taken out a firm with hardly a punch thrown. I swung my brolly at a black geezer whose face was so contorted with aggression that I thought he'd explode.

'You're shit, Wednesday,' one screamed.

'We're not Wednesday. Come on.'

Kav went towards them. Police came in and surrounded Chelsea. I put my brolly up to show them my true colours. It was embarrassing that Wednesday represented Sheffield and were all over the pitch, only returning to their seats once police had moved in. Chelsea were taken to the away end and at half-time we had a chat with a few of their boys through the fencing. Sheffield United hadn't played Chelsea for years so we had not had the chance to do battle. We told them what a good firm we had and that they wouldn't be able to take the piss with us.

The game was great. Wednesday led 3-0 before a tremendous Chelsea fight back saw them take the lead 4-3, only for Doug Rougvie to trip local Wednesday hero Mel Sterland in the last minute to concede a converted penalty. It ended 4-4. Chelsea went through in the replay.

# HUNTED THEN FRONTED

A ruck with some black guys who associated themselves with the Wednesday firm turned into a nightmare for me. One Saturday evening 10 young United boys, myself included, had been drinking in our usual haunts on London Road. We always had the last couple of sherbets in the Lansdowne. Inside, we were surprised to see three black and three white lads who had links with Wednesday. The blacks guys were well known to us and their reputations went before them. It was obvious from the start they were out to cause some bollocks and bollocks is what they got. Yifter, an older Blade, had been challenged to a fight by one of the said blacks. He took up the challenge and as everyone went outside, more threats were made towards us. I was last out and there was a bit of a stand off, with both sets squaring up and offering threats. I ran towards them and, bang, one was out for the count. The lot went up and although the intruders were outnumbered they had a right pop. One was shot point blank with a distress flare. He reeled back and everyone steamed him. To cut it short, four were left unconscious and taken away by ambulances.

I knew there would be repercussions. I also knew that my name would be top of their hit list. Two weeks later, ten blacks went up to two Blades, informing them that Cowens and a lad called Lowie were dead meat. For the next year, they tried to find me. I never hid or stopped doing the things I always did. I drank in the same pubs. It was going to come on top for me, but I wasn't going to run. I had too much pride.

Then one day, I found them. United had played Huddersfield away and we returned in high spirits after chasing Huddersfield's firm. Back in Sheffield we met up in the Penny Black. After a drink, our lads started to drift up town. I was about to go when Eyes came over.

'Steve, I'd fuck off if I was you. Harrison's in and he's asking who you are. I've told him you're not here.' Eyes knew Harrison well. He was one of the hospitalised blacks from our fracas on London Road.

'Cheers, Eyes. I'll get off.' I had no intention of going now. I went in to the other side of the bar and got another pint. Once all our lads had moved on, I walked through and sat next to

Harrison, who was chatting with Eyes. I had deliberately let all our lot go: I wasn't one of these 'mob behind me' boys. Eyes looked at me 'gone out' as I interrupted their conversation.

'All right mate?'

I looked at Harrison. He was six foot three and a very handy lad. He half smiled and continued to chat to Eyes, then turned to me.

'Had a good ruck, then?'

'Yeah not bad. They didn't have much of a pop though.'

We chatted and he stared at the enamel BBC badge attached to my Diesel duffle coat. Then it came out.

'What's your name then?'

Eyes looked uneasy, as he'd told Harrison I wasn't around.

'Steve Cowens.'

'Cowens! You're Cowens?'

He jumped up. 'Fuckin' outside,' he demanded.

'Look, I knew you were here for me so I've come over and I'm not going outside.'

He sat back down looking a bit stunned.

'You cheeky bastard,' he said, then informed me that his mate Macka was going to rip me to bits when he caught up with me. Macka was another of the blacks beaten unconscious in the fight earlier.

'Tell Macka we've drawn your team in a cup game and play you in two weeks, so he can see me then.' My football team had drawn the Earl George in a Sunday cup competition. They were well known in Sheffield not for their footballing abilities but for terrifying teams into defeat. I ended up having a couple of beers with Harrison. I think he admired my front. Sheffield is no doubt different to many other cities around the country. Although the people we had hurt were serious players in our city, they also sorted out their problems at street level. In Manchester, Liverpool or Glasgow, this kind of dispute could lead to your door being kicked in or even guns being used. Sheffield is, and I hope remains, a city where that level of payback is very rare indeed.

Two weeks later, the cup game arrived. Most of our team were Blades and three or four were boys. I had broken my right hand in a fight in town a week earlier, but I was determined to play so I wasn't seen as bottling it. I tapped cotton wool around the pot and showed the referee, who passed it. The game was at

11 am. At 10.55, no opponents had arrived. I joked to my uneasy team mates that they'd bottled it as we ran about the pitch trying to keep warm. Then, eight cars came screeching into the leisure centre car park. Around 25 geezers, mostly blacks, came storming up to the pitch. Accompanying the posse were a Rottweiler and a couple of Staffies.

A huge black guy who ran all the bouncers in Sheffield barked out, 'Which one's Cowens?'

I put one hand on my stomach and one behind my back then bowed towards them. Many of them stood, staring at me.

After they had got changed, the game kicked off. My mate Macka was playing in central midfield, the area where I was on patrol. I was determined not to be intimidated as I copped for the verbals, so the first challenge with Macka, a header, I went in full steam. He threw an arm out as I clattered him, heading the ball way back into their half. The game finished 4-0 to us and I was pretty surprised how many of them came and shook my hand at the end of the game. I thought it would come on top at this point, but nothing. Macka headed over to me and stuck out his hand. I shook it with my plaster cast. I was relieved that Macka had respect for me; I had plenty of respect for him.

We got changed in a small wooden outbuilding. Their room was next to ours. Most of our lot were dressed and gone in record time. Shotgun and me were sat in our pants when Mitch threw an air-bomb at their changing room. An almighty bang nearly blew the roof off the hut. Shotgun and me looked at each other as they went shit-pot crazy next door. Then angry lads came steaming round.

'Who the fuck did that?' one screamed. I got up and pointed at Mitch as he disappeared into the distance.

'That's him there. Him who's just broke the hundred-metre sprint record.'

A few laughed and after nearly two years the ice had been broken. I know all of them now and have a beer with a few if I see them in town. Macka was one of the gamest boys ever. A few years later, I saved him from a bad beating when he stood on his own after Wednesday had disappeared in a major ruck. All of them have since stopped running with Wednesday's mob.

# SHAME AT FRIENDLY GAME
## 6 MAY 1986.

The lowest I've ever felt at being run by a football firm was undoubtedly after Tony Kenworthy's testimonial at Bramall Lane. Any football thug who says he's never been run, or never been put on his arse, is either lying or he's seen nothing. I have been run and I have been dropped, even knocked clean out once. That's the way you play the game: give some, take some. But sometimes getting seen off is harder to take.

The testimonial for Kenworthy, who had come through our youth system and played for United for 12 years, was against Wednesday. Even testimonials and benefit games were a good enough excuse for the rival firms to have a *tête à tête*, such was the rivalry between them. In the years prior to this game we had had Wednesday off on numerous occasions, so we were confident. It never entered our heads that we'd end up on the back foot.

Neither of our firms went to the game in large numbers and the crowd was only 6,822. At the end of the game, United's fans invaded the pitch. I got Kenworthy's shirt and was pleased as punch as I tucked it into my Barbour jacket. Then I headed to the Lansdowne pub, from where 70 of us set off for town. There seemed to be a lot of 'divs' in the mob but we still had 35 good lads, enough to take care of business.

To avoid the police we took the quiet back streets and came into town past Henry's Wine Bar. We bumped straight into Wednesday, who had a decent firm out, perhaps the same numbers as we had. The usual pre-brawl roar went up and we ran at them. They backed off a little as punches were exchanged. I saw one leading Wednesday boy brandishing a knife in front of him. Hilly was fronting him up, calling him a wanker. A distress flare was fired at Wednesday, who by now looked as if they were ready for off. I was at one side of the brawl when I realised that only our 'faces' were doing the business while all the passengers we had with us were 20 yards back up the street, just prancing around and shouting. Why they had come along is beyond me.

A five-yard gap had opened up between the two warring factions, then Wednesday had a charge, United's lads started backing away whilst shouting, 'Stand'. This was too much for the pretend boys, who turned and legged it. I was still on one side as Wednesday chased United. Herman an older Barmy Army top boy from the Seventies, stood on his own. He got a bit of a ragging from Wednesday's vultures, until me, Hilly and Frankie ran to his aid. Herman was furious.

'That's it, I'm never turning out again, when we run from them dickheads it's time to pack in,' he mumbled as he walked off in disgust. He was as good as his word and was not seen out again with our mob.

Hilly, Frankie and myself ran up behind the Wednesday, who had run by us. We could hear the sound of more brawling as United tried to get themselves together. When we reached the end of the road, around six of Wednesday's boys came into view.

'Come on, these here,' I said.

I wanted to hit someone. We ran at them. Flem, a mixed race Wednesday boy, dipped in his pocket to pull a knife out. I fronted him. Hilly knew him well and ordered him to put the blade away, which he did. I ran at him and he backed off. Lewis, a tall Wednesday dresser, fronted me. I punched him with a decent shot causing him to stumble back. I went at them again and they ran. That was the end of the night's hostilities. Despite our minor victory at the end, I went home totally dejected. To show you how important it was to me at the time, I couldn't sleep that night, such was my despair. I vowed it would never happen again.

A young United fan was slashed that night in the fracas and six arrests were made.

# WEST BROM ON THE RUN
## 22 AUGUST 1986.

The first game of the 1986-87 season saw a 1-1 draw with Shrewsbury at Bramall Lane. Our next fixture was West Brom away. West Brom aren't exactly in everyone's top ten hooligan-wise but our night match at the Hawthorns saw our coach overloaded with 65 boys. Our driver, Hammer, used to do a bit with the boys and didn't care about the extra passengers.

We alighted the coach bang outside their kop and, in a spontaneous decision, we went in. Going on the opposition's kop had been a hooligan trend in the early Seventies but had died out within a few years. That's probably why the police didn't even bother us as we queued. West Brom fans knew the score, however, and looked on as we filed through the turnstiles. In a queue adjacent to mine, a total 'plank' was looking at me, dipping his hand in his jacket pocket and nodding, that old I've-got-a-concealed-blade chestnut.

'Wait through there, ya muppet,' I said and pointed through the turnstile as he entered just before me.

Surprise, surprise, when I got through he'd disappeared up his own arse and was nowhere to be seen. We waited just inside and got everyone together, as it was obvious our intrusion had been sussed. We got onto the kop without any problems and filed to the back, which meant they had to come up at us. It kicked off straight away as 'Sheffield' was chanted to let them know we had arrived. They were no match for us as everyone steamed in, in a heaving mass of flailing fists and bodies. West Brom got legged down their kop and, as panic set in, loads of their fans spilled onto the pitch. It came on top for me at that stage, as a few Brom boys had got behind us. I sussed the situation and went up towards them. Then it kicked off again at the other side of our firm. The main bulk of our lot ran in. This left a few of us to face these sneaky bastards behind us. They ran into us, we stood as a mass of arms and legs traded blows and I copped a few punches. We stood firm, then Morksy and more of our lot came up to help and we ran them along the top of their kop.

The police came in numbers and rounded us up. At first they were going to walk us round the pitch to the away end, which would have been a good pose, but they decided to take us out of the ground. They then made us pay again to watch the game. It's bad enough having to pay to watch United once.

Three United boys were arrested and charged with threatening behaviour.

# RETURN TO VIOLENCE: THE ZULUS 6 SEPTEMBER 1986.

I had started to play football on Saturdays with a semi-professional side. My uncle used to play for Wednesday and, after watching me play on Sunday mornings, decided I was wasting my talent.

He persuaded me to try out for Crookes FC, who played in the Central Midlands League. I went along for training, then played in a trial match. Two Man City scouts were there watching one of our players. I played like a demon and scored the winner with a bullet header in a 1-0 victory. After the match I signed for Crookes, picked up my club jumper and tie and was told I would be in the squad to play Heanor Town on Saturday. I would be paid £25 for a win and £15 for a draw or loss.

I felt like a pro when we set off on the coach that Saturday morning. It would keep me out of trouble, I thought. But after only five games – including one where a certain Gary Crosby, who later signed for Nottingham Forest, gave me the runaround at Lincoln – I was missing the buzz with the boys. They had been to Leeds and had a good ruck on a stretch of grass known as Ambush Park and I was gutted to have missed it. My addiction to the whole scene was total.

The final nail in the coffin came with a visit from Birmingham City. Our lot were meeting in the Penny Black in Pond Street near Sheffield train station. I popped in early to have a quick drink before going to play football. I had just arrived when Nudger shouted that Birmingham had left the station and were heading into town. It was early and only 30 Sheffield had arrived. Nevertheless, they went to meet Birmingham head-on. I followed from a distance. I had my club tie on and was carrying the essential item at the time, a Head bag containing my 'togger' stuff.

Inevitably, it went off. Birmingham had the numbers and, as our lot tried to stand and trade, my mate Nudger was smashed to the floor. I lost it and ran through, swinging my Head bag around. It was a useless weapon but I couldn't just drop it. Police arrived just in the nick of time. We would have been battered, no doubt.

I still played football that day but my mind was elsewhere. All I could think about was the lads at war with Brum. Football violence is addictive and the buzz had caught hold of me again.

# THE NAMING OF THE BBC
## SEPTEMBER 1986.

Another testimonial at Hillsborough had been arranged for that September. The evening game was just another excuse for us to have a ruck. Sixty United lads turned out and, acting on a tip-off, we headed to a pub which we knew Wednesday were in. After our previous encounter, I was in a determined mood.

'No one runs tonight boys. If they do, they'll be remembered,' I told our firm.

To our dismay, Wednesday had left before we arrived at the pub. With them at the game, all we could do was sit and wait. Quite a few of our lot drifted back into town leaving 40 hardcore boys in a pub around one and a half miles from Hillsborough. While we were there, that something happened that was thankfully never repeated. Two lads went to a filling station and made two petrol bombs. This wasn't a Blades thing: we were strictly fists 'n' style. I wasn't happy.

The police came in and politely told us to 'fuck off or you're nicked'. We headed into the city centre and waited on the route we knew Wednesday would walk. The 40 of us hid in a quiet alleyway, smashing the streetlights so we were in darkness. Nevertheless, when Wednesday's firm of around 70 boys finally approached, we were rumbled by one of their lads walking ahead of them. A couple of police vans then approached and chased us into town.

We managed to keep together, then bumped straight into Wednesday on High Street. The two petrol bombs were thrown but thankfully did not explode as Wednesday ran. And a new chant rang through the city streets:

'BBC! BBC!'

The name BBC – short for Blades Business Crew – had finally been adopted. Most football gangs by now had names, oftened shortened to their initials: the DLF (Derby Lunatic Fringe), the LTE (Lincoln Transit Elite), the ICF (Inter City Firm), and so on. Around six months earlier, 12 United lads, including myself, had sat around a table in a pub on London Road and discussed what to call our crew. The name Blades Business Crew had actually been mooted before and BBC had been shouted in three previous fights. Others, however, preferred alternative names: the Blades Firm Force, Sheffield United Tricky Crew, H Block, and Bulldog Blades were all put forward. Finally, though, we settled on the BBC. Some of the crew had calling cards made up: 'Congratulations, you have just been tuned in by the BBC.' I had 280 enamel badges made with the Yorkshire Rose replaced by a skull's head placed above the two swords of the club crest. It looked pretty good. To be honest, I sold them to anybody who had £1.50 and made a few hundred quid.

Wednesday, too, got in on the act and the name Owls Crime Squad was made up by one of their boys I know well. It was actually adopted from the initials of Ocean Cleaning Services, a firm that has quite a few vans driving around with OCS written on the side, though of course they knew nothing about it.

# HAMMERS IN THE CUP
## 9 FEBRUARY 1987.

With the help of Nudger, I ran two coaches to the FA Cup fourth-round tie at West Ham. It was an evening game but our crew turned out in numbers; in fact so many turned up it was chaotic trying to sort out who would travel. I tried to make sure all our top boys got seats but some were left and another coach was hired. In all, five 'unofficial' coaches went, three of them with boys on.

We rendezvoused in a pub about four miles from Upton Park and decided to continue to the ground by tube. Around 150 boarded at Wanstead while the rest stayed behind drinking. I sensed an air of apprehension as our firm sat on the rocking train. I don't know what it is but I never feel at ease on the London tubes. A lot of northern people feel the same. I walked up and down the aisles, telling all who would listen that we were going to run one of the best firms in England. 'I'm going straight in, this is what sorts the men out from the boys.' I was trying to put people at ease, as everyone sat there staring out of the windows into the darkness.

A few West Ham got on at the next stop and started smirking and taking the piss. If we had let these mingle in when we stopped at Upton Park, we'd be in trouble. So as we alighted we punched a couple to let them know we meant business. Around 30 of our top boys headed up the stairs. Me, Titch and Sep were fronting. 'Just get into them early and everyone will be all right,' I said.

Our mob's mood changed dramatically as we piled out of the station into the main road, giving it, 'BBC, BBC.' Ten or so West Ham black lads across the road were scattered. However, the Met were onto us quickly. Within 60 seconds, West Ham had produced a large firm. They were amazed we'd had the front to come on their manor and tried to get at us but police horses and dog handlers reinforced the escort. We had got 30 good lads at the back and 30 at the front. West Ham always try to infiltrate these areas. I strutted at the front of the escort; it was a good pose. Although not much had happened, we had gone down to West Ham and walked a firm through their main area. We had put on a show and sometimes that's all that happened at football, it's all about showing face. I have got a lot of respect for West Ham, they're a tough mob and a close-knit group, as most of their Inter City Firm come from in and around the East End.

We got to the ground without further trouble. At half time, punches were thrown at each other through a small segregation gate by the away-end toilets. A minibus-load of Blades were banging on the gates outside. We could hear them and they sounded quite distressed. They had been fighting and quite a few had been badly beaten, but the police just ignored them. The game finished 4-0 to West Ham and there was no further trouble apart from another minibus of Blades who kept jumping out of their van as it moved through the traffic and chasing West Ham stragglers, until the Met arrested a couple of them who were carrying bats. It was the first and last time I ran a coach: there was money to be earned but the hassle wasn't worth it.

# WEDNESDAY BOTTLE
## COCKNEY CONFRONTATION
### 21 FEBRUARY 1987.

Wednesday's home fixture with West Ham coincided with Plymouth's visit to beautiful downtown Bramall Lane. The police let both games go ahead, probably due to the low security risk of United's visitors. No arrangements had been made among United's boys for the Londoners, as West Ham were seen as Wednesday's problem, not ours. However, we arranged to meet up after the game in the Penny Black, knowing West Ham would have to walk through Pond Street to get to Sheffield train station. It was a chance to have a pop at the infamous ICF.

With Plymouth a non-event on the hooligan calendar, I drove to town around midday to see if West Ham had arrived. I knew a few of our lot would be in the Dodgers pub close to Sheffield station, so I popped in for a Coke. In the Dodgers sat 12 to 15 Blades, so I went for a drive around to see what was happening. As I drove along Arundel Gate, I saw a group of 120 boys. They were heading away from town. It was Wednesday's firm. Alarm bells rang in my head. It was pretty clear that they were on a Blade hunt and London Road was their port of call. It was only just turned midday and Wednesday knew no United firm would be around in numbers. To me, it was a cop out to avoid West Ham.

I tracked Wednesday as they got to the bottom of London Road, then sped around to the back of the Lansdowne pub, our boozer at the time. Raggy was in a corner on his own, pint in hand, reading the paper. I grabbed him and we just got out of the back doors as Wednesday came in the front. We both jumped in the car and headed back to the Dodgers in town. Only a handful more Blades had turned out. I explained to the boys that Wednesday were on London Road in numbers. The odds against us were overwhelming but I argued with other Blades that we had to turn up, as they were on our patch. Bear had the idea of parking at the Sheaf pub and walking the short distance to London Road. We did just that. As we approached London Road from a side street, the landlord of the Pheasant, another pub we frequented, was at the doors nodding his head up the road. His body language told us Wednesday were heading straight for us.

'Stick together and we'll be all right, start running and we'll get battered,' I said, trying to get every one of the 23 Blades to defend our manor. I ran onto the petrol station and emptied the sand out of a heavy steel bucket. Someone else got a fire extinguisher. I zipped up my hood and led our lot around the corner. Wednesday were only ten to 15 yards away as we ran at them. They were taken by surprise. I charged in, swinging the bucket around wildly. Everyone else piled in and we backed Wednesday away. Our numbers didn't matter as Wednesday didn't know how many more would be coming around the corner. A few of our lot were bluffing, pretending to beckon invisible Blades from the road.

Wednesday came back at us, bricks and bottles rained down and one of our boys copped one straight in the face. I stood but it was bang on top. A few got around my side and I was in that bad situation where, had I tried to run, I would have been caught, but if I stood much longer I would be done for. I threw the bucket to give myself a yard, then turned and ran. Someone clipped my legs. I stumbled and then hit one as he tried to grab me. Our lot were legging it down London Road.

'OCS,' the Pigs chanted as they gleefully chased us.

Our lot ran into the Lansdowne and were immediately issued with bats and pool cues from the landlord standing by the door. Howie and I ran around the back and loaded up with rocks as Wednesday smashed the pub windows. An old man in the pub was hospitalised as the windows crashed in on him. Our lot were beating Wednesday back from the doors as me and Howie launched a two-man assault by hurling our stones at the Wednesday masses. A police van arrived, followed by more officers and Wednesday were escorted away. Insults were exchanged over railings. I spotted a Wednesday lad I knew.

'What was that all about? West Ham too big for you?'

'Cowens, you're shit,' one of their main boys shouted back.

'What does that make you, you mug?'

Meanwhile West Ham had been all over town, unchallenged. Perhaps Wednesday's showing up in the television documentary on the ICF had put them off. In the 1985 documentary *Hooligan*, 30 Wednesday boys gathered on High Street in Sheffield were shown turning on their heels at the sight of one black ICF youth and a few of the Londoners' youngsters, known to their colleagues as the Under Fives.

'Sheffield Wednesday came towards us, a few of us jumped over the fence and they just ran,' was how one of the West Ham lads summed it up to camera. The narrator of the documentary went on, 'Disappointed by the feeble opposition, they head for the match.'

'Just mugs,' was how another paisley shirt-wearing Londoner described Wednesday.

The programme was a talking point for hooligans around the country for weeks. Some of West Ham's lads were proper characters, who came out with their own analysis of what hooliganism could encompass, although I took exception to the baby-faced Lacoste boy who claimed, 'Northerners wear the same clothes but don't carry it off as well as us, they always look scruffy.'

Casual's the word mate; he was one to talk, complete with a Bee Gees haircut.

After the match against Plymouth, word went round for the BBC to mob up, but with only 6,982 in the crowd we did not have a good firm. Those that had turned out gathered outside the Lansdowne, then walked to the Penny Black. Wednesday were nowhere to be seen. A few West Ham were about but we left them. Around 70 Blades had assembled, but only 35 to 40 were boys to be trusted in a major off. I went for a drink with a geezer I hadn't seen for ages.

Word came that Wednesday were in the Yorkshireman pub. It was a strange place for them to be, on a quiet back street at the top end of town. All 70 Blades headed over. They sent 15 good lads up to try to get Wednesday onto the street so they could fight without having to attack the pub. The rest of United's crew got twitchy while hidden in the inappropriately named Peace Gardens. As the small group of Blades shouted and bounced around outside the pub trying to get Wednesday out, everyone got too eager and charged up. An attack on the pub took place for some five minutes in which all the windows went in and the double doors were ripped off their hinges. Wednesday threw glasses and other objects out. Most of the Blades got fed up and had started to wander off by the time the police arrived. Four Blades and one Wednesday were arrested.

A week later, a coachload of Blades was stopped on the Sheffield Parkway on its way to Grimsby. Four more Blades were arrested for the Yorkshireman incident, including me. After being fingerprinted, photographed and interviewed, I was released without charge six hours later. I joked with our boys that I had sung like a canary in the cells.

The cops had done me a favour by pulling me in, as Grimsby turned out to be a bad day all round. After a drinking session in Cleethorpes, the lads had headed for Grimsby's ground and chased some of their boys. One of them ran into a tree and knocked himself unconscious. He was rushed to hospital. The police arrested everyone on the coach. The charge was going to be bad one, possibly manslaughter, the police said. The Grimsby youth came out of his semi coma an hour later. All credit to him: when the police informed him they had everyone locked up for his assault, he pissed on their bonfire by telling them what had really happened and said he was going home. Good effort mate!

# DONCASTER TOWN CENTRE
## 20 APRIL 1987.

While returning by train from a game at Hull – where we had run the Hull City Psychos during the day – we stopped off at Doncaster. It was a spontaneous decision and a good crew of around 60 entered the town centre. The first pub, opposite the Frenchgate shopping centre, was half empty. A few black youths were in, looking very uneasy. Around seven or eight of our lot were black; race and colour never came into it with our boys, a Blade was a Blade. They got talking to the Doncaster blacks, who explained they were always having trouble with the Donny Whites, a large group of Leeds fans from the Doncaster area. Leeds were a very racist crew. We drank up and headed deeper into town.

We ended up in a boozer near the markets at the bottom end of town. We had clocked a few lads monitoring our movements but ignored them, as we had a big crew which included most of our main actors. Everyone was chatting and playing pool when a cry of 'Leeds, Leeds, Leeds' went up.

Me and Sep were nearest the door as they came down the entrance towards us. We slung our drinks at them, Sep picked up a stool and we steamed in. The pub echoed with the chant, 'BBC, BBC.'

They backed out into the street. In the scramble to get into them Sep threw the stool, then we jumped over it and ran into the street, trading punches. We then realised the stool had wedged the door and only the two of us had got out. We were chased down the road for 20 yards before they stopped and concentrated their efforts on the pub doorway. Sep and myself looked back up the road. Fifty Leeds were trying to steam the doors. I didn't expect our lot to get out, as it is difficult in a situation like that and the first few through the door usually end up in casualty.

A roar went up. Pool balls, glasses and bottles were hurled at Leeds and created enough room around the doors for everyone to steam out. We ran back up as our boys poured out and a full-scale battle erupted in the street. Leeds backed away, then ran. A few got a beating but the bizzies were there in minutes. Two of the Leeds boys ran to a cop van to seek refuge but were kicked and punched right under the bizzies' noses. One Blade was arrested but gave the usual load of bullshit, anything to get let off. 'We've just been attacked by them bastards,' he pleaded.

It kicked off again an hour later near the market stalls as our boys chased their prey. We were eventually rounded up and escorted back to the train station. A chant went up that echoed round the near deserted streets. It was the first airing of a song that became well-known in Sheffield pubs:

> *Fight, fight, wherever you may be*
> *We are the firm from the steel city*
> *And we'll fight you all, wherever you may be*
> *Coz we are the famous BBC*

Like soldiers returning after victory in battle, we marched back to the station. That was when the bizzies decided they had had enough and took liberties. As we were escorted through the Frenchgate centre, they started pushing us and kicking the backs of our legs. A few were bitten by police dogs. It seemed our black lads were singled out and given a real hard time. As we got to the other end of the Frenchgate centre, which leads out to the train station, Kirky, a mixed race lad, was pushed. A scuffle between the police and us began and truncheons were drawn. I'll never forget what happened next. A bizzy cracked Kirky over the head so hard that the truncheon broke in half and rolled across the marble floor. Everyone went nuts. Kirky was out of it, slumped unconscious with blood running down his clock. We tried to get the copper's number and pick up the broken piece of truncheon from the floor. Quite a few were nicked, including Kirky, who needed 12 stitches in his head.

In court the usual happened, the police won the day. Kirky and a few others were found guilty and no action was taken against the officer. Kirky got 80 hours community service.

# POMPEY                    9 MAY 1987.

The last game of the 1986-87 season was Portsmouth away. They had won promotion and the game was irrelevant to both teams.

Kav hired a large van and we planned to make a weekend of it. Bournemouth, an altogether more salubrious stop then Portsmouth, was our destination and 20 of us set off on Friday morning. More of our lot were heading down the same day in cars, and more travelling down the next day.

Diehard football fans will be familiar with the tedium of these long journeys. The miles and miles of motorway seem to stretch on forever. We supped dozens of bottles of cider and amused ourselves with tales of football violence, which usually started with the line: 'Nar then, remember when Stoke (or whoever) came.'

And usually ended with the comment: 'That was a great day.'

At Bournemouth we sorted our digs and went out. Rotherham were playing Bournemouth next day and Bournemouth needed a draw to clinch promotion. The first pub we went in, four lads from Toy Town came over and tried to tag along with us but we were having none of the woollyback tramps. Later, we bumped into more of our boys and the 40 of us moved from pub to pub. While everyone sat and talked of the plans for Portsmouth the following day, I played a quiz machine. This scruffy barfly lounging against the machine kept telling me the answers, which I ignored at first. Then I realised he knew all the answers. I won £28 and then another £30. After that, I watched him win £50. I bought him a drink and he explained he was from Norfolk and went around the coast playing the quiz machines.

'I get sussed after a bit, then move on. In a good week I can earn two thousand pounds,' he said.

The genius didn't spend his money on clothes, that's for certain, but that might have been part of his act. I admired his scam though and shook his hand. Nothing much happened that night as we split into smaller groups to save on hassle getting into pubs. Bournemouth is a sound enough place for a good bevy and the only trouble was a brief skirmish with some bouncers.

Next morning, feeling a little groggy from one or two lagers too many, we set off, three vanloads in a convoy. Our van led the way and Kav drove like a maniac, as usual. Approaching Portsmouth's Fratton Park ground, we spotted a large group of Pompey lads. The side door of the van was flung open, Kav drove up the kerb and punches and kicks rained down on them. Pompey did one as the other vans emptied behind us.

The police had clocked us and a motorcycle cop shot up to the side of our van and pulled us in, *Chips* style. He was on fire.

'You stupid bastard. I'm going to take you around the back of the ground and drive vans at you all afternoon, you clever twat,' he politely explained to Kav.

We were then escorted to the game. United pissed on the Portsmouth party bonfire by winning 2-1. Three pitch invasions held up the game as Pompey's lads tried to get at us. It seemed that all 28,000 in attendance that day were on the pitch. I took photos of Pompey's firm and impressive it was, more than 1,000 lads trying to get at us. We scaled the perimeter fences to signify we wanted it, but the away end at Portsmouth is cut off by a moat, so it was bravado on both sides. Police dog handlers formed a snarling barrier in front of us and most of the 1,500 following from Sheffield were relieved at their presence. The final whistle saw thousands of Portsmouth swarm the pitch and once the players had left the field they concentrated on us. Police wanted us out of the ground, so we got our crew together and left mob-handed. It would have gone off outside but for police, shouts from Portsmouth of 'Get the niggers,' directed at our blacks, making us close ranks and stick together.

Some of our lot got word to Portsmouth's lads to come to Bournemouth that night. When we got back to Bournemouth, everyone met in a pub called the Lansdowne, which was appropriate as our main pub in Sheffield was named the same. Around 150 had gathered and we all hoped Pompey would show, as we had a good crew out. That night was hilarious. While the restless ones went searching for Portsmouth's mob, the 6.57 Crew, we got rat-arsed. This poor Irish folk band did their best to do a gig, but Blade after drunken Blade had hold of the mike. It was all good spirits without a hint of trouble. If anyone got too out of hand they were pulled down by the rest of us. The landlord loved it, as did the old glass collector. He had a knacked old straw sombrero on his nut, braces and sandals. Every time a few empty glasses had gathered on a table, he appeared from behind the bar to a rising chorus of, 'Ooooooh.' This then reached fever pitch until he touched a glass. The whole boozer went up. 'Oh this year we're off to sunny Spain, y viva España.' The old man had a grin like a Cheshire cat. Imagine, 150 thugs made his night.

Scouts came back with news that a few Pompey had been seen but not a mob. Fifty went out on the hunt. Paul got hold of the mike and sang My Old Man, everyone's favourite at the time. We all jumped up onto tables.

*My old man said be a Wednesday fan*
*I said fuck off, bollocks, you're a cunt*
*He said, come on, we're going to the game*
*I said, fuck off, I'm going down't Lane*
*And so, I went down to John Street*
*Found myself, a good seat*
*Saw the lads go two up at the break*
*Then went to the bar, for a pint of Magnet,*
*and a meat pie filled with steak*

Last orders went. We had drunk the place dry. The few remaining bottles and cans were bought and 150 pissed-up Sheffielders headed for the beach. As we walked down a precinct, a mob of Bournemouth lads threw bottles out of a bar but our numbers ensured they stayed inside. We went at the pub but police were monitoring us and arrested a few of our lads. Pud ended up bent over in a rubbish bin, arm up his back, after being nicked. I pulled at him pleading his innocence. It was ironic really, as I had punched Pud a few weeks earlier for calling me a 'pig lover'. I had been out for a drink on Rippy's birthday, despite the fact that I was bang at it with Wednesday at the time. Rippy was a well-known Wednesday boy who I got on well with. He had trained with our football team and travelled to a few Blades games with us. I'd had the balls to show my face among their lads on his birthday and didn't need fellow Blades pulling me down over it. Nevertheless I risked being arrested trying to get Pud free. The bizzy let him go, Pud thanked me and we shook hands, our quarrel forgotten.

Me, Vince and Housey got split from the rest and bumped into three lads. 'We're Portsmouth. Come on,' one shouted. I punched him and we chased them. They ran across the road to a police car and as the copper got out, he must have been bemused as we chased them around the car. Housey chinned one right under the copper's nose. As the officer radioed for help, we did one. I reckon a few Pompey came that night but not a serious mob. It would have been a top war if they had shown.

Down at the beach, Jimmy, a Rotherham Blade, stripped off at the end of a jetty and jumped into the freezing sea shouting, 'Rotherham Blades.' Pud, not to be outdone, ran down the jetty, booted Jimmy's clothes, and dived in fully-clothed screaming, 'BBC.'

Next morning my hangover dulled the anger at the tyres on our van being let down. 'Rotherham' and 'Sheffield wankers' was written in the grime on the van.

Rough fuckers, those Rotherham lads.

# VILLA PARK
## 26 SEPTEMBER 1987.

Fifty of our boys travelled on a coach to Villa Park. As soon as we were near the ground, we stopped and headed for a boozer. After a couple of hours drinking we headed for the match. Somehow we got split up and 30 of us went and sat in the stand that ran along one side. The rest ended up on the away end behind the goal. During the game insults were traded with a few Villa boys at the other side of a partition. The game was an entertaining 1-1 draw.

At the final whistle, we headed outside. I was one of the first out and it was obvious a welcome committee had been formed. It looked like 300 boys but was probably more like 150, as the street was packed with fans making their way from the ground. I clocked the police Hoolivan surveillance vehicle just to my left. I also saw the camera on the side of the stand pointed towards our exit point. As we tried to get everyone together, Villa's boys were moving in. My first thought was, Fuck it, let's have a go. The adrenaline pumped around my body and I ran into them, as did a few others. My arms and legs were going like the clappers. Villa were caught by surprise. They must have thought we would bunch together and stand outside the exit next to the bizzy van but instead we moved them back. A full-scale battle erupted and now Villa steamed in traded blows, all under the lenses of the two video cameras. I'd have loved to watch the tape recording.

I ended up across the street with Pud, one of our boys. We went for it as our poor numbers held their own. The bizzies came in and three of our lot were nicked (and later banned from attending football games for 12 months). Villa continued to pour at us. Pud and myself were separated and, oblivious to what was happening around us, as we fought like crazy. It came right on top for us both so we scrambled across the road to the rest of our lot who were still bang at it, no one knew who was who. I punched out at anyone who came near me. As police gained order we jogged through the gates. A bizzy booted me, causing me to stumble. Then we found our coach. All our lot were buzzing and Villa must have been impressed by our gameness.

Boxy came over to me. 'You all right, windmill? How come you didn't get nicked.'

I interrupted him. 'Windmill?'

'Like an out of control windmill, man,' he explained. I laughed. He has called me Windmill ever since.

We had a body count: three arrested.

'Where's Howie?' I asked.

He slid out from the driver's sleeping quarters under the coach seats.

'I'm here, mate.'

A good day, all in all.

# MIDDLESBROUGH: THE FRONTLINE

## 7 NOVEMBER 1987.

Boro came to the Lane with a growing reputation. We had been on their patch a few years earlier and done the business. An article about that day's events appeared in *New Society* magazine in May 1985 under the title 'Blades Day' and was written by Gary Armstrong. Gary had studied Sheffield hooligans for years, culminating in an anthropological book called *Football Hooligans, Knowing the Score*, published in 1998. He has also written articles in about Blades in other books: one, which detailed Sheffield United v Leeds confrontations, was entitled 'False Leeds'.

On this particular day, I had been to Manchester in the morning with Kav for clothes. We used to go shopping about once a month, travelling to London, Leeds, Leicester and Nottingham but Manchester was our favourite. There was Cecil Gee, Wardrobe and plenty of other shops where you could buy designer gear. Hurleys near Piccadilly Station was another good shop and is still going strong. I was once in Hurleys when 30 West Ham steamed in and robbed a few items.

Kav and I finished our shopping and returned to Sheffield, where we went straight into town to meet the boys. We bumped into them heading towards a bar called Legends. Boro had been seen and word around the campfire had it that they were in there. Sure enough, as we crossed the dual carriageway and climbed over the five-foot railings in the middle, they came to the windows. I thought they should have come out but they just threw glasses as we went for the doors. Sep threw a sign through the window. In the next second, the police arrived and chased us. Thirty went one way and about the same number the other. I ran around the block to meet the others at the bottom of a series of steps and walkways. As I got there, I looked up to see about 80 Boro steaming down the steps onto one of the walkways. I could see a lone figure battling with them.

'Who the fuck's that?' I shouted, as the rest of the Blades reached the bottom of the steps. I didn't wait for an answer but just ran up to help him. It was Kav, my shopping pal. He wouldn't run whatever the odds. He was handy as well, having done years of boxing – I called him One Punch, as that was all it usually took him to finish a fight. Boro had him backed into a wall where he was covering up, releasing vicious punches when he had the chance. As I got to his side, I copped an accidental punch from him as I grappled with his attackers. I took a few more blows from the Boro. The odds were bad. A big, well-dressed Boro boy with his coat zipped up and the hood pulled tight to his face gave me a cracker on the temple.

Suddenly it all stopped. I looked up and Boro were moving away. It was pretty obvious the bizzies had arrived but I was on one and ran over and punched the tall lad who had just hit me. Two coppers grabbed me. I protested my innocence, even though I was bang to rights, but they threw me in a van.

'I've been to Manchester shopping,' I tried to explain. 'We've just got back and we were attacked.' I took the receipts out of my Burberry wallet. I could see doubt creeping into their minds.

'I saw you fighting.'

'You'd fight if your mate was getting hammered.'

They took my address, gave me a warning and let me go. 'If I see your face around Bramall Lane, you're nicked.'

What a result. I went to the car, drove home, got changed, put on a baseball cap and headed to London Road. I bumped into Kav.

'Jesus, Stevie, I thought you'd been locked up,' he laughed. We shook hands and he thanked me for backing him up. I explained what had happened. He agreed that I'd used up another life.

Boro had been told earlier where to come for a pop. Not many firms ventured onto London Road, which had 13 pubs in under a mile. Ten of us decided to go back into town to see if we could locate Boro. We had gone about a quarter of a mile when we bumped into them drinking in The Pump, a pub on a back street just out of town. They were straight into us. We had a bit of a pop then backed off and returned to London Road to gather our boys. Boro had followed; it was going to go off big time. Only a few firms have been on London Road and they usually don't last long.

Both sides ran at each other. The bizzies then steamed in before the actual combat commenced and chased boys all over the place: the truncheons were out so it wasn't time to hang around. Sheffield cops don't mess about. I think they are probably the strictest in the country. Hard but fair. Mess them about, you get messed about, that is the game.

Boro were escorted to the ground, a few of us shadowing their movements. They tried to get in our stand but the bizzies threw them in the away end. After the game, they played up again. A few split from the police and we had a 15-a-side toe-to-toe until the arrival of Johnny Law curtailed our war-polling activities. Hats off to Boro, they came and had probably the best result an away mob has had at Bramall Lane for years.

# FIGHT, FIGHT, WHEREVER YOU MAY BE

## GOD REST YE MERRY HOOLIGAN

## WOLVES

## STAY OFF THE GRASS: BRISTOL CITY

## WEDNESDAY CENTENARY

## LEEDS AWAY: LOW FLDS ROAD STAND

## HOUSEY'S STAG NIGHT

## TOTTENHAM OFF-SPURS

# GOD REST YE MERRY HOOLIGAN

## CHRISTMAS EVE 1987.

Christmas in our family was a time when we all got together. My aunt and uncle had a huge converted barn, complete with four-hole miniature golf course, snooker room with bar, gymnasium and sauna. The barn overlooked the picturesque Derbyshire countryside and the beautiful Hope Valley. Christmas and New Year was always spent there. We have quite a large family who are all keen Blades, except my Uncle Dave who once played for Wednesday and has kept his allegiance ever since. I was a bit of a black sheep among my relatives, totally different from my well-educated cousins.

It wasn't unusual for United and Wednesday boys to go out on Christmas Eve dinner and have it away. These get-togethers started around 1979 and died out in around 1989-90. I never used to turn out for them. Firstly, I didn't want locking up. Secondly, it was a time for family, not friends. Boxing Day was the same, it didn't matter who United were playing, I went to the match with family and violence was far from my mind.

Usually I bought all my presents well in advance but for some reason I had left my wife's present until Christmas Eve. I met Nudger and we had a couple of drinks together in Gossips before walking to the Fargate shopping precinct. I planned to get my wife a suit from Next. As we walked down Fargate, I saw a group of around 20 lads. I recognised these as a group of Blades who called themselves the Suicide Squad. These lads were all from the same estate in Sheffield. They went to most games independently from the main Blades firm but were no strangers to trouble and had quite a few handy lads. As we passed them they rushed over to the other side of Fargate. I could see they had somebody surrounded and were giving him a slap or two. Nudge and me headed over. I recognised one of their targets as a Wednesday fan called Winky. He was a young, game lad whose elder brother was one of Wednesday's main actors. I knew them both pretty well and although you couldn't say we were bosom buddies, I went to his aid and stood between him and the Squad.

       *Fight, Fight, Wherever You May Be*

'Leave it out, there's only two of them,' I said.

The Squad were flummoxed. Although three or four of them knew me pretty well, one twat grabbed my hat. It was a cricket cap with BBC embroidered on one side and the United badge on the other. I loved it.

'Who the fuck are you?' the geezer with my hat asked politely.

'Gimme my hat back, dickhead.' I reached out.

He was a menacing figure, a well-built skinhead whose aggressive manner told me he was trouble. The lads I knew with him did nothing, as they were completely pissed. Plus, they probably didn't like me sticking up for a Pig. I had a plaster cast on my right arm after breaking it in a fight and so I couldn't chin him. My left hand was all right as a swinger in fights but I'd have to get a good one in first. I walked up close.

'Give me my hat back...' Last chance.

'Fuck off.'

I butted him with a beauty. He reeled back as blood spurted from his nose. His mates threw a few haymakers at me, which I dodged. Police were over straight away and grabbed me. I pleaded innocence, saying my hat had been stolen and I was trying to get it back. The bizzies let me go with a warning to behave or else. I could see the geezer with my hat. He was using it to stem the flow of blood from his nose. I ran over, threw a left and kicked him. I was promptly arrested and thrown into the meat wagon.

At the station I was charged with drunk and disorderly. That was a laugh; I hadn't even had an alcoholic drink. One officer, who later became one of Sheffield's football intelligence team, sat in the van. He looked at me and smiled, I smiled back.

'Luck run out has it?'

'Looks that way.'

I was arrested at four o'clock. Time always goes slowly in the cells but I couldn't believe it when a bizzy shouted through the slot.

'Cowens.'

I bolted upright. 'What time is it?'

'Twelve fifteen.'

'Fuckin' hell. Our lass will go mad.'

'She's here to pick you up.'

Oh no. My family. What will I say? I picked up my gold chains and money. My wife, as you can imagine, was not happy. We headed out to Derbyshire at 1 AM on Christmas morning. I was hoping everyone would be in bed, but as I walked through the door I heard laughing. They were still up playing cards. I walked into the lounge, head bowed, ashamed. My mum and dad looked up at me.

'He's here, Reggie Kray.' You could rely on my Uncle Dave for his usual tact. I slunk off to bed.

That was the end of it as far as my family were concerned but it wasn't the finale of the stolen hat matter. At the end of that season we played Huddersfield and took a large firm. After the game, we headed up the road leading to Huddersfield's town centre.

'Cowens.'

A shout came through the busy crowd. It was Beck, one of the Suicide Squad.

'My mate wants you.' I looked to his side and the lad I had butted stood there.

'I'm going to kill you,' he growled.

'Where do you want it then?' I replied.

'Back in Sheffield. Up on the Friary balcony.'

'No problem, see you as soon as we get back.'

'You'd better be there.'

'I'll be there mate, don't worry about that.'

A few BBC had heard the conversation and wanted to come with me. I insisted on going alone, as I didn't want to be seen taking any back-up. Once back in Sheffield, I headed for the Friary balcony, which overlooked the Penny Black pub in Pond Street. As I walked towards it I saw Sep, a good lad from the BBC. He knew what was happening and insisted on coming. We had just walked through the underground on Arundel Gate when I saw the Squad.

'Willy,' one shouted. It was the first time I had heard his name. Willy looked up and came at me. He threw a wild one, which I ducked and then I sent him reeling with a punch straight into his face.

'Come on then.' I bounced around as blood started to trickle from his nose again. He came back; we scuffled and grabbed each other. The Squad were moving close. I didn't trust them after what had happened on Fargate.

'Keep back,' I protested.

They continued to close in so I headed back. Willy followed.

'Tell them to stay well away, it's just me and you.'

To be fair, he shouted for them to keep their distance. We battled again. He was a strong game lad and I knew I would probably have to knock him out to end the fight. The Squad came in close and again we walked further away. It went on like that for what seemed like forever. The next thing I knew we were outside the City Hall, some 700 yards from where we had started. We fought again. The bizzies went by the bottom of the road and then slowed as they saw us fighting. We both clocked them.

'Look,' I said, 'we're both going to get locked up here. This is stupid.'

'Shake my hand.' He stuck out his mitt. I took it and we shook.

'You're a good lad, Cowens.'

I was a little taken aback that the lad who for ten minutes had wanted to rip my head off would come out with a statement like that.

'Lets go and have a beer,' I said, and Sep and I headed to the Domino pub near West Street.

'You've done him,' Sep said.

'Sep, I didn't do him. I had to fight like fuck. He's a handy lad.'

I hadn't a mark on my face but the top of my head was a bit bruised. He had a bloody nose and a mark underneath his eye. I talk to him now and we were involved in a brawl with Wednesday a few months later. This time we were together doing what we did best, fighting for the Blades. My court appearance for the Christmas Eve caper produced a £100 fine and £40 court costs.

For the next two years I flitted in and out of the violence. For the first time, I started to look at my life from a different perspective. Running with the boys was no longer the be-all and end-all of my life. I was now married, to Debbie. We took on a mortgage and planned to start a family. I had been with Debbie for six years now, and my week-in week-out involvement with the BBC became just a big game thing. Having said that, I was still involved in fighting at Huddersfield, Newcastle, Port Vale, Wolves,

Barnsley, Leicester, Sunderland, Stoke, West Ham, Portsmouth and Bristol City!

## WOLVES                9 MAY 1989.

United took over 5,000 fans to this crucial end of season promotion game. One point and we were up. Wolves had clinched the Third Division championship and the evening game was a complete sell-out. I travelled without a ticket, as did many others. I was lucky to get one at the ground, along with Tiler, for Wolves' main stand. The game was just about to kick off when Tiler and me headed there. Around 15 lads hung about and we were sussed. One came over.

'Where's yeow from?' he said in that gormless Midlands accent.

It was on top, as we were backed on to the turnstile wall. Then quick as a flash, Tiler chinned him and waded in. I was slow compared to Tiler and to think he'd served his apprenticeship under me. Police came, including Sheffield's football intelligence. They saved us really, as 15 against two is bad numbers.

United got the draw required and we were promoted to Division Two. Everyone was in good spirits. This didn't stop around 100 of us chasing a large group of Wolves boys up the steps and across the main road afterwards.

## STAY OFF THE GRASS: BRISTOL CITY

### 13 MAY 1989.

Bristol City away always guaranteed trouble. At the end of the 1987-88 season we had visited Ashton Gate for a relegation play-off. There was trouble between the two factions before, during and after the match. Play-off games are a recipe for disaster with feelings running so high. The potentially-explosive fixture lived up to expectations with police struggling to keep the sell-out 25,335 crowd under control. We took a massive firm down and gave Bristol's Intercity Robins a torrid time. Bristol won the game 1-0 and we could only manage a 1-1 draw in the home leg, thus sending us down to what was then Division Three. Bristol City soon followed us, as they lost their next match.

In 1989, we had already secured promotion back to the Second Division (barring a 10-0 defeat in our last game) with the 2-2 draw at Wolves (see above). So the game at Bristol would be a party for our fans. Dave Bassett (the best manager Sheffield United will ever see) had produced a minor miracle in his first full season in charge. We had been relegated the season before and to turn things around so quickly was testament to Harry's motivational skills and his eye for a bargain. The signings of Brian Deane for £40,000 from Doncaster and Tony Agana on a free from Watford was nothing short of a masterstroke. Deane and Agana's goal return for the 1988-89 season was 30 and 31 respectively. Bassett also put together a team that would run through a brick wall for the club. Sir Bob Booker, Mark Todd, Martin Pike, Tufty Wilder, and Jock Bryson were all players who with respect weren't world beaters but they had hearts as big as buckets and Blades supporters love to see players who give their all on the pitch.

I travelled down in a hire car with Ian, Rats and Binzo. Ian couldn't believe it when he pulled up to pick me up. I had massive flares on, complete with orange floral design down the sides. My long baggy shirt complemented my trousers perfectly with more orange flowers and ten-inch collars. To complete the ensemble I had a brown suede tasselled waistcoat, John Lennon sunglasses and purple platform boots. I haven't a clue why I dressed like that for a fixture that was certain to involve bother at some point, but there you go. Ian and the lads pissed themselves as I clambered into the car.

'What the fuck have you come as?' Rats asked.

'Jealous, your jealous coz I'm a trend setter. Fuck your Armani, this is all the rage.'

'In your dreams mate,' Binzo replied.

Arriving in Bristol we parked near the away fans' coaches and went in a pub, which was chocker with 200 United boys. We had got tickets for the seats and knew that, with our numbers, we could have a right beano.

In the ground, Bristol's boys sat on the other side of a police imposed no-go area about 15 yards from me. Ten police and a number of stewards lined the gangway to keep both sides apart.

The game was barely ten minutes old when we surged across the seats. If the Bristol boys had not been up for it, we would have struggled to get at them but they came at us, so the police and stewards were unable to control the situation. Punches and kicks were exchanged as we battled it out. I was struggling to stay on my feet and began to regret my ludicrous footwear but I loved the look on their boys' faces as I waded in, flares and all. More Bristol boys came across the terracing in front of us when they realised it had kicked off. Calm was restored, then Bristol scored and it kicked off even worse. We went at their mob in the stand then steamed down the steps to the terrace below. Stewards were knocked out of the way and everyone was bang at it. The brawl spilled onto the pitch and the game was held up.

Two United players, who shall remain nameless, shouted encouragement. 'Go on Blades, give it 'em.'

Some fans later wrote to our local paper to complain about their behaviour. I thought it was sound. We cheered United on while they were playing, so why shouldn't they cheer us on when we were at play? Woody took a classic photo as we fought with Bristol on the pitch. I looked like an early Seventies freak caught up in a time warp; all that was missing were six scarves tied round my waist, neck and wrists.

Bristol gave as good as they got for a while, then we managed to back them off. Police on horseback restored order and after five minutes the game resumed. It was a complete disaster on the pitch as the team lost 2-0.

After the game we got everyone together and headed for the coaches. As we walked down the road a copper stood on a wall opposite, shouting instructions to us as we left the ground. Behind him was a massive park. I still laugh at the events, which unfolded.

Bizzy with loudhailer: 'Your coaches are to your left, stay off the grass as there's trouble in the park, so go to your coaches.'

Trouble in the park? Great. Thanks for telling us. We ran across the road and jumped over the wall where the bizzy stood

'Stop, stop. You're a disgrace to your club, to your city and to football,' belted the bizzy through his loudhailer as United's boys poured past.

'Bollocks,' Pud shouted back.

The bizzy span round sharply. 'I heard that,' he said, sounding rather hurt.

On the grass it had already kicked off, with around 30 Blades struggling to hold around 100 Bristol. Everyone ran over to help and we managed to chase Bristol, now themselves outnumbered. Dog handlers and police on horseback charged into the park. They took no prisoners and Titch was knocked flying by a horse, which ran into him full pelt.

The fighting continued. We chased Bristol, who were heading up to a dual carriageway parallel to the park. It went off again as Bristol ran at us. The police made three arrests and Bristol ended up on the other side of the carriageway. Shane and me jumped over the railings, which separated each side of the road. We didn't last long as a few of their lads ran at us, one flashing a craft knife. We just managed to get back over before one of us was striped. A United supporter had been slashed before the game.

The bizzies got it sorted and we headed back to the cars and coaches. Ian had to go and see one of United's players, so we drove into the car park at the back of the stand. Around eight Bristol lads were walking through the car park toward us. Ian sped up and drove at them and they jumped out of the way. Rats opened the car door as we sped past, knocking one of them flying. Ian got out and went for a one-on-one with a lippy Bristol boy. I headed towards the other Bristol lads with my arms outstretched.

'Come on, then.'

I must have looked like some Woodstock throwback. United's players, sitting on the coach, looked on in amusement. A few bizzies came over and things calmed down.

Around 40 BBC had agreed to meet up later to have a night out in Weston-super-Mare. I got changed and felt human again. The first pub we went in had 25 Blades in, all the worse for drink. I knew a few of them. They weren't BBC but used to show their faces at big games. A few years later I moved into Mosborough, the area where they all live, and many have become good mates. They are good lads, 100 per cent United and love a good time. On this occasion, though, they were a bit too loud and over the top, so we supped up and left. The only trouble we encountered was with some dickhead bouncers who tried to stop us entering a lively pub.

'Not tonight lads.'

'Not tonight?' We were hardly going to come back next week. 'Why, what's up?'

'I've told you, not tonight.'

'Fuck off, we're going in.'

With that, we waltzed past the bouncers, who thought about stopping us, then thought better of it. They must have realised it wasn't worth it.

Later that evening, we heard a commotion up a side street. The pissed-up Blades were scrapping with some biker types. I went up and tried to calm them down, as they were all getting nicked. One by one they disappeared into various police vans. We beat a quick retreat before we added to the tally. Out of the 18 Blades who were there, 18 were nicked: 'all for one' and all that.

They hit the headlines of the local newspaper back in Sheffield. For their first appearance in court they hired a van but only got as far as the American Adventure theme park in Derbyshire. As they were running a little late, one of the lads phoned the court, told them they had broken down, then they spent the rest of the day in the theme park on a bender. The drinking session ended with all the lads betting Scratch he couldn't swim across the lake in the middle of the park. Pissed, he took the bet on and as soon as he began his epic swim, all the lads went back to the bar. Later Scratch told them that as he was getting out of the other side, two old ladies on a bench eating their lunch gave him a round of applause. He never did get his £50 bet money.

# WEDNESDAY CENTENARY 1989/90.

The 1989-90 season was United's 100th since being formed. To celebrate, a pre-season friendly was arranged with Sheffield Wednesday. The game was to be played at Bramall Lane in August and would be a nice warm-up for the boys as the forthcoming season meant guaranteed trouble with the likes of Boro, West Ham, Stoke, Leicester, Pompey, Leeds, Wolves and Barnsley, who were all in Division Two. When the fixture list is printed, hooligans always look for the fixtures where there is a possibility of trouble.

On the day of the game, we met at the usual place, The Pheasant on London Road, about a mile away from the ground. When I turned up, there were only about 40 of our lot basking in the sunshine outside. Wednesday had met at the Arbourthorne Hotel, a pub on a tough housing estate three-and-a-half miles from the Lane. A few phone conversations went on, with the usual threats and insults. I wasn't interested in the chat.

At around 1 pm, one of our lot came over.

'Steve, Wednesday have just been on. They say they've got 150 out and are coming down here to give it us.'

'They won't come down here,' I replied.

By now we only had around 60 out but it was enough, as most of them were our top boys. A scout in a car pulled up outside the Pheasant.

'Wednesday are on the move, they've got a big team out, they've gone in the Earl of Arundel,' he reported. leaning out of the car window. Everyone supped up and headed off for the Sheaf in twos and threes so the bizzies wouldn't catch on.

The Sheaf was around 500 yards from the Earl but neither pub was visible from the other. Our numbers swelled to around 100. More reports came back that Wednesday had a major firm out with all the faces there. Everyone was buzzing.

At 2.30 pm we headed down and around the corner to a long straight road which led to the Earl. Wednesday, on seeing us 200 yards away, poured out and ran towards us. They had a great mob and looked the part as they bounced toward us.

I was at the front with Tiler. We looked at each other. 'Straight in, don't stop,' I yelled. Tiler didn't need telling.

'BBC, BBC,' the chant went up.

Wednesday completely filled the road and pavements. Around ten black lads were fronting for them. I knew most of them; they were well-respected hitters, most of them bouncers at nightspots around Sheffield. Glasses, bottles and bricks filled the air. Then Wednesday slowed to a stop. Big mistake: it's the first sign of a loss of nerve.

We went into them. Wednesday backed away screaming, 'Stand!' at each other as we piled in. Everyone got into them and as they turned and ran we chased them down the road. Two Wednesday had stood and were getting battered. I recognised one as Wak, a game black lad who I had had some trouble with. He used to be a Blade but went with Wednesday because all his mates were Pigs. I ran over.

'Leave him, he's the only one with the bollocks to stand,' I said. I grabbed him and took him to the trees on the side of the road where he shook my hand and muttered, 'Shit Wednesday.'

We had proved in one 45-second brawl that we were the top boys in Sheffield. They had turned out all the faces but our young casuals were too strong and too game. A lot of their faces disappeared from their ranks after that. The police marched the dejected OCS up to the ground. We mocked them as they tried to break from the bizzies to save some face. They had had their chance and lost it.

The game was a dull 0-0 draw, before a crowd of 17,951. The only good thing about it was that Wednesday's Carlton Palmer was sent off. Most of Wednesday's lads didn't go to the game; those that did heard 'Run, run, run, Wednesday, run,' being chanted from our stand. After the game we scanned the streets for Wednesday but found nothing. Small mobs of our lot headed into town then on to Silks, a lively disco/rave type pub which we often frequented after home games; nothing to do with all the drinks being £1. As I entered, it was packed with around 250 Blades, although only 150 were boys. I was also surprised to see Wak and around six black lads who had been chased with Wednesday's firm prior to the game. Our lot weren't pleased with their presence but if everyone had given it them it would have been bullying. Wak once again shook my hand, we had a brief conversation and they left. Our lot were arguing.

'We should have given it them.'

'No, that's not our style.'

'But they'd have given it to us, if it was us outnumbered.'

'Look, they'll be back with the rest of their firm and we'll give it them again, okay?'

Around ten minutes later, the large windows in the pub came crashing in.

'Wednesday, Wednesday,' was chanted in the street.

We all piled to the door. Silks had only one entrance and it was impossible to get everyone out at once. We were packed in the doorway and the front lads got smacked with all sorts, as

Wednesday were well tooled up with ready-made weapons from the roadworks around the corner. What didn't help was the fact that Tony's rottweiler was biting us in a frenzy as he tried to get out.

A surge saw around 15 of us get out. It was suicidal as bricks and bottles bounced off us, so we backed off down the road. Then to top it all, the black lads that had been in Silks and hadn't been touched came up behind us. Around 20 of them attacked us in a pincer movement. I managed to get through with just a punch landing on my shoulder. We turned at the bottom of the road and looked up. Wednesday were going to town on the pub, throwing everything through the windows.

Then something happened which I'll never forget. Tony, the well-respected black lad who had the rottweiler, came out of the pub into the barrage. Around 20 Wednesday tried to do him but he waded in with one hand, the other holding the 12-stone dog. That kept them back. We ran back up but the police came from everywhere, causing us to scatter. The Wednesday blacks and around 15 more of their lot headed towards us. Forest, one of our main actors, squared up to Wak and, as Wak tried a punch, dropped him with a roundhouse kick. We steamed them and two or three Wednesday were chewed up a bit by the dog.

The hospital was full of wounded soccer thugs; it even kicked off in casualty to end the most violent get-together United and Wednesday had had for years. I have since got to know Wednesday's black lads well and most of them stopped bothering after that day. One called our lot 'a screaming mad load of wild banshees,' which I take as a compliment, I think.

# LEEDS AWAY:
# LOWFIELDS ROAD STAND
## APRIL 1990.

This game at Leeds saw the Business Crew at perhaps their best in terms of organisation. The BBC had no leaders or organisers; word of mouth usually saw everyone get together. The top boys all had a say about the day's events but what decisions or action to be taken was in the lap of the gods most of the time. Many times, especially at home, our firm was in disarray, with 30 going this way, 20 that, and so on.

The Leeds match was a vital one, with both clubs going for promotion to the old Division One. Leeds had given United a measly 1,800 tickets, consequently many of our boys travelled to Leeds and bought tickets for the Lowfields Road stand, where many of their boys sat. Credit cards were used to get tickets via the phone and, in all, around 350 Blades had tickets for the stand. Of these around 250 were our boys, and most of the rest would get stuck in if need be. Every club has fans who don't class themselves as hooligans but will have a pop if it comes on top.

We set off around 11.45 am in a convoy of cars and vans, heading for a pub just off the motorway. Around 200 of our crew gathered and after a few drinks we set off. Cars pulled across the road to block off traffic and keep everyone together. I was buzzing: we had no sightings of bizzies and were heading in the back way. About a mile from the ground we parked on the bottom of a small housing estate and walked *en masse* to the ground. Via an industrial estate we managed to get onto the top road that led directly to the ground, totally undetected by police.

The Leeds fans looked shocked as 200 boys bounced to the ground. We were giving it the big 'un, posing, strutting along, and a brief fight took place outside the Peacock pub right outside the ground. Our numbers were too strong for the 40 Leeds who came out. A few got clipped. By now it was 2.30 and we went straight into the ground so we could all get together and take some shifting. To our surprise the bizzies just searched us and let us in.

We took our seats well pleased with ourselves. As the Leeds fans came in the stand, they looked well pissed off to see 350 smirking Blades in a huge block. Fights broke out and police were slow to respond. A few Blades were nicked including Daz, a lad who had bought 80 tickets for the game. Leeds lads were moaning, showing the bizzies their tickets as we sat in their seats. Six Leeds boys came on our row showing off. We told them where to go. Then Eyes, one of the older and more experienced Blades, had a marvellous idea. Because the police stood down the gangways at the side of us, it was impossible to attack Leeds without being arrested. Eyes shouted for everyone to stand on their seats, blocking out the police's view. This was done and the six Leeds boys got a thumping. After three stand-ups no more Leeds ventured in.

The game itself was the usual Leeds v Blades away, i.e. a Blades defeat, this time 4-0 to Leeds, with their centre forward Bobby Davidson becoming top of my most hated list for standing on our goalkeeper Simon Tracey every time he had the ball in his hands. (Bobby would be forgiven after scoring two goals for us in a 3-1 win at Hillsborough a few years later).

Afterwards we filed down the steps. A mob of 1,000 Leeds stood around, waiting with the bizzies trying to move them on. We headed out. I bounced across and tried to walk through the line of police only to be shoved back. I smiled and winked at ten Leeds who were going demented.

'We're the boys mate, lets do it,' I shouted, only to be pushed hard by a copper who kindly told me, 'Carry on and you're nicked, twat.'

The police didn't know what to do as we walked out in the opposite direction to that they expected. All the other Blades fans headed left, toward the coaches. We went right. As we passed the Peacock another skirmish kicked off but was quelled by police. As we walked further away from Elland Road, Leeds shadowed our movements. A few sly punches were thrown as a few of our lot escaped the escort. A coach pulled across our path and as all our lot went one way around it, Shane (a big game mixed-race Blade) and I went the other. Shane turned and threw punches at the following Leeds boys. I ran to help him as the bizzies had followed our main crew. Shane turned and laughed as we headed to the rest of our boys.

On our way home, I remember wishing we were always as co-ordinated as that but with United's boys it was never a possibility, as no one really wanted to be seen as the organiser. A few internal squabbles happened because of lack of organisation, some including myself, but to me it was all bollocks. I just wanted to be a boy who was well respected.

# HOUSEY'S STAG NIGHT
## SUMMER 1990

The 1989-90 season was probably the best that United fans will ever see. No one expected United to gain promotion for a second year running, no one except a certain Dave Bassett. The season had gone well both on and off the pitch. There had been trouble at the Stoke, Sunderland, Barnsley, Hull, Newcastle, Middlesbrough and Leeds games. The United team continued their upward march with a spirit and commitment that made you proud to follow them. What made promotion back to the top flight even more remarkable was the fact that throughout that season boardroom squabbling over ownership of the club hit more headlines than the team. Reg Brealey, United's chairman and no stranger to controversy, had put his share in the club up for offers.

The outcome was pure pantomime. The name Sam Hashimi may not mean much to a lot of people but the Iraqi businessman entered the fray with a bid for our club. The Gulf War was just around the corner and although this problem may have been embarrassing to the club, it would have been nothing compared to what could have followed. A Sheffield businessman called Paul Woolhouse thwarted Hashimi's bid and this intervention was a relief for most United supporters. A few years later, Sam returned to England, only this time as Samantha! The sex change was even more embarrassing when he/she appeared in national newspapers with a United scarf covering her charms. What no one realised was that Woolhouse had no money and his business practices were a tad suspect. Not long after, Woolhouse went missing with thousands of pounds of ticket money taken from the club.

Our final match of that season was at Leicester. United needed a win to gain promotion and over 8,000 Sheffielders made the trip to the Midlands. Trouble erupted all around the ground as United's fans infiltrated home supporters' areas. The match was won 5-2 and more good news reached the celebrating hordes: Wednesday had lost 3-0 to Notts Forest, thus sending them down from the First Division. Wednesday down and United replacing them in the First: life doesn't get much better.

After the game, twelve BBC walked to the train station and bumped into the Baby Squad. Leicester ran at our lot who, despite being outnumbered, stood and traded. When the police arrived quite a few Leicester came over to our lads and told them they were the gamest boys they had ever seen.

Back in Sheffield, the party began. Over 2,000 Blades drank the London Road dry. The street was closed to traffic as the celebrations went on. Around 10pm, the BBC turned their thoughts to an old foe, the OCS. Five hundred boys headed up to West Street in search of Wednesday. Police blocked off roads and drove United lads back. Raggy and myself managed to get through the blockades and, entering West Street, bumped into a few Wednesday lads.

'Don't go down there Steve, there's two hundred Wednesday out for blood,' one informed me.

'Cheers, but five hundred of our lot's on the way,' I replied. As I spoke, 100 BBC came around the corner. The Wednesday lads shot off to tell their firm but police shut off the road and avoided a major confrontation.

We looked forward to the summer in the knowledge that next season we would be up against England's best teams and boys. But first of all I had a stag night to sort out for my friend Housey.

Housey was a good mate and a United boy I had known for years, the kind of younger brother type you tended to look out for in dodgy situations. Not that he needed much looking after. I was chuffed when he asked me to best man at his forthcoming wedding. It did, however, put me in a difficult situation. I knew all his family and his future wife, so when the subject of the stag night came up I knew the onus would be on me to get him through it unscathed. I knew all the lads who would be going were football boys, and a cocktail of boys, beer and seaside is a recipe for disaster. A few places had been discussed and Skegness, being the nearest seaside town to home, seemed to be favourite. It would be easier to get back home if or when any of us were locked up.

I hired a van and 20 of us set off on the day in question, to be joined later by a couple of carloads. The afternoon passed peacefully enough, apart from Housey being stripped naked and left wandering around the amusement area of the seafront with only a police traffic cone covering his pride. The coppers who nicked him were all right when I explained it was his stag night and I was supposed to be looking after him. I assured them there would be no more trouble. Little did I know.

After a few younger Blades had been thrown off a bridge into a smelly pond, we headed for Ingoldmells, a busy resort about four miles from Skegness. I had 'suggested' to a younger Blade that he stayed sober to drive home and under protest he agreed, leaving me to continue my lager onslaught. We had been warned of the bouncers' reputation at Raffles night club but thought nothing of it as we sat outside a bar that joined onto the venue. As the night drew near to a close, there was no hint of trouble. A lad called Steve and I went for a bite to eat.

As we returned, we realised something had gone off. Eight bouncers were now standing where we had sat. A couple of our lot came over to us. Then Sam came around the corner with his green tee-shirt wrapped around his head and blood pouring down his face.

'What happened?'

'The bouncers came over acting the cunt, one's hit him with a walkie-talkie.'

I asked which one did it and the biggest motherfucker of a man was pointed out. I told everyone to get ready and walked over. The menacing bouncer didn't seem too impressed.

'What the fuck you done that for?' I quizzed the 20-stone giant.

He looked at me like I was a piece of shit and smirked. I jumped in and butted him with all my might. As he reeled back, the other bouncers attacked me. I was getting battered over a wooden table as all the boys steamed in to help. I jumped up and punched one of the retreating bouncers. We backed them into the pub doors where several regulars joined in on their side. They probably hadn't seen football thugs at work and were shocked as we laid siege. A few of the regulars that ventured too far out were dropped and kicked. I picked up a large litterbin in the shape of a white rabbit, then ran in and hurled it at the doorway.

I was just wondering if these bouncers were really the animals everyone said they were when from round the back of the club came eight of their colleagues carrying luminous baseball bats.

This didn't look good. I hurled a bottle at them, then shouted to our lot who were still steaming the doors to 'fucking run'. These doormen meant business.

As our lot turned and ran down the road, more bouncers came up towards them from another pub called the Villager. Our lot fought past them. I had been left behind and was now running behind the bouncers who in turn were chasing the boys. I stopped to break a plank from a fence. It was pitch dark as I ran down, with holidaymakers all around and was impossible to tell who was who. I was nervous.

The bizzies came. I dropped my weapon as two cop vans hurtled down the road past me. A few officers ran down on foot, so I jogged behind them. The bouncers were walking casually back up the road. It was then I realised that these bouncers must be the bollocks, as the coppers looked terrified and one mumbled to a bouncer carrying a lime green bat, 'Get back to the club.'

If that was Sheffield, they'd be nicked, but here they were a law unto themselves. There was no sign of our lot; I thought they had run clean back to Sheffield. Our van was parked on the other side of Raffles and my mind was working overtime. There's a definite charge of affray here if we get collared. I bumped into a few of our lot and managed to get everyone together. We all had sticks and planks as we made our way back to the van via a darkened caravan site. Almost everyone was wounded in some way.

When we got to the van we realised that Housey, the groom, was missing. I told everyone to keep their heads down and went looking for him. I had walked ten paces when he came round the corner, covered in blood, with two bizzies. He pointed to the van, the dizzy bastard – he's sometimes a bit daft and once had a misspelt tattoo saying BLADES BISINESS CREW; it's covered up now with a panther. We tried to ditch our weapons but the bizzies were on us like ants. I asked Housey if he was all right and explained that I was going to 'do one' as I was on a bad charge back in Sheffield and didn't need another. Getting away was going to be difficult.

'Can I have a piss, mate?' I asked one of the bizzies.

'Yes, over there.'

I couldn't believe my luck as he pointed to a bush five yards away. I clocked the two bizzies watching me. They took their eyes off me for a second and I leapt head first over the fence and ran through the pitch-black caravan site. I must have fallen over four times I was that kettled, and wasn't sure if they were chasing me. All of the caravan plots were separated by ten-foot wide moats. I came to one, felt along the fence for a gap and ran down the bank then tripped and went into the stagnant water. I got up the other side and realised I wasn't being chased; no copper would have waded through that shit anyhow. I stunk like a skunk's backside.

All our lot were locked up for the weekend and I had to get a taxi home at a cost of £60. The taxi driver wouldn't let me sit down, so I had to lie on the floor. He drove with the window down, complaining about the smell. I finally got home at seven in the morning, to be greeted by an annoyed wife who helped me out of my faded Diesel jeans that went straight in the bin.

All the boys were charged with violent disorder. After four court appearances all charges except Sam's were dismissed. He copped a £240 fine for the lesser charge of threatening behaviour. I had failed miserably in looking after Housey and wondered if the wedding would go ahead with me as best-worst man. Housey is still married today, has a son, and is godfather to my son.

# TOTTENHAM OFF-SPURS
## 20 OCTOBER 1990.

Around 100 Blades met at Swiss Cottage before our fixture at Tottenham's White Hart Lane. It was our first season in the First Division for a long time and we wanted to show the big boys that the BBC was a force to be reckoned with. After catching the tube, we stayed on at Seven Sisters, figuring it would be heavily policed, and instead got off at Tottenham Hale over-ground station, which was nearer to the ground. On the way to the ground it kicked off outside a pub but Tottenham didn't have the numbers. The game itself was a write-off, with the Blades on the receiving end of a 4-0 hammering. This made our appetite for an off even greater.

We got together outside the exit. It was clear that the Yids, as Spurs' mob is known, had grouped up at the bottom of the road. There were plenty of police around, including Sheffield's football intelligence officers, who kept a close watch over us. Tottenham started to walk towards us, so we headed for them. The Yids had a steady firm numbering around 100. I was at the front, then I noticed Raggy, one of our boys, was actually walking toward us with the Tottenham. What's he up to? I thought. A tall black guy was fronting the Spurs mob.

'Cam on then.'

He had just got his words out when Raggy dropped him with a sidewinder. That was the signal. We ran at Tottenham despite the large police presence. The usual shout of 'BBC' went up. To my surprise, Tottenham backed off then turned and ran. Three or four Blades were arrested and sporadic fighting broke out on the Seven Sisters Road. Raggy and myself ended up split from our main group and on the wrong side of a bus with Tottenham all around us.

'You're shit, man.' I gave them the verbals and a few came at us but stopped when we fronted them. Then I saw the ugliest football thug I've ever seen.

'Fuckin' hell Raggy, how ugly is he?' The Neanderthal stared at me.

'Fack off, wanker.'

The police came to our aid and we joined up with the rest of our lot who were still showing off. One hundred Sheffield boys walked down Seven Sisters Road in a police escort. The Yid firm tailed our movements from across the road. Then a couple of our boys from the Suicide Squad broke from the escort and ran at Tottenham. A roar went up and, as we broke away, a few punches were thrown and a couple more arrests were made. We had shown off big time and were well pleased with ourselves. When we eventually got to the tube the police would only let ten of us down at one time, thus splitting us up. We teamed up back at Swiss Cottage and then stayed drinking around Leicester Square all night. Tottenham's feeble firm surprised me. I had expected a blood and snot rumble.

In 1984, when Spurs played a pre-season friendly at Sheffield United, they had brought 50 boys and we had two offs with them.

I remember it really well: I was hit by a brick outside Sheffield Station then, in a successful but painful bid to avoid arrest, I ran into a small wall and broke my toe. The Spurs lads that day were game. It shows how as the years go by, some mobs are not what they used to be. Or is it that you tend to fight with more conviction when you're away from home? United's firm has held a steady hooligan mob together for 20 years now, which not many teams have. The reason for this is unclear. Birmingham are another firm that have held together over the years. Others come and go. It was not long ago that Man City's firm were one of the best in the country; nowadays Man United run the show over there. I think that most people in the country see us, in football terms, as the poor relations of Sheffield. This seems to gel United's lads together. Although our hooligan element don't turn out at every game, when the need arises there can still be 250 boys out on patrol.

# STRICTLY FISTS 'N' STYLE

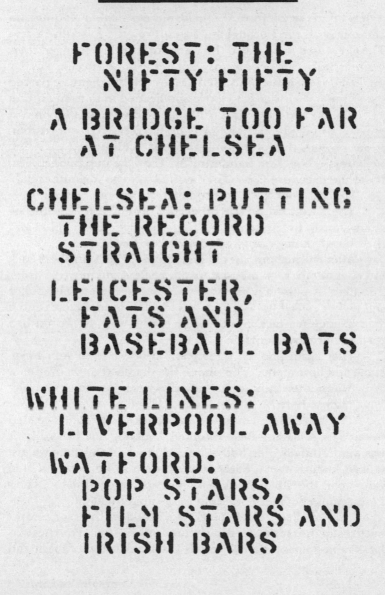

## FOREST: THE NIFTY FIFTY

## A BRIDGE TOO FAR AT CHELSEA

## CHELSEA: PUTTING THE RECORD STRAIGHT

## LEICESTER, FATS AND BASEBALL BATS

## WHITE LINES: LIVERPOOL AWAY

## WATFORD: POP STARS, FILM STARS AND IRISH BARS

# FOREST:
# THE NIFTY FIFTY
## 1 APRIL 1991.

A fleet of cars set off from Sheffield, our destination Nottingham and our rivals the Nottingham Forest firm, the Executive Crew. The Crew used to be called the Naughty Forty but changed their name as Stoke City's hooligans went by the same title. On this day we renamed them the 'nifty fifty'. Once in Nottingham, we parked up on the outskirts of the centre and headed in to town around 11.30am. We had a tidy firm if 70 with no divvies. A spittoon of a pub was found, with the landlord only too pleased by our custom. It was obvious the local hooligan scouts had spotted us. A few well-dressed boys kept wandering by. Then the pub phone went. It was the Executive Crew. They wanted us to go to another pub.

'We're in your town, you come to us,' was the reply.

The Forest lad on the other end promised they would be along shortly. Everyone was buzzing – a quiet area, no plod and their boys heading our way. It couldn't be better.

After half an hour, they hadn't showed. Tiler rang them back but after another ten minutes we got restless and moved further into town. A pub on a side street was our next stop. The police still hadn't sussed us. The pub was ideal, two pool tables and a load of cues in a rack that could be used if need be. Forest had tracked our movements.

Tiler again phoned their pub. 'Look we're in your town, come and have a pop.' The phone was slammed down on them.

Another ten minutes had gone by when the shout went up: 'They're here.'

The pub emptied onto the quiet back street. Forest headed towards us. A leading Blade shouted, 'Nobody run, just walk.' It was weird: usually everybody would charge but this time we just walked towards them. Forest slowed, then as we were only ten yards apart the 'BBC' shout went up and everyone ran in. I knew Forest would do one. They didn't look up for it at all.

One of them, a tall black lad, stood at the front, arms outstretched, as his mates disappeared around him. Punches and kicks rained in and they were off. The black lad got caught and took a kicking. Job done, we were then rounded up by the police and escorted to the ground.

After the game, which we lost 2-0, we mobbed up again and headed back to town, only to be sussed by police and escorted all the way. Once in town, the 40 or so who didn't manage to escape the escort were penned in a small precinct. The bizzies videoed us and took photos as we sat around. Names and addresses were also taken. I didn't know half my mates had changed their names by deed poll. I was asked if my name had been taken and said yes, even though it hadn't. On the way back we were well pleased with ourselves, even the strict policing had failed to dampen our spirits at putting the nifty fifty on their toes.

# A BRIDGE TOO FAR
# AT CHELSEA
## 15 FEBRUARY 1992.

By 1992, our boys had been through everyone we met and had established a reputation through the country. There was no one we feared. So when we drew Chelsea in the FA Cup quarter-final, we viewed it with great anticipation. The Chelsea Headhunters were possibly the top firm in the country. If we could get it on, I was confident we would do the business. Our firm had around 100 core boys but could easily amass 250 for big games. The core lads were all game and good mates.

For the first time, a few of our boys received menacing phone calls during the week prior to the game. London accents told Wasser that we would be cut up, and so on. It didn't need Inspector Morse to work out who had supplied the Headhunters with our with phone numbers; it was Errol, a Wednesday boy who knew Chelsea's firm. He went way down in my estimation for that, even though he had been on the wrong end of a couple of kickings from us. Errol and a couple of Wednesday lads had once visited my workplace because some loser had phoned them claiming to be me and saying he was going to do them. They knew it was not my style. I still think it was one of their own lads who had phoned them, trying to get me into a ruck. Rumours did the rounds that

Chelsea were going to team up with Wednesday, who were at Arsenal the same day. I couldn't see it happening. Chelsea didn't need any help.

Various modes of transport culminated in a meet at the World's End, a large pub opposite Camden tube station. It was no secret we were heading there and we knew Chelsea would be around. All our main actors were out in a mob of 90 good lads. Everyone was in good spirits; it's a buzz when all your top lads are together and your crew is almost div-less. A few Blades on a scout came back with news that a couple of Wednesday boys had been seen. Surely Chelsea hadn't teamed up with them? It turned out that three Wednesday were with Chelsea. Drinks flowed, then one of the Wednesday lads was again spotted, this time with two Chelsea. They were across from the World's End, beckoning our lot down a road.

I tried in vain to get everyone to stay in the pub. It was obvious to me that we were being set up. 'Stay in here, let them come to us,' I shouted. No one was listening. They were too eager and headed down the road after their prey. My reasoning was that if Chelsea came to us, we could steam out with glasses, bottles and anything else that came to hand. Instead our firm walked out with nothing more than clenched fists. This was London and we were going for a ruck with Chelsea: I couldn't believe how naive our lot were.

As I walked down behind the boys, I'd got the hump on. 'Stupid, this,' I said to anyone within earshot. We had walked 400 yards when a roar went up. I couldn't see what was happening except for our lot running and bouncing around, as I was 60 yards further back. I ran down. A distress flare was fired at us. Chelsea had it sussed. It was times like these that I wished that United's boys were a bit more clued in.

In the ensuing off, punches and kicks were exchanged. Then just as I had got to the front, our lot started to back off. I ran through shouting, 'Stand!'

The first Chelsea boy I saw had a long Bowie-type knife, brandishing it like Zorro on speed. I realised why we were backing away; Chelsea were well tooled up. Although we had the numbers, our Queensbury Rules attitude had done us.

'Cam on you fackin mugs,' a Chelsea boy brandishing a wooden bat screamed. Seconds later a pool ball hit me on the shoulder. Raggy steamed in and got captured. A Chelsea boy sat on him like he had caught a big game trophy. A few Blades ran in to help and Raggy managed to get away. As we ran everybody was screaming, 'Stand. Fuckin' stand.'

But I knew that once you have backed off, it is virtually impossible to get your act back together. I also knew that no one was going to fight against these weapons. After our 400-yard dash back to the World's End, I ran in through the side door and picked up a stool. Mad Dog did the same and the two of us stood in the doorway waiting for Chelsea to come. Our lot had run to the main doors, Chelsea ran past the side door which me and Mad Dog guarded. Errol, the Wednesday lad, glanced in at me, stool in hand. He nodded my way and smiled. I knew him pretty well and it is the only time he's ever seen the back of my head.

'You wankers, we'll see you in Leicester Square later and we'll be tooled up,' Mad Dog shouted at a few passing Chelsea. Police swarmed in from everywhere. We were herded onto the tube and set off for Stamford Bridge. As I sat on the tube I took comfort in telling others, 'I told ya, we should've let them come to us, these are always carrying. We're too naïve.'

A few Blades sat there nodding at me. At the next stop, Drib came running down the platform screaming, 'They're on here, come on.' We piled off and ran up. Sure enough around 20 Chelsea were in a carriage, going mad bouncing around as we stormed through the sliding doors. A fist to fist brawl kicked off. Our superior numbers didn't really count for much, as only so many bodies could do the actual fighting. Chelsea held their own; these must have been some of their top boys, as there were no youngsters with them and they looked the part. Two Wednesday lads were with them, one being Errol. I couldn't even get on the tube, never mind throw a punch. I ran up to the next carriage and a few followed me and we came at them from both sides. I steamed in and Chelsea ended up back to back as they tried to repel our attack. They were dropping like flies, a big pile of bodies trying to protect themselves. The two Wednesday had managed to get to the bottom of the pile.

The beating Chelsea took was a bad one. One lad was unconscious in his seat with only his head sticking out from the bodies laid on him. A Blade had one of those balls you hang on to when stood up on the tube, with a flexible steel arm and a solid plastic globe on the end. This formidable weapon was brought down on the Chelsea fans time and time again. A few of our lot tried to pull Errol from under the bodies. His back was exposed and a Blade was going to give it him with a broken glass but I stopped him. The beating went on for ages. Sweat ran down my face and my white Chevignon sweatshirt was covered in splashes of blood. We ran back to our seats as the Met arrived. I took off my sweatshirt and tied it around my waist. After about five minutes the police and ambulancemen took Chelsea away.

I saw Errol on the platform. 'You all right?'

'Yeah,' he replied, looking a bit shook-up. I felt like telling him I had saved him from certain stitches but didn't bother.

When we finally arrived at Fulham Broadway station we hit the streets and a few of us tried to head off in the opposite direction from the ground. The police sussed us and rounded us up. I managed to get away from the escort along with about six others. Quite a few Chelsea were across the road and we went into them. They weren't going anywhere. These were game lads and a brief fight ensued before the police intervened. United's 6,000-strong following were disappointed as we lost 1-0 in an acrimonious match. Chelsea's Vinnie Jones was booked after all of five seconds as he booted Sheffield-born Dane Whitehouse, who had just dribbled round him (when Vinnie got booked at Man City playing for us a couple of years earlier, he was a bit slower off the mark – he took seven seconds). I always thought Vinnie was very limited as a footballer but I admired his will to win.

After the game, we went back to Camden in the hope that Chelsea would be around. Most of our lot had cars parked around there. The World's End bouncers wouldn't let us in, so we had a drink in a little boxing-themed pub across the road. Two hours later we had all moved on to Leicester Square and Chelsea came. We had let them know where we would be drinking and they were good enough to give us a chance to even things out. A few of us went into them and started to get the better of things but the police arrived in less than a minute. That was the end of an eventful day. I thought as we drove home we could be among the elite boys of this country but I also knew that running around with knives and weapons simply wasn't our scene.

**Left** Me with my back to camera in light coloured jumper – and leg-warmers – mobbing one of our players on the pitch after a goal. I might have been a hooligan in the making but I was also a massive football fan.

**Above** My little mob of young guns with compulsory 'tache in 1981s. The casual soccer fashion had just kicked in.

**Above** The author, aged 17, with Sheffield United goalscoring legend Keith Edwards outside Bramall Lane.

**Above** Me (centre in cap) and some of the bys celebrating a 2-0 win over Sheffield Wednesday in 1992. By now I was a fully fledged top boy.

**They came, they saw, they ran. Bristol City away.**

**Top** Bristol City's boys come across the pitch towards us as the nervous stewards wonder what to do.

**Bottom** The two mobs square off. I am at the front (circled) in Seventies style fancy dress.

Blades Business Crew

**Top** In we go – the BBC in action. The photographs were taken by one of our boys in the stand.

**Bottom** Bye, bye… the Bristol mob retreat. Job done and another feather in our cap.

**Above** On the beer and on the town. A typical post-match evening, this time after playing Portsmouth away.

**Above** Me (centre) with some of the boys at a pre-season game with Skegness. Unlike some mobs, the BBC was tight-knit and the core of lads stuck together for two decades.

Blades Business Crew

**Above** Paul Heaton of the Beautiful South singing unaccompanied at a charity event we arranged at Bramall Lane for one of the lads who had been paralysed after diving into a shallow swimming pool on holiday. He sadly later died.

Blades Business Crew

The trappings of a hooligan firm: **above** one of the lads on his way to Poland with the all-important BBC/Cross of St George flag, and **below** calling cards produced by the Business Crew over the years.

**Above** Portsmouth away and the notorious 6:57 Crew come across the pitch to say hello. They are kept back by a line of police with dogs.

**Above** A surveillance picture taken of me (in scarf) at a match against Derby County.

**Above** Debbie and I on our wedding day, 1 August 1987.

**Above** With my son Jack, shortly after his birth in May 1993.

**Above** When in Rome: football fans get everywhere. Sadly the occasion was not Sheffield United playing in Europe, but an Italian Serie A match.

Blades Business Crew

The days events were without doubt a blow to our crew's reputation. We thought we could take on anyone in the country. If we had done Chelsea that day, as we should have, the BBC would have taken some stopping. We had been taught a lesson. Organisation and leaders that could make decisions were needed but no one wanted to step into that role; it brings the Law down on you and the clanging of jail bars.

# CHELSEA:
## PUTTING THE RECORD STRAIGHT

In a recent book by Martin King and Martin Knight, called *The Naughty Nineties,* the events of that day have been related from a Chelsea perspective. A 16-page section is entitled 'The Blunting of the Blades'. I feel I must put the record straight on a few things. For a start, the BBC have been run before and I personally have been knocked out before at football, unlike King and his Chelsea mates, who must be supermen if you ask me. He goes on about how Chelsea phoned some of our boys prior to the match, which is true, but then he says that one of the conversations was interrupted by, 'Come on son, your tea's going cold.' Leave it out.

Numbers are often exaggerated in stories, that is accepted, but 200 Blades chasing two Chelsea down the street? I don't think so. Next, King goes on about 'unarmed combat'. I'd hate to see them when they're really tooled up – they'd put Arnold Schwarzenneger to shame. He mentions a mixed race boy sparked out: we had two mixed race guys with us, both good lads, and neither of them was touched. Another falsehood appears when he tells the story of his mate 'Tony' and six other Chelsea lads getting hammered by our lot on the Underground. How around 20 lads can suddenly become six is beyond me. I had better go and get my eyes checked because I must have triple vision. Then we learn that they laughed about their beating later, maybe they did but at the time the terror in their eyes told a different story. The beating they received was one of the worst I have seen in football.

Finally he goes on about later that night in the West End and uses the word 'apparently' when he says that 'Sheffield United stood and fought and narrowly came off worse'. Secondhand info, mate. I was there, I know who came off worse. Perhaps it was the only crumb of comfort on a bad day. Don't get me wrong, King's books are okay and he has definitely done a bit, but all this about 'we are the invincible Chelsea', well I'll leave it there.

# LEICESTER, FATS AND BASEBALL BATS 1993

Wimbledon away is not a glamorous fixture. Crap ground, crap fans and for United always a crap result. I went down in a minibus with Blades from the area where I lived. They were a motley crew of non-BBC spliff smokers. After the game, we met in Covent Garden with other Blades, two BBC boys, a few Rotherham Blades and five ex-Barmy Army blokes who now called themselves the BDS (Blades Drug Squad), for reasons best not explored. A certain Mr Heaton also met up with us, along with a Blade from London. In all there were 26 of us, a rag, tag and bobtail outfit if ever there was one.

By 8 pm most of us were at the stage where sea legs take over, when a large group of well-dressed boys came through the pub doors. They looked the part and I immediately felt apprehension as they filled the pub. There were no kiddie-mugs among them. I asked a couple who they were.

'We're Leicester,' came the reply.

I was relieved that they weren't Cockneys; at least with people north of Luton you can hold a conversation. I knew a few Leicester boys from many years ago when four of us used to stop off there on our way home from away games and meet up in their boozer at the time, the Snooty Fox. We had some good nights until one evening we ended up in a dodgy part of town where they had taken us. They had some sort of trouble with local black lads although nothing major happened. Later a few Leicester turned on us, so that ended our nights out with their boys.

I mentioned a couple of names I knew, one who for the sake of anonymity I will call Brady. Brady was a long term Leicester hooligan who'd been locked up with one of our boys. He wasn't with them but was meeting them later. Our lot and Leicester got on quite amicably. They told stories of how they had been to Portsmouth that day and had run Pompey's firm. Leicester had taken two coaches and told me, 'We're the top boys in England at the moment, we've been through everyone.'

It was about this time that it all went pear-shaped. Max, a tall, solid youth from our van, who was normally quiet, chinned a Leicester boy. I later found out he was off his nut on speed and had been egged on by Scratch. The atmosphere turned ugly but what happened next was unreal. I pulled Max.

'What the fuck are you doing?'

'Sorry mate,' he put his hands up, palms out, toward the fuming Leicester lad. 'Give me your best shot,' said Max, sticking his chin out.

'You what?' said the Leicester fan, stunned.

'Go on, give me one.'

The Leicester lad drew his fist back and pretended to hit Max, stopping short. He obviously thought Max would move but the daft twat just kept on standing there with his chin stuck out. A tall, mixed race youth with Leicester then jumped through the crowd and chinned Max. That was it, the lot went up: tables, chairs, bottles, glasses. I fought like a demon; we all had to. I thought we'd get leathered for sure but to my surprise Leicester backed away. Our frenzied onslaught packed them into the exit doors as they tried to get out; the ones at the back were battered with stools. We chased them into the street and down the road, then most of our lot doubled back to the pub as Leicester disappeared into the night.

Scratch and about five or six others continued chasing despite my shouting them back. I jogged up behind them. As I turned a corner into a precinct, a few Leicester boys ran at Scratch and the few Blades that had followed. The brain-dead bastards steamed in, thinking everyone was there. Scratch fought with the mixed race lad who had punched Max and they wrestled each other to the floor as everyone battled it out. The police came from everywhere and Scratch and the black lad were nicked along with Fats, a young lad from our van. On being arrested Fats pretended to cry, protesting he had lost his dad. He got away, nice stroke (a few years later Fats got life for murder after a fight outside a local chippy – he was hit over the head with a golf club, which broke in two, and when he grabbed one end to fend off his attacker, the jagged shaft plunged into the man's heart and killed him).

Eight of us decided to head for the quieter back streets to find a pub and sit tight. None of us could believe we'd got a result with the numbers we'd had out. Eyes told us that he had been leaning at the bar with two Leicester boys telling him how they were the country's top firm and had done this and that, only to watch them cower in the corner as their lads got steamed out of the pub. 'Different league mate,' Eyes explained as he escorted them out of the back door. We moved on after one drink and walked up a dimly lit road to another boozer. As we were about to go in about ten casuals came out. One of out lot said, 'They're Leicester,' so we bounced up. 'Come on boys, let's have it.'

'We're rugby fans,' they pleaded.

We let them go. After we had been served and sat down the general opinion was that they were Leicester boys but just bottled it. We were all completely kettled, singing United songs, ignoring the landlady who told us to be quiet or get out. Fats, who didn't go to football that often, wouldn't shut up:

> *Forever and ever, we'll follow our team*
> *Sheff United we are supreme*
> *We'll never be mastered*
> *By no Wednesday bastard*
> *We'll keep the red flag flying high.*

A few boys came through the entrance doors.

'Fuckin' hell, they're here.'

We jumped up. If they had got in, we'd have been slaughtered. They backed out and we stood around the doors. Every window came in. I looked through the broken glass and 70 Leicester were going mad in the road.

'Fuck off, Dexy boys.'

The night air was split by the sound of sirens. The Met arrived and Leicester scattered. We sat down to finish our drinks. The landlady was sound as the police steamed in expecting another firm to be in the pub.

'It's not these lads, they were only singing,' she told them.

She was right but she had every reason to be annoyed; if we hadn't have been there her pub windows would still be intact. We drank up and moved on after police advice. As we went outside, a few cuffed-up Leicester lads were sat on the pavement. We gave them abuse as we passed. After asking an officer which station our arrested mate would be in, we headed off in search of the cop shop. It really dawned on me how sad London is as we walked by. Shop doorways were taken up by scruffy homeless people with only cardboard boxes and tatty blankets to keep them warm. I told everyone to check the homeless people's feet, which was greeted with laughter and some blank looks. I explained that Scratch had once given a tramp his new Nike trainers after feeling sorry for him. Scratch did things like that when pissed. We checked at the police station and found he had been released, so we headed for the nearest tube station. A sad figure was leaning on the tiled wall; it was Scratch and was he pleased to see us. He looked like Julie Andrews at the beginning of *The Sound of Music*, running towards us with his arms outstretched.

'I didn't know where to go,' he mumbled.

We jumped on the tube and set off, saying goodbye to Harry, our mate from London. We were all off our nut and didn't realise we were heading in the wrong direction; typical northerners really. Four Cypriot-looking geezers got on at a stop and sat opposite us. They were right lairy bastards. Two of them had empty wine bottles and were banging them on the sole of one foot. I ignored them at first but they stared at us chewing gum like Danny Zuko in *Grease*.

'Bang that bottle once more and I'll smash it on your head,' I said to the one opposite me. He continued and I was about to get up to him when Dave punched him from the side. It was a beauty, knocking both of his front teeth out. We jumped up and punched a couple but they didn't want to know, so we took the bottles off them and sat back down. They jumped off at the next stop and mouthed some shit at us as the tube pulled away.

At the next stop the police got on. We explained what had happened and they left us with a warning: 'Behave yourselves or it's a night in the cells.'

As we travelled on to the next station it finally dawned on us we were heading the wrong way. It was also the last tube. We jumped off at the next station and found a phone in the dark car park outside the station. I rang our driver on his mobile and was just explaining where we were when out of the station came the Cyps we had battered. One was carrying a fire extinguisher. I dropped the phone with the words, 'Hold on, it's going to kick off again.'

As they approached I punched the one brandishing the extinguisher. Scratch picked it up and hit him with it. A fight broke out and it was fun for a while; though they had a right pop they couldn't fight very well and were easy to drop. Then two cars screeched up behind us and out jumped seven or eight of their mates armed with baseball bats. Two of our lot ran. For the rest of us, the only way out of the car park was to go through them, which we all managed to do, with a few of us getting clubbed. We ran for our lives as they chased us.

We got clear and ran under a bridge, then I heard a shout of 'Help'. It was Scratch. He was on his hands and knees getting battered. I shouted to our lot and ran back, arming myself with a brick in the process. I ran up and punched one while pretending to throw the brick. Scratch managed to get up and run while I lobbed the brick at them and then joined him. We caught up with the rest of our lot who were busy dismantling a fence. I emptied a wheelie bin on the pavement. There was nothing I could use inside, not even a Cornflake packet, so as they approached I stood there with the wheelie bin in front of me like a crazed bin man.

They overpowered us and we did one again. I had to swerve across the road to avoid capture. Mart was running parallel to me on the opposite side of the road with the geezers chasing him. He was caught and felled by a sickening blow to his head from a bat from behind. He went down and I knew he was in big trouble. I shouted to the rest of our lot but they had disappeared around the corner. It was a desperate situation: your mate is getting battered and you know you're going to get it as well but you have to go in. I couldn't look a mate in the eyes again if I left him. I ran across as they kicked and clubbed the limp body of Mart like hyenas round a zebra carcass. I punched one, who fell. As they came for me I kicked and lashed out. Then like the cavalry Dave came back around the corner with a brick in each hand. He came beside me and threw a brick, hitting one in the chest. We grabbed at Mart who was covered in blood. He stumbled to his feet as we dragged him, while trying to fight at the same time.

For the second time that night the noise of police sirens filled the air and for the second time it was more than welcome. The Cyps cleared off. Mart kept collapsing and blood was pumping from his head as I tried to locate the wound. The police came and were brilliant. Mart was taken to hospital, our van driver was phoned and they let us sit in the police van to wait for our lift. Scratch wouldn't get in, protesting with his charge sheet in his hand, 'I've been nicked once tonight.'

'You've been busy mate,' one copper replied.

Max and Scratch both had large cuts on their heads but refused to go to hospital for stitches. Our van arrived, and everyone in it wanted to know what had happened as we headed for the hospital to pick Mart up. On arrival, me and Eyes walked in and located Mart, who had numerous stitches in two deep head wounds. His back was also covered in welts and bruises. But he was all right, dropping his trousers to expose his dick and asking the nurses what they thought of it. We arrived back in Sheffield at around 5.30 in the morning, what a proper mad day. So much for 'boring' Wimbledon.

Incidentally, four years ago, Max, the lad who had caused all the bollocks in Leicester Square, went to Amsterdam on a stag night with the lads from our area. Something weird happened to him as he went missing for 24 hours. He then turned up at five o'clock in the morning at the hotel. All the lads were still up having a smoke and took a photo of Max stood in the doorway. That's the last anyone has seen of him. The photo shows him with his eyes bulging and his white Stone Island jumper covered in mud. If anyone knows his whereabouts, get in touch.

# WHITE LINES: LIVERPOOL AWAY
## 2 APRIL 1994.

United's Premiership plight hung in the balance as 5,000 fans travelled to Anfield. We'd hired a coach. Of the 54 on board, 40 were boys, the rest my mates from where I lived. The plan was to spend all day in Liverpool: off to the match, more beers, then on to see the *Beautiful South* play a gig at Liverpool Civic Centre. Everything went to plan. We even set off on time, which was a minor miracle for our lot. Our rendezvous was The Crown pub near Liverpool train station. There we met more Blades, a few Everton lads we knew and Paul Heaton, the Beautiful South's singer/songwriter and a fellow Blade.

Our first pint was necked at 11.45. It would be the first of many during a 13-hour binge. I was surprised there were no Liverpool boys around but we had never gone mobbed up into Liverpool centre, so why should we this time? As kick-off approached most of our lot got taxis to the ground, leaving six or seven on an all-day binge. We agreed to meet back at The Crown later.

I never expected United to get any sort of result but a superb defensive display earned us a 2-1 win. Even more surprising was that both our goals came from Jostein Flo who was, in the opinion of most Blades, useless. Even his fellow players called him the 'pantomime horse'. After the game around 50 of us met in the Arkle pub near the ground. The scousers were a friendly lot, saying they hoped we stayed up and that our fans were brilliant. They also had a moan about their side's plight. They ought to have been born Sheffield United, then they could moan.

The atmosphere was sound until a loud slap interrupted the peace. Raggy had given a stocky, balding geezer a clip. Apparently he had been trying to stoke the scousers up to have a pop at us. Twenty minutes later, I went outside to assess the taxi situation. As I stood, rather stoned, looking left and right, the trouble-causing scouser was walking toward me. He stopped to pull on a pair of leather gloves and stared at me. I couldn't take this fuckbrain seriously but I knew he'd have to go.

'What the fuck's up wi thee, daft cunt?' I asked.

'Come head,' he replied arms outstretched.

I went for him and he reeled backwards. A few of our lot came out of the pub and he retreated further across the road.

'What the fuck's up wi' that dick, has he got a tile loose?' one asked.

We decided to have a laugh. He was quite hefty, in his late thirties and obviously not very fit. Six of us chased him up a long road. We had no intention of giving him a beating, even though he deserved one. He ran like the wind at first, then after about 60 metres slowed. Another 60 and he was ready to collapse. We turned and went back down, laughing. We jumped in a waiting taxi and were still laughing as we headed down town. The lippy scouser was leaning on a wall, hyperventilating. I pulled the window down and shouted.

'Oy, twat, I bet you're still there in the morning.'

He looked up red-faced and walked into the road putting two fingers up at us. The taxi behind contained more of our lot who, on seeing him, jumped out and chased him back down the road. Once again we cracked up. I bet he hates Sheffield United with a passion. He must have been close to a cardiac.

Back at The Crown everyone was in good spirits and the lager tasted better now our Premiership future was brighter. Our Everton mates snorted coke like it was going out of fashion while our lot made do with endless joints topped up with a wrap or two of billy whizz. A few close mates and myself had become (and still are) good mates with the Everton lads after Bally had met one on holiday. One Evertonian is now godfather to a Blade's daughter. Strange that in 1983 we'd had an off with the same lads before a League Cup game at Bramall Lane. Our Scouse mates were there and admit they were on their toes.

By eight o'clock the 60 of us were well out of it and the inevitable singsong disturbed many people's night out in various pubs and bars. I loved days like these, 60 happy Blades singing songs in that Sheffield twang and sense of humour. Paul Heaton was as drunk as anybody. He had been out all day and was due on stage in twenty minutes. I don't know how he managed to sing that day but it was a brilliant concert, so maybe drink relaxes the man.

Once inside the venue I weaved my way to the front despite it being full. Five others joined me and we went for it as the concert started. Raggy's trainers had come off in the crush and he banged them on my head in time to the music. It got on my tits after a while so I grabbed one off him and threw it at Heaton, who dodged it even after consuming 15 pints.

Five tracks into the gig, Heaton looked at me. 'Steve,' echoed through the mike.

It seemed like a dream as mid-concert he beckoned me onto the stage. As security helped me over the crush barriers I thought,

I've got to sing one. Me, Steve Cowens, a mere pawn in the great chess game of life. No such luck.

'Steve all the boys have kicked off at the back with security, sort it out or they're going to stop the concert,' Paul informed me.

I went down a corridor with two security men. At the end of it stood 25 nervous-looking colleagues. Through the doors stood our lot, starring menacingly at the bouncers.

'Is it you that can sort this lot out? They've attacked us twice,' the lead geezer said.

'I don't know about that but I'll have a go.'

I went to the lads. 'For fuck's sake this is a concert, not a football match.'

One or two told me the security got clever and started pushing, so our lot steamed them. I calmed the situation and the gig went ahead.

Afterwards, we went for a few beers in several bars. Liverpool was sound. The Everton lads took us to a bar that had an upstairs room with a singer. The bouncers didn't look too pleased but were powerless to stop us going in. Me three mates and the Toffee boys sat in a corner out of the way. One Evertonian produced a small bag of charlie.

'Steve, juwana line? Fucken sound gear.'

The singer, a young lad around 21, was into his act belting out some miserable pop dirge. No one was listening except his mother on the table next to us. Four Blades put everyone out of their misery by throwing their pints on him. To top it off the poor guy jumped five foot in the air as he got an electric shock from the microphone. His mother gathered his things and they both beat a hasty retreat. A brawl broke out at the bar but the locals didn't stand a chance really. Things were starting to get out of hand so it was time to head back to the coach which was due to leave at 2 am.

When we got to the rendezvous point I saw Scratch but no coach.

'It's fucked off,' he mumbled.

'Fuck off,' I retorted.

'Straight up, the driver got off the coach for a piss and Tom jumped into the seat and drove off, he nearly crashed it. Coppers came and ordered us off. Budge has got nicked for shouting,

"What's the fuckin' charge man?" (a local joke taken from a *Sid the Sexist* video). All our ganja is hid in the seats.'

Five of us got a black cab back to Sheffield at a cost of £55. I borrowed £10 from Tom to pay my share. It just shows the state I was in that day, as around a month later I went out in my leather jacket that I'd worn at Liverpool, in the pocket was £80 and I'd borrowed a tenner to pay my way home.

Despite the Liverpool result, we were relegated at the end of the season after four years in the Premier League in a bizarre twist of fate. Dave Bassett had performed a minor miracle in keeping us up for so long. He had no money but his shrewd use of the transfer market and the fact he could get his players to run through a brick walls for him kept the club afloat. United fans loved him and he loved being at the club. The affection for Bassett was evident right from the start of United's return to the top flight. The Blades went 16 matches without a win and were rooted to the bottom of the league. Not once through all those games did the crowd boo or call for anyone's head, there was an inner strength and the fans' loyalty was repaid when, at the 17th time of asking, we beat Nottingham Forest 3-2. The final whistle was greeted by thousands of fans invading the pitch and carrying the players off the field. It was a remarkable gesture by fans that appreciated a team of triers and a manager that cared.

United climbed the table and finished the season in 13th place. For the next three years we stayed in the Premier League until the final game of the 1993-94 season. United travelled to Stamford Bridge needing a win to be certain of survival. With five minutes to go United (who were drawing 2-2 with Chelsea) were actually sixth from bottom when, in a bizarre twist, the results involving Everton, Ipswich and Southampton all turned against us. When Mark Stein scored for Chelsea in the very last minute the writing was on the wall.

I left Stamford Bridge that day feeling empty. My team, the team I had supported all my life, had gone down. The club and supporters will always feel cheated at that relegation: there have been claims that match-fixing influenced it. Everton scored the winning goal in the last minute against Wimbledon. In goal for the Dons that day was Hans Segers and his attempt at keeping out Graham Stuart's 25-yard trickler was dismal. Later Bruce Grobbelaar, John Fashanu and Segers (who had actually played for United in 1987) were charged with match fixing. The Everton-Wimbledon game was one of several under scrutiny. All three walked free from court though Grobbelaar's libel victory against the *Sun* newspaper was later overturned. The cost of relegation to Sheffield United FC would run into millions of pounds. Graham Stuart signed for us a few years later and I got talking to him at a friend's barbeque. I asked him about the goal and he just smiled. The truth may come out one day but this I know: Hans Segers is no longer welcome in Sheffield.

# WATFORD: POP STARS, FILM STARS AND IRISH BARS 17 DECEMBER 1994.

I had been to Watford three times in ten years and never even seen a boy worth kicking off with, never mind any trouble. We once lost 5-0 there in a pathetic FA Cup showing when Watford's three black forwards, John Barnes, Luther Blisset and Worral Stirling, tore our defence to pieces and our keeper John Burridge came out with the classic line, 'It was like Rourke's Drift out there today.'

In 1994 our game at Watford coincided with a *Beautiful South* concert at Aston Villa's leisure centre. The plan was to watch the Blades then travel to Birmingham to see the *South*. All we needed was a van and a driver. Somebody suggested Andy, a bloke from our local who had a minibus. He had taken us to Wimbledon once and the lot went up (see earlier). After half an hour I managed to persuade him, with two factors swaying his decision.

'Look Andy, there won't be any trouble, it's only Watford, they don't have any boys. And I'll get you a ticket for the Beautiful South.' Sorted.

We set off with 15 lads in the van, half local Blades and half from our Sunday football team. No BBC travelled that day. When we arrived we found an Irish pub near the ground. A few other Blades were in there, including Mr Movie Star 100% Blade Sean Bean. He was with his mates from Handsworth, an area of Sheffield where he was brought up. In the back room of the pub was a pool table. Our lot settled down, played 'killer' and smoked endless joints.

Nothing happened until a few of us headed to the ground. As Raggy, Bally, Eyes and myself approached the stand. I clocked around 25 boys, all geared up. At first I thought they must be Blades, but as we got closer they came across the road towards us. Three of us had Stone Island tops on and, as all boys know, you can spot a fellow thug; their mannerisms and clothes make them stick out from normal football-goers. The usual verbals went off.

'Fuckin' Watford, you've never been boys.'

'We're Tottenham.'

A few bounced about as if they were going to steam us. One was punched and police hurried over. As we headed for the away end I was puzzled. What were Tottenham doing here? Was it because we had taken the piss at White Hart Lane a few of years earlier? Or did they know some Watford lads and had come to help out?

After the game we headed back for the Irish bar. Around 40 lads stood outside the ground, obviously looking for it. I bounced towards them but just as it was about to go off the police rushed over. Sheffield's football intelligence officers followed us as police kept us on one side of the road and them on the other.

At the pub, our vanload and the Handsworth Blades continued our drinking binge. Our plan was to stay there until 7.30, then set off for Birmingham. We had a good time and the Irish people were very hospitable. One football intelligence man came into the pub a good hour and a half after the match. One of our lot went up him.

'What you hanging around for? There's not going to be any trouble is there? We're going to a concert soon.'

The officer nodded and went. Our driver was sent to pick the van up. I went to the bar for a few more bottles. Nipper nudged me.

'Who are these?'

I glanced to my left. A few boys were coming into the pub, looking apprehensive.

'It's them.' I went at them and they backed out the door. Nipper went to get the rest of our lot. I stood in the doorway with 50 Watford and friends bouncing around in the road. Our motley crew quickly arrived behind me.

'Get out,' yelled Raggy.

I turned around and looked at our lot. Half had the bleary-eyed, stoned look.

'I'm going out but for fuck's sake everyone follow.'

They did. We chased them up the road, one got dropped and too many of ours jumped on him. This left just six or seven of us chasing them. They raided a skip and came back at us. We stood in the road. Ian copped a large brick to his forehead. He was in a proper Frankie wrangle. We backed off trying to help Ian get away but he had the old Bruno legs on. The rest of our lot came running to help. Ronnie, a young lad from round our way who didn't go to football, came running up with a long plank. We got ourselves together and realised this was our chance to run them again, then the daft bastard just threw it at their feet and ran.

We backed into the pub doors and Scratch got hit over the head with Ronnie's plank. All the windows went in as they attacked the pub. We returned fire, led by a mad Irish geezer who stood on the seats right in front of the smashed windows throwing pint pots out.

'Come on ye dirty feckers,' he bawled. Bricks bounced off him and still he stood there.

'Seamus, get down, you'll be hurt for sure,' a bartender shouted at him. Seamus was having none of it.

'Ya barstards.'

We ran back out with pool cues and once again chased Watford. Raggy and a couple of others chased three who ran into a house and locked the door. So three Blades smashed every window in the place. The police arrived and our newfound Irish friends explained that we had been attacked and had been in the pub all day causing no trouble. Seamus, top man, picked up his Guinness from the bar and continued drinking, blood running down his head. He mumbled something about always having trouble with them 'barstards'. Everyone later enjoyed the Beautiful South concert, except Ian who needed several stitches to a bad head wound. The hero of the day was definitely that mad Irishman, Seamus.

# THE WASTED YEARS

## THE TROUBLE WITH WEDNESDAY

## SUNDAY, BLOODY SUNDAY

## MY TOWN IS DRAGGING ME DOWN

## THE SHEFFIELD DOUBLE - PART 1

## THE SHEFFIELD DOUBLE - PART 2

## DEATH AT THE DERBY GAME

## THE STEEL CITY CUP

## DIRTY DO FROM A MOTLEY CREW

## BACK TO A BAD LAD

## SUFC V SWFC

## A BLADE'S STORY

There are many difficulties in sharing a city with your deadly rivals. The hatred that exists between Sheffield's two clubs will match any other rivalry in the country: only the Glaswegian derby surpasses it and that's more to do with religion than football. After one United lad was attacked whilst shopping with his wife by so-called Wednesday top boys, it made me think what it would be like to live in a city that is not shared. Other big cities like Manchester and Liverpool are but don't have the problems that Sheffield has.

Over the years, I have been arrested four times for fighting against the Snort Beasts. They have phoned and visited my place of work and attacked me twice playing football on Sunday mornings. I never did the dirty one back and I've saved many a Wednesday lad from a bad beating. I actually got arrested for fighting against my own club's followers because they were beating up a well-known Wednesday lad and I thought it was out of order. It's just the way I am. There's no result in 20 Blades ragging ten Wednesday. If it was the other way round then it's a buzz, outnumbered and well on top, that's how I liked it.

I could write a book on my encounters with Wednesday alone but I have stuck to a few stories that span the years. Wednesday's boys have in recent years tried to get their crew on the go again. After several years of relative quiet, the city centre has once again seen trouble between the BBC and OCS. It does not, and will not, involve me any more.

# THE TROUBLE WITH WEDNESDAY 1985.

As I have already outlined, the balance of power between the two firms shifted in the winter of 1982. October 1985 saw the Blade/ Owl violence take a turn for the worse with a new and ugly weapon, the petrol bomb. Wednesday had tried to march a firm up London Road twice in the previous two months. This resulted in the OCS being chased both times and some of Wednesday's top lads taking bad beatings. One Wednesday lad of mixed race had his dreadlocks yanked from his scalp. The dreads were pinned up on a wall in a pub on London Road for two weeks.

We heard through the hooli-vine that Wednesday had planned another attack on our London Road territory. We had also heard that they would be tooled up and had a surprise in store for us. Touching 100 Blades turned out this particular Friday night. I made elaborate plans. I bandaged my leg, even though it wasn't injured, and carried a crutch. I intended to run into Wednesday like a runaway windmill. If arrested, I would point to my bandage and claim to be an innocent lad attacked by hooligans.

A couple of cars patrolled the streets on the lookout for the enemy. The police had got drift of the impending riot and London Road was heavily patrolled. Getting at Wednesday wouldn't be easy and we knew a few arrests would probably have to be sacrificed. News of Wednesday's whereabouts came through an unexpected source. Some officers entered the pub and one of our boys overheard a police radio message that Wednesday were heading up St Mary's Gate.

Four of us went down in Frankie's car to suss out their mob. We saw around 120 of them. As we drove past, two lads leant out of the car window and fired distress flares at them. They cheered as the flares rose above their heads and crashed into the pub wall. Wednesday had gathered in the Sportsman Inn and our lot were 350 yards away in the Pheasant. On our return, we sent 20 down London Road as a decoy. The rest headed off in dribs and drabs. It worked. The plod followed the 20, allowing the rest to mob up and walk down the dark streets towards our goal. 'Quiet, walk don't run,' was the word.

Wednesday saw us and poured out of the Sportsman. They looked good and bottles and glass crashed around us and quite a few of our lot were injured by missiles coming through the gloom. Once the ammo had run dry I steamed in, my crutch connecting with a Wednesday boy. We chased them back to the pub. Then police steamed in from everywhere. I limped away as they went to work with truncheons. Three of our lot were arrested.

As I hobbled around the corner, I bumped into Sam. 'Run again,' he said gleefully, referring to Wednesday.

Then, ten black Wednesday boys came out of a side street. They had missed the off.

'We've just run your boys, you mugs,' I yelled.

I had all the mouth of a cockney on acid and after getting over their initial surprise they came at me. I simply tucked my crutch under my arm and ran off, laughing, with Sam.

'Cheeky bastard,' one shouted.

It seemed to echo in the darkness, then round a corner and straight into four coppers on foot. Shit. I limped and put the crutch to the floor again. To my amazement the bizzies just told me to clear off and gave Sam a clip. Later that night a Blade was blinded in one eye as United attacked a pub with a few Wednesday in. A shard of glass hit him and lacerated his pupil.

Many people outside of the violence may well wonder why we would follow a course that could lead to injuries like that. Of course it is not worth losing your sight in a fight over football but such events never put the hardcore hooligans off. Injuries were just accepted; no one cried about being hurt in a fight. And the lad in question was soon into the violence again.

Ten boys were arrested that night, all Blades except for two young Wednesday lads. They had been carrying petrol bombs. The Molotovs had not been used but this was a dangerous development. Over the years, I saw some actions that in my eyes were out of order. Once after Wednesday had been run, a lad called Bacon was caught and sprayed with lighter fuel by a Blade, who then proceeded to put a cigarette lighter to him. I dragged the Wednesday lad away and then walked him up to the Limit nightclub. Bacon deserved some respect for being game enough to stand when everyone around him had disappeared. I ended up going into the club with him for a drink and inside were 40 pissed-off Wednesday. They could have given me a hard time but didn't. Although I was bang at it, they knew I had a code of conduct.

The two young Wednesday lads got two years prison for the petrol bombs. One year later, petrol bombs were used for real.

# SUNDAY, BLOODY SUNDAY 1988.

I was in the thick of all the trouble on Saturday nights, but as far as I was concerned, the streets were where scores were settled, not people's homes, work place or anything else. Yet three times while playing football on Sunday mornings, I was singled out by Wednesday's non-churchgoers. This particular morning could have been quite nasty if it hadn't been for my front and a Wednesday boy called Chirpy. I had been tipped off in the week that Wednesday were coming after me. It didn't need a brain surgeon to work it out, as we were playing the Arbourthorne Hotel, a pub that Wednesday drank in. On top of that, the pitch we were due to play on was bang in the middle of the Arbourthorne Estate, a Wednesday stronghold.

Two days before my match, some United boys asked me how, where and when they should turn up. I insisted that no BBC should turn out.

'We're playing football. I don't need all this shit Sunday morning.'

There were several reasons I didn't want a pitched battle on my behalf. Firstly, I didn't want our team kicked out of the league. Secondly, if it went off the team would be targeted even more. Thirdly, I saw it as totally out of order and believed it to be Wednesday's problem.

A few weeks earlier I had been sent off for chinning an opponent, so I would be suspended for the game and would therefore be stood on the touchline. The Sunday morning came and our team were not their usual jovial self. The tension could be felt as they changed into the kit.

'Look, it's me they're coming for, just win the game.'

I wasn't exactly carefree but it didn't bother me too much. If I was going to get it, then someone was going with me. The game kicked off and we quickly took a 3-0 lead. As halftime approached, I glanced up towards the Vulcan pub, which overlooked the pitch, and saw around 30 Wednesday coming around the corner accompanied by a rottweiler and a doberman. I glanced at my dad (who was our manager). He looked like he had seen a ghost.

'Steven, fuck off now,' he demanded.

As Wednesday reached the touchline, Holder, a Blades boy who played for us, chinned one of their players. A lot of players got involved and Wednesday ran onto the pitch shouting, 'Uh-uh-uh.' I ran on from the other touchline and headed over. The referee restored calm and I trudged back to my dad. Wednesday were pointing across at me, then started to walk around the pitch towards me.

'For fuck's sake son, go.' My dad was distressed.

I was concerned he would get hurt if he tried to intervene in the beating I was about to get, so I headed away from him and walked straight towards Wednesday. There was no way I was going to do a runner. The adrenaline was pumping as I walked past the first few Wednesday lads.

'Wanker.' A lad with one of those shitty Gabbicci jumpers shouted at me. It was Quinny, who I later got to know. Another lad booted me from behind.

'You're shit,' he snarled.

'I'm shit? Thirty of you lot for me?'

I shrugged my shoulders and headed over to the main bulk of Wednesday's nasty mob. They must have been stunned at my front. One of Wednesday's main actors was a lad called Chirpy. I didn't know him to talk to at the time, but knew who he was.

'What's happening Chirpy, thirty of you for me?'

'We thought Luey and Shane played football for you.'

'They don't play football, for fuck's sake, man.'

'Oh we heard they all played for this team.'

'No, just me.'

I couldn't help thinking his comments were bullshit and he had dropped a few names to excuse their actions.

'Come on, let's go,' he said. Fair play to old Chirpy; I was signed, sealed and delivered but he called the hounds off. It was something I would have done in his shoes but then again I wouldn't have turned out in the first place.

As they left I shouted, 'Nice one, Chirpy.' I was relieved but still angry that they had turned up in the first place. My dad was shaking like a leaf when I got back around to him.

'Jesus, son. What did you say?'

'Just forget it pop, it's sorted.'

Another day living life on the edge as a football hooligan. We won the game 6 –2, incidentally.

# MY TOWN IS
# DRAGGING ME DOWN
## 1989.

Most Friday evenings, Raggy and I could be found drinking in various city centre bars. We didn't know that on this particular night United's boys had clashed with Wednesday, who were out celebrating Chirpy's stag night. Chirpy had been a front-runner with Wednesday for years and around 50 of them were in town. As Raggy and I headed for Sinatra's night club, suited and booted, we bumped into an out-of-breath Wednesday lad called Tesh. He explained that they had been chased all over town. We offered to walk Tesh up to the Limit nightclub, where Wednesday would be going.

As we got up there we bumped into their lot hanging around on a street corner. They came around us. I had been looking for one of their lads for a few months and spotted him. I went at him and they steamed us. It was on top and I lost my Armani jacket in the struggle. Raggy managed to retrieve it and we retreated. I now had a fat lip for my troubles and was on one.

We jumped into a taxi and headed for the Leadmill nightclub in the hope of getting a few United lads together. We found five and walked back up into town. The magnificent seven bumped straight into Wednesday outside the Wapentake pub. I screamed at our lot not to move an inch because I knew I wasn't going anywhere. They came at us and I just ran into them, kamikaze-fashion. I was engulfed in knuckles and boots.

The next thing I knew, I was being thrown into a police van with five Wednesday lads. Down at the station I was slung into a cell. The scuffed up Burton-type shoes outside the cells should have given me a clue, but the sight as the door opened was unmistakable. It was Chirpy, fast asleep on the wooden bench. The door slammed behind me and I walked over to him. Leaning down I shouted in his ear, 'Chirpy, the Berties are here.'

Chirpy jumped from his slumber. His face was a picture as he gazed up at me.

'Cowensy, what the fuck you doing here?'

'I'm your solicitor, what do you think? Your mates have just mullered me in town.'

We sat and chatted for the next three hours. He was all right was Chirpy, one from the old school, code of conduct and all that. It was nice to hear Chirpy concede that Wednesday couldn't touch United's firm. I shook his hand as he was released.

In court I was fined £120 with £40 costs. A good night out, not.

The violence between the two rivals continued for the next two years. The Woodthorpe Arms was targeted by 20 BBC one Friday night. They were after the Wednesday firm, and one lad in particular. Bats were used that left their target needing stitches and other Wednesday lads were hurt. Although I knew of the plan, I stayed away. It was not my scene going tooled up and storming a pub. I also knew and got along with the intended victim. He was a main face who had grown up with my wife and I had a bit of time for him. The attack provoked outrage in the local media.

Another city centre pub hit the headlines: 20 of us were drinking in there when it was stormed by Wednesday. Pud was attacked until we came running to his aid. We backed them out of the pub; the 20 or so Wednesday had a bit of a go then turned and ran. Two lads were captured but surprisingly they weren't ragged; instead our lot held them down and shouted, 'Come back, we've got your mates.' Wednesday continued to run.

West Street was increasingly the battlefield. One Saturday evening saw a 150-a-side fight outside the Hallamshire Hotel. Twenty-two people were arrested and several boys visited hospital casualty. Another interesting story from around this time involved a black United hooligan called Nathan. He had been one of the leading protagonists in the attack on Wednesday in the Woodthorpe Arms. Nathan went with his girlfriend to an Indian restaurant. Just as the bhagis arrived, so did around 15 Wednesday boys. Nathan was attacked and fought them off with a pickle tray. The incident took place in Pitsmoor, an area in Sheffield with a predominantly black population. Fifteen white lads attacking a black lad is not the thing to do around those parts. To make matters worse, one of United's main actors passed in a car as the fracas spilled into the streets. In minutes, 20 blacks were chasing Wednesday all over the place. BMWs screeched around and two young lads were caught. One started crying and was released, the other took a bit of a beating.

Recently Wednesday's firm have, for some reason or another, gone down the racist avenue. The lack of blacks with their crew may have something to do with it but I know one thing. The blacks that have fought for Wednesday over the years have more respect than those little pumpkins can ever hope to gain.

# THE SHEFFIELD DOUBLE – PART ONE
## 17 NOVEMBER 1991.

The build up to this derby game was electric. It had been almost 12 years since the last competitive game between Sheffield's two clubs. United made the game a noon Sunday kick-off on the advice of South Yorkshire Police. Sunday drinking hours at the time were 12 until 3 pm and after the match police refused permission for pubs to open within three miles of the ground. It was hoped that trouble could be minimised. It had the desired effect as both sets of fans and boys had nowhere to go before and after the game.

I took my seat in the South Stand. The atmosphere was unbelievable. Our boys were scattered all around the ground, with the largest group of around 250 situated in the John Street terrace. The players were on the pitch and the game was about to kick off when a young United boy came running down the steps of the stand.

'Wednesday are in't back o't stand.'

I was sitting with two long-term friends who had nothing to do with trouble. Without really thinking, I was off up the stand, pausing briefly to shout to around ten BBC who were sitting in the next block to me. As I went down the steps into the back of the stand it was deserted. A quick look right, nothing, and then a look left. Around 40 Wednesday were gathered at the end of the stand. I jogged over towards them. Wednesday stood around on the concourse eating pies and supping Bovril. When I got 20 yards away I knew this was all Wednesday's main boys, with no young mugs. I then had a quick glance back and realised I was on my own. Wednesday had spotted me and a few fanned out with arms outstretched.

I had two choices: stop and maybe retreat or just continue my one-man attack. I chose the latter and just waded into the mass of bodies. I did well for a while, but with the sheer number of kicks and punches raining in on me, not to mention the pies and Bovrils, I went down. They put the boot in as I tried to get back to my feet. Then to my great relief I heard the shout of: 'Come on.'

Tiler, Luey, Pud, Feaney and six or seven more of our lot ran into Wednesday. I jumped to my feet and went back in again. We were well outnumbered, but the lads we had were good ones. Fist and boots were flying as we battled it out, no side giving an inch. Although I had been ragged a bit, I had no apparent injuries. The sheer number of Wednesday in the confined walkway seemed to restrict their punches as they got in each other's way. We had room to manoeuvre and I got at least three good shots in. Through the corner of my eye I saw someone about to hit me. Just in time, I lashed out with a peach that smashed into his face. He reeled back through the throng. It was Mifter. I knew the lad well. He's a handy guy who does a bit of boxing. Still, no love's lost in a war.

Stewards and police ran in, quelling our fun. At half-time news had travelled through the stand, and we got 50 together, weaving our way through the mass of fans having a half-time break to try to locate the Wednesday. The police were there before us so the verbals went off.

'You're shit, Wednesday.'

'See you later, up West Street.'

'Me and you, let's take a walk,' and so on.

All this took place right under the noses of Sheffield's football intelligence. Six plain clothes men tried to mingle and look like fans, but they may as well have had uniforms on they were that obvious. I saw Mifter and his eye was shut thanks to my right cross. I apologised and said that there was no offence. He looked pissed off but nodded. If I had taken one, there wouldn't have been any grudge. It's just one of those things. I knew nearly all Wednesday's top lads, so things like this were bound to happen.

The game ended 2-0 to us and we were ecstatic. A hundred Blades headed up Ecclesall Road straight after the game. It was reasoned that Wednesday might be up there. The other reason was we would be able to get a drink thanks to plenty of licensed burger restaurants. The drink flowed and before long everyone was up singing anti-Wednesday songs.

*Walk tall, walk straight and look the world right in the eye*
*That's what my momma told me, when I was about knee high*
*She said, Sonny you're a Blades fan, so hold your head up high*
*And as you're walking down the street, poke a Pig fan in the eye.*

Everyone was in great spirits. This didn't stop 80 per cent of the dining Blades leaving without paying. Later that night we went looking for Wednesday up West Street and town, but found nothing.

# THE SHEFFIELD DOUBLE – PART TWO
## 11 MARCH 1992.

The return game had much more promise of a set-to between the two firms. The match was an evening kick-off plus hundreds of United followers had tickets for the Wednesday seats and kop. At teatime, around 300 United boys gathered in two pubs in town. The plan was to drink our way to Hillsborough and hit the back of their kop ten minutes before kick-off. The bizzies had it sewn up though, as ten riot vans backed up by police on horseback and dog vans monitored our movements. We tried to split into two mobs, with our main boys hanging back but once again the bizzies had it sussed.

The march to Hillsborough was on, an impressive mob stretched out 200 yards from front to back. I knew when we hit the crowds at the ground it would be easier to shake off the plod and more importantly easier to plant a few Wednesday. As soon as we hit the back of their kop on Penistone Road it went off.

'BBC, BBC,' rang around the streets and fighting broke out everywhere. To be fair, a lot of Wednesday had a go, which surprised me. They didn't stand much of a chance as huge mobs of seasoned hooligans went about their work. I ended up at the end of their kop where quite a few Wednesday had gathered as they headed for the game from the various pubs at the top end of Hillsborough. Me, Shammy, Holder and around 20 other BBC ran into them. A couple of game lads stood. As one was beaten to the ground, Wednesday charged back. We stood and traded. Police steamed in and the truncheons were in full flow, a sign that they were struggling to contain the situation. Seven Blades were arrested and later banned from Bramall Lane and other grounds for a period of one year.

It is worth noting that though it was only ever the BBC's intention to fight with rival hooligans, in melées against Wednesday a lot of 'normal' fans tended to join in. It was rare to see them get involved but at a Sheffield derby I suppose the normals despise each other as much as the hooligans do

(The local press carried a front-page photo of Samuel coming out of court after the hearing and the Star reported how United's hooligans had attacked Wednesday fans and how these hardcore football thugs were the main instigators of the trouble. I sometimes wondered if South Yorkshire Police wrote articles for the *Sheffield Star*, although on this occasion the reporting wasn't far off the facts. Some of the reporting of incidents over the years has been laughable. Leeds once got the front-page headline in the local press: '300 LEEDS THUGS SMASH UP CLUB'. The fact was that 50 BBC had attacked Wednesday in a pub.

United had been given 6,200 tickets, which had sold out in hours. I had a seat in the Cantilever stand along with 25 other been-there, seen-it, done-it Blades. The stand is Wednesday's main seating area where quite a few of their lads sit. We made our way up to the top, so any attack could be more easily repelled. We also had a good view of a fight involving 400 Blades on Wednesday's East Bank kop. As the police waded in, masses of United followers were ejected and gathered on the pitch behind the goal. I'll never forget one bloke with his two sons dressed in United tracksuits. The two boys must have only been around nine and eleven years old, but as they trudged around the pitch in front of Wednesday's baying kop, they were giving it the wankers sign and the two-fingered salute along with their proud dad. I know it sounds pathetic that young lads should be encouraged this way, but I thought it was sound.

When the teams took to the pitch I gazed with admiration at our fans on the Leppings Lane end: a sea of red and white balloons, two massive flags, a dozen red distress flares lighting up the away end. It was awesome, the kind of thing you only see on TV footage from games abroad. The Wednesday scarfers sat around us openly admitted that they had never seen anything like it. The atmosphere was electric, something really special that makes the hair on the back of your neck stand up.

The game was a Blades dream. Bobby Davidson made himself a permanent place in Blades hearts with two goals in a 3-1 win. The other goal came from Dane Whitehouse, a Sheffield lad and Blade through and through. Dane had scored in both games and you could see what it meant to him.

After the final whistle, we hung around at the back of the stand. As the crowds vacated the ground we could see the movement of boys heading up towards us. Quite a few Wednesday had sussed us; not hard, really, as we were standing on seats going crackers. As they approached, we stood together, smiling. Wayne went forward and round-housed one straight in the side of the head. He went crashing over seats as he fell. That was the signal. We poured forward and they were off, trampling over seats and pulling each other out of the way.

Outside the ground we mobbed up at a nearby petrol station. Then the 200 of us made the three-mile walk into town. No Wednesday were around and everyone headed off to various clubs in town. The clubs were packed with United followers drinking and dancing celebrating the Sheffield Double.

Forty-two fans were arrested that night, 37 Blades and five Wednesday.

# DEATH
# AT THE DERBY GAME.
## WEMBLEY, 4 APRIL 1993.

The worst possible scenario surrounding football violence is the death of a rival or of one of your own. Although boys go into each other with the aggression of a 'survival of the fittest' mentality, the thought of killing an opposing boy never enters a hooligan's head. Having said that, I've seen some merciless beatings.

The year 1993 saw probably the biggest game Sheffield football has seen. The FA Cup semi-final had drawn the city's two bitter rivals together for a game which only Wembley Stadium could house, such was the demand. Each club had sold 35,000 tickets and could easily have sold more. This was Sheffield's day out and rivalries and passions were high. Pleas for a trouble free match from both clubs and the police were well intended but to be honest there was more chance of Rangers-Celtic, Spurs-Arsenal, Newcastle-Sunderland and Portsmouth-Southampton sitting down and having a nice tea party together.

In a heartrending moment prior to kick-off, Sheffield's football fans were for once united. Mel Reece was another one of Dave Bassett's great goalkeeping buys. Add Simon Tracey and Alan Kelly to the list and Bassett had three quality keepers. Tragically Reece developed cancer and his painful walk around Wembley brought a standing ovation from both sides of the city. It brought home that football was after all, just a game and that life was much, much more important. Mel died not long after but he will never be forgotten for his brief but brilliant displays for our club.

United boys took without doubt the biggest away crew I've ever seen to that semi-final. The evening before the big match saw 400 Blades boys packed into a pub near Leicester Square. Rumours did the rounds that Wednesday were meeting Chelsea, if they had showed (which they didn't) we'd have gone straight through both of them. The frustration showed later as our mob skirmished with police who'd completely circled the boozer, a few of ours were then arrested for nothing.

Next day, United had a massive mob of 600. It was an awesome turnout, which included a crew of 50 black lads. Wednesday's firm were seen before the game, they had 60 lads out. Wednesday won the game 2-1after extra time. It would have been six or seven if it wasn't for an outstanding display by our goalkeeper, Alan Kelly.

After the game we mobbed up and walked down Wembley Way. I stood on a wall and took a photo of our huge mob. Wednesday's firm had been held back by police, so I waited on a wall. They looked a bit lost, huddled together and surrounded by police. One of their main boys saw me and came over. I pointed to our lot further down Wembley Way. He acknowledged that it was a massive crew and Wednesday couldn't get a firm out to touch us. The BBC disappeared down into the tube station, with most heading for Victoria Station in the hope of meeting up with Chelsea.

The semi-final had been a magnificent spectacle but was overshadowed by a fatal incident in the Wembley car park after the game. Sonny, an older, well-known Wednesday boy who had been around long enough to know better, punched a peripheral Blades follower in an altercation. Sonny will regret that punch for the rest of his life. The non-hooligan fan had a lifelong heart condition; when he fell from the punch he cracked his head, causing heart failure, and died. Although everyone knew it was a tragic accident, a few United boys vowed revenge. I saw Sonny a couple of months later and he was devastated by the events. He later received a two-year custodial sentence for his part in the death. What should have been a brilliant day for Sheffield football was overshadowed. Football is life, not death.

# THE STEEL CITY CUP 1994.

The now defunct Steel City Cup was the brainchild of Reginald Brealey, United's chairman between 1981-95. The idea of a pre-season competition between the two sides was, in theory, a good one. Little did Reginald know that both sets of hooligans would be rubbing their hands at the thought of a ruck.

This particular game was at Bramall Lane. Nothing happened before the game, and afterwards we headed into town 70-strong on the lookout for the OCS. Everyone met up in Silks. Wednesday knew where we were and kept phoning the pub telling us to come down to Ecclesall Road and have a pop. I wasn't interested really and had not been in any United-Wednesday rucks for ages, but by 6.30 pm everyone had had enough of the threatening phone calls. Raggy jumped into a taxi with Holder and a couple of others. The plan was to meet up in Champs bar,

50 yards from the Nursery Tavern, where Wednesday were thought to be. Unfortunately for Raggy and the three other United lads, Wednesday were in Champs. They chased our four lads down a side street.

When we arrived in seven more taxis, 50 Wednesday were in the street. We bumped into the bulk of them returning after chasing Raggy and Co. I punched the first one to come my way and he went down, glasses flying across the tarmac. My victim was Jamie, an older face who I actually got on well with. I had hit Jamie twice before in fights and he had dropped both times, a proper Frank Bruno of the hooligan world.

Next up was a tall rasta; in an embarrassing scene I chased him around a parked car. More Blades arrived and Wednesday took flight. Tiler, game as usual, ran past a few of the retreating Wednesday lads when he copped for a sidewinder from Granville. Stunned, he went down and as a few Wednesday went for him, Housey and I ran in. Tiler stumbled to his feet and despite being very dazed, continued to try to fight, bless him.

Wednesday turned around outside the Nursery and picked up bottles and glasses from the tables. I ran at them and two Pils bottles crashed into me. As I went in again, another bottle crashed into my chest. This hurt; I'm sure Eric Bristow was out with their mob that day. In again and Wednesday backed into the pub doors, then tried to close them. I yanked the door open and waded in.

Police sirens told us it was time to split the scene. Further up Ecclesall Road there had been more fighting and a huge Wednesday lad called Teeney had been knocked unconscious. A United lad had got too carried away and threw a lump of concrete into his face. Later that evening, Teeney was in intensive care. The TV news, radio and Teletext reported the incident. I considered going to see Teeney in hospital but thought better of it. He wasn't to know I was not involved in the incident.

Eight Blades were 'dawn raided' by police as a result of that incident. There had been rumours for several years that United had a police informer amongst them but this incident proved that there were no grounds for the rumour, as the culprit was never arrested. He did, however get punched by another Blade who thought his actions were out of order. Teeney thankfully recovered.

# DIRTY DO
# FROM A MOTLEY CREW
## 12 SEPTEMBER 1999.

For the previous three years I had gone to Hillsborough for the visit of Everton. As mentioned earlier, we have got good mates among the Everton lads. Also, my mate played for Everton and got us free tickets. I would never pay to see Sheffy Wendy unless the Blades were involved.

We met our pals in the Howard Hotel, which was chockfull of Everton cheering on Man United as they beat Liverpool 3-2 in a televised mid-day game. Through my new job working for a local contractor, I had become pals with an older Wednesday lad called Zack. He was a huge bloke but sound as a pound. He worked the door at the Masons Arms, a Wednesday stronghold in the middle of Hillsborough, and I arranged to meet him for a drink before the game. I told him I would bring a couple of Everton lads for a bevy but not a big firm, as that wouldn't be on. So seven of us went up including a Wednesday fan.

All told we were three Sheff United, three Everton and one Wednesday. We had a couple of beers with Zack, then made a move to the game. As we headed up the Hillsborough shopping precinct I heard the unmistakable sound of fist on jaw. I spun around to see around 25 Wednesday attacking us. After a brief scuffle we did one towards a skip further up the road. The poor Wednesday fan with us ran away that fast that I thought his trainers were on fire. The skip had little in it except for a few house bricks. I picked three up and ran at Wednesday, who were screaming, 'Cowens, you're taking the piss.'

Taking the piss? If I'd marched 40 boys down there, that would have been taking the piss. We were an easy target. The golden rule when you've got something in your hand is to keep hold of it but I was on one and ran at Wednesday. I threw a half-charlie at a fat lad. It smashed into him. A Wednesday lad picked it up and screamed, 'We've got one now.' He lobbed it at me, missing by miles.

The rest of our lot were scrounging in the skip and, as scouse Moz said, all he could find was a couple of little pebbles. Police came as it was coming on top. Robert, Everton through and through, was arrested as he stood in the middle of the road with two half-charlies in each hand. I went and remonstrated with a couple of top Wednesday lads I knew.

'You're out of order. If he gets nicked I'm holding you two responsible. It's typical of you, this is.'

One Wednesday lad named Jester made out he wanted to take a walk but it was all mouth in front of his mates and the police. A Wednesday knife merchant came over and said, 'Steve, I'll try and help get your mate off.'

I told him to fuck off but, to be fair, he did help out. Robert was released because the bizzies knew we'd been attacked. Everton won 2-0 to cheer me up.

We caught the tram back to town and went to the Hallamshire Hotel on West Street for a drink. I told Raggy that Wednesday were bang out of order and if we bumped into them tonight I was going to 'wade into the lot of them'.

'That little crew Wednesday have now haven't a clue about how to conduct themselves,' I went on. 'They know I've packed in with all that shit now. Why don't they start showing their face in town and have a pop at our lads, instead of pulling strokes like that?'

'Look Steve we've spent most of our lives chasing them around, we shouldn't have gone up there in the first place,' Raggy reasoned. I suppose he was right, but I go where I want and don't need the assurance of 30 lads behind me, unlike some.

One of Wednesday's lads has actually recruited his girlfriend as a lookout for their firm. She goes in pubs and susses out what is going on before reporting back via a mobile. When she's got the day off she sits at home listening to police conversations on a scanner and again she reports what's going off. This is the way it has gone with them. There'll be women playing for their team next!

We met 30 BBC and at around 10 pm found out that 40 Wednesday were drinking in a pub just down the road. I never go in town with our boys any more but I'd been dragged back into it by a dirty 'do' from a motley crew. Rather than just attack the pub, we wanted Wednesday in the street so our main bulk held back. I walked through the doors and informed ten Wednesday, 'We're here, get outside.'

A Wednesday lad called Tesh said to me, 'Steve don't do anything stupid.'

They never even made an attempt to get out nor to attack me. The rest of our lot came up and police started to arrive in numbers. I looked through the window and had to laugh as Jester and his mates started throwing glasses at the windows from inside. Police moved us on and I got my third and final public warning.

'Move it Cowens, or you're nicked.'

Police ended the day's events. I couldn't help asking myself what was I doing, risking getting nicked for these mugs again? But it was like a rash I had to scratch.

# BACK TO A BAD LAD

United lads have flitted in and out of the England scene over the years. Most dramatically, England's Euro 2000 qualifying game in Poland saw a few of our lads attend. They had got friendly with some Darlington hooligans and met up with them in a pub called Legends in Poland. Around 100 lads were there, mostly from northern clubs, including Huddersfield, Forest and Man United.

A well-known German go-between called Ronald told the English that the Poles wanted a ruck in Monument Park, Staski, at a designated time. The English obliged, only to be ambushed by 200 tooled-up Polish hooligans. In the vicious brawl which ensued, only Sheffield, Darlington and a few Millwall fronted for England. This led to two Blades being hurt. One was hit on the head with a hatchet; he suffered a six inch wound and is lucky to still be here. The other was stabbed. A couple of Darlington were also badly injured.

Soon after, England played Belgium in a friendly at Sunderland's Stadium of Light. Sunderland and Newcastle were out for a row with each other. Our lot drank in a pub near the ground with their new Darlington mates. Sunderland had a big crew out and one asked Sep if they fancied teaming up against Newcastle.

'We're Sheffield mate, we don't team up with anyone.'

The police got between Sunderland and Newcastle, thus preventing any shenanigans. Sunderland then turned on United, who obliged and had a bit of a skirmish with the Mackems with help from the Darlington boys.

There had been talk of United taking a big firm up to Scotland for England's Euro 2000 play-off game with the 'sweaties'. On the day of the match, I went to the Players Café in Sheffield's Attercliffe district to watch the game along with 20 mates. Ten minutes before kick-off, 40 BBC strutted in. It's always nice to see a few old mates and handshakes were aplenty. Scholes's brace in England's 2-0 win sent the place barmy and the beer flowed.

Afterwards we decided to go for a drink in the Wellington pub in the Darnall area of Sheffield. Darnall is a Blades stronghold, with a good set of lads who have all done a bit for United over the years. As we left the Players Café, one of the United lads was shouting down his mobile.

'I'll give you "wog", fat boy, the roughest toughest wog you'll ever meet.'

Jack was on his mobile to a pub on the outskirts of Sheffield. Wednesday were in there and Jack had got on to a Wednesday main face.

'I'm coming for you now, fat boy, so get ready coz I'm gonna smash your fat face in.'

I knew the Wednesday boy on the phone. I couldn't believe he was signing his own death warrant. Jack is a boss boy and has everyone's respect. I told him not to go up, as Wednesday would never let him have a one-on-one with the guy he had been arguing with. We jumped in taxis and went to the Wellington. United's lads followed. We were all in there when I noticed Jack was missing, so I went up to Luey.

'Where's Jack?'

'He's gone to sort fat man out.'

'What, on his own?'

'No, Farlie and two others have gone with him.'

'Fuckin' hell, they'll get turned over.'

Luey shrugged. He knew as well as me that Wednesday would see it as an opportunity to do four Blades in. Sure enough, news came through on the mobile that 30 Wednesday had attacked them and that one United lad was in a bad way. An ambulance had rushed him to hospital where he had over 20 stitches in a head wound. Taxis were ordered and the BBC were mobilised. I could not make up my mind what to do, as my mates were on their way into town. I had two choices: go into town with my mates and keep out of trouble, or head off for Wednesday with the rest. The red mist came down as I remembered how a few months earlier those Wednesday had attacked me in Hillsborough. I also thought about Jack being game enough to go to their doorstep, only to be attacked mobhanded. I made my decision.

The 40 BBC re-grouped in a pub about a mile away from where Wednesday were. We knew that the bizzies were around and that they knew we were on the move. Police monitored us then drove off. A bus pulled up and we piled on. Jack was there and told me on the bus what had happened.

'It was brilliant Steve, we had a right pop. I smashed fatty's face in and at first they couldn't touch us, then it came on top.' He had broken the Wednesday lad's cheekbone.

The bus stopped 30 yards from their boozer. I put my Paul & Shark baseball cap on and jumped off first. Four police vans were parked across the road. I headed straight for the pub. Twenty lads stood outside. Three dog handlers and a few riot police were also in the car park.

'Who are these, are these them?' they said as I walked past a dog handler.

I got to the doors where Wednesday stood.

'Come on, boys.'

I swung at them. They threw glasses and bottles at me and backed inside the pub. Our lot, who had gone across the road to the wrong pub, came charging to help. I was just beginning to think how well I had done not to get hurt with the bottle attack when a riot bizzy smashed me across the head with his truncheon. To make matters worse, I had a police dog hanging from my arm. It had a good chew, then bit through the flesh on my hand. The riot police systematically kicked the shit out of us. A few of our lot ended up in hospital for stitches in head wounds caused by truncheons.

I escaped up the road and watched on as the bizzies continued to batter our lot. A bus pulled up, so I jumped on and

I was on my way home. I had let myself get involved again and was pissed off at myself but to be honest it was like being 20 again, with the buzz that nothing can replace.

# THIRTY YEARS ON: THE WAR CONTINUES

On 16 December 2000, Sheffield United entertained Wednesday. Later that same evening saw the inevitable trouble between the two rival hooligan groups. Police on horseback, dog handlers and the riot squad used CS gas to break up the marauding gangs of football thugs. Thirty-three were arrested.

It is impossible to explain why the rivalry between the two rival clubs borders on hatred. Other cities are shared by two clubs or have rivals close by but they don't have the year-by-year problems that Sheffield has. Wednesday's demise from the Premier League has once again seen the return of derby games, which are always potentially explosive fixtures. It is often asked, sometimes by our own lads, why United's firm still go after Wednesday when they can't match United in the hooligan stakes. The answer is simple: the two sides hate each other with a passion.

# SWFC V SUFC HILLSBOROUGH, 1 NOVEMBER 2000.

A Worthington Cup game saw a turnout touching 400 United boys. The United supporters had snapped up their 8,000 ticket allocation within three hours, so many had gone to Hillsborough and obtained tickets for Wednesday areas of the ground. The police launched one of the biggest operations Sheffield had seen. 'Anyone arrested and convicted would face an automatic life ban from football grounds,' came the warning. Unbelievably, after we had walked through the Hillsbrorough precinct on the way to the ground, police left the main firm of around 200 core hooligans to their own devices, concentrating on keeping the singers, beer-heads and hangers-on in check.

A group of 80 Wednesday were chased outside a pub, but on the realisation that they were normal fans the pursuit ended as quickly as it began. The 200 United lads arrived at the back of Wednesday's kop around ten minutes before kick-off. The streets were packed with fans. Wednesday fans looked on nervously as the firm walked by but they needn't have worried; it was only the OCS that our lot were looking for. After walking right around the ground, everyone headed into the turnstiles in various parts of the stadium.

Despite the warnings of a life ban, as the two teams took to the field fighting broke out in the Cantilever stand. Around 500 United supporters were in there. Wednesday won the game 2-1 in extra time; United's goal being greeted by sporadic fighting all around the ground. Two lads actually slugged it out in the goalmouth in front of Wednesday's kop while the game went on.

On the final whistle 300 BBC mobbed up and walked through Hillsborough and into town. Wednesday's firm disappeared. A total of 36 people had been ejected from the game and six arrested on various charges. In six weeks time Wednesday would be visiting Bramall Lane for a league game.

# SUFC V SWFC
## BRAMALL LANE,
### 16 DECEMBER 2000.

Due to Sky TV's live coverage, the game was scheduled for kick-off at 11.30 am. This prevented fans from drinking prior to the game but also made it a long day for the South Yorkshire Police. As everyone already knew, Wednesday's firm would not be coming to the game but a little mob of 20 waifs and strays did get escorted to and from the Lane. Credit to that little mob, they showed, which is more than their main boys did. United once again turned out a massive firm and between 5-600 boys sat in H block of the South Stand. The match ended 1-1.

The potential flashpoint was later on in the city centre. United's firm headed off into town after the game and around 300 settled in the Stonehouse. This still left a couple of hundred drinking on London Road. It was argued that Wednesday might show up and a reception committee would need to be there to greet them. Everyone knew Wednesday's movements, as they were tagged by United lads in cars.

A massive police presence made any violence between the two groups seem impossible but the excitement level rose when news came through that over 100 Wednesday were on the move. As the United firm tried to vacate the Walkabout pub at the bottom end of West Street, police in riot gear beat them back. The bar suffered substantial damage before the hooligan gang forced their way out. The police then tried to keep United's mob from gaining entry to West Street but the BBC split into two groups and ran around the block to get at Wednesday. Police seemed to lose control of a very volatile situation.

The two groups of hooligans caught sight of each other and the roars went up. Police had managed to get in-between the rivals but United broke through the lines of bizzies and, 100-strong, steamed at the OCS. A couple of older Wednesday boys stood until the last minute before turning to run. One was captured and pulled to the ground. Police used CS gas to break up the United firm, which had by now split into three groups.

Later a group of 30 Blades were arrested, locked up for the night and released in the morning without charge. My part in the night's violence was zero. United don't need me anymore and I don't need the violence, so that chapter of my life is over for good. But for others, nothing has changed.

# A BLADE'S STORY

The following is written by a United hooligan called Tiler. I first met him in the early Eighties, when he was 16. Even then, he was a game lad. I took him under my wing for a while and now he is a main face with United. This is his story:

> My love of football started at around six years old. I was living in Mossley, near Manchester, and used to watch the older lads play football at the top of our cul-de-sac. They wouldn't let me play because I didn't have a Man City shirt; everyone had to have one, so I decided to become a City fan. My grandad had been staunch City

all his life and started to take me to matches home and away.

In my early teens I began to notice the violence between rival crews. At one match at Maine Road, City were playing Cardiff. The Kippax had a segregated area for away fans and I noticed around 200 Cardiff fans, all between 18 and 30, dressed in a similar style: Tacchini tracksuits, Ellesse, Lacoste, Nike and Adidas trainers. I thought to myself, this is a football firm. I started to follow the same fashions, always watching what the other lads were wearing.

My family moved to Sheffield and I didn't get to as many City matches as I would have liked but I still followed their fortunes. I attended a Catholic school on the side of the city where there were more Sheffield United supporters. I went to a match at Bramall Lane to see Man City; outside the ground before the match there were quite a few scuffles and running battles. I went on the away end and stood near the City lads, at that time called the Mayne Line Service Crew.

To be able to afford the style of clothes I wore, I used to shoplift with a friend of mine from school who was a Blade. This brought me into contact with the Sheffield United firm, because we used to sell the clothes we had stolen to them. My first actual involvement in football violence came in the winter of 1986. Sheffield Wednesday were playing Man City at Hillsborough. I was in town with a couple of black lads, both Blades, and we met up with a couple of others, one Blade, one Wednesday. We decided to the go to the station to see if there were any City lads around. We bumped into six of them, they squared up to us and a fight ensued, both sets of lads running into each other. I had never been involved in anything like this before, the adrenaline started to pump, a couple of the City lads ran into me, I got a couple of decent punches in. The fight lasted a couple of minutes. We managed to back them onto the platform before the police arrived and I disappeared sharpish.

The buzz was immense and that initial feeling I had experienced was to become a way of life for me. I started to go to as many United matches as I could, tagging onto the firm which later became known as the Blades Business Crew. I got to know most of the lads through my schoolmate and started to meet up with a few of the boys my age for a drink before the games. It soon led to trouble with the police. Before one pre-season United-Wednesday friendly, I was nicked and charged with threatening behaviour. It didn't deter me.

My first away match was on a Tuesday night at West Brom. About 60 of us went on a coach. We bounced around West Brom's ground thinking we were the business, then managed to get on West Brom's end. The inevitable happened – a group of lads gathered around us and a mass brawl broke out. In my endeavours to make a name for myself, I ran straight into them while there was a gap between the two crews. Big mistake. I was arrested straight away. One of our main lads tried to get me away but only succeeded in getting himself arrested.

By this time I was beginning to get noticed, I knew who the main lads were but I thought most of them reckoned I was just a kid. During that same season, United played West Ham in the FA Cup. All the United crew were turning out. I took the day off work and hoped I would be able to get onto one of the coaches. There were a lot of people hanging around and it was tight as to whether everyone was going to get on the coaches. I was running around getting my name on as many coaches as I could to ensure a place.

Then one of the main actors who was running the coaches said to his mate, 'Make sure this lad gets on, he'll have a go.'

That man was Steve Cowens, the author of this book. He was well-respected even then. So I was on my way to West Ham. This was the time I felt that I was accepted as one of the lads.

Over the years to come there were many fights, many arrests and many court appearances. We could always get a few witnesses together and generally get off with the more serious charges. I should have done a few years at Her Majesty's pleasure but always managed to do well in court. We had some great times. Being outnumbered and getting a result is the best feeling of all.

The best day for violence away was at Leicester in 1990. United won promotion to the top flight with a 5-2 victory. A dozen of us went on the train with the aim of meeting more lads around the town centre. As soon as we got there we bumped into 25 local lads and ran them off straight away. Later, as we walked down a side street near the ground, we heard chanting. Seventy boys came round the corner.

One of United's top lads turned and said, 'Anybody who runs gets it from me later.'

We decided that whatever happened, we would stand. They looked good, screaming and shouting but as they neared us and realised we weren't going to run, they stopped. The police arrived, took us to the ground and left us. We then met up with the same lads again, there was just a wall separating us, off it went, fighting everywhere. Both gangs, trading punches, then the rest of our lads came. They didn't stand a chance. Then we just bounced around the ground slotting their boys as we went. Kick-off came, all went well, United were promoted and news came through that Wednesday had been relegated. What a day!

After the game we had to make our way back to the train station. We bumped into around 20 of Leicester's firm, the Baby Squad. They beckoned us to follow them, which we did, even though the police were escorting us. As we walked along a main road, a pub immediately emptied and around 100 Baby Squad began to follow. The police left us but we were in no mood to run. We crossed the road and turned to face them. They were straight into us but we stood our ground, then inevitably the bizzies intervened.

The Leicester boys couldn't believe we had stood and were shaking our hands, saying we were the gamest boys they had seen. The police escorted us back to the train station. When we were on the platform a train full of Luton fans pulled in opposite us. We all cheered them for completing our day by sending Wednesday down. Our result was to take us into the top division where we were to meet bigger and better firms.

We went everywhere, not always meeting our rivals but when we did we always did the business. We ran Tottenham down Seven Sisters Road, Arsenal bottled it at Highbury, Man Utd brought a big firm to Bramall Lane but we were just picking them off and giving it to them. We had a great fight at Villa, we took a big firm to Forest and phoned their main pub to inform them where we were, they turned up and got ragged.

One weekend when we played in London, Wednesday were also in the capital for a game at Arsenal. A couple of Wednesday's boys are pals with a few Chelsea lads and we'd heard rumours of a meet up between the two groups. We were having a drink and a call came through to the pub asking for me. A bit surprised, I took the call; it was Wednesday telling me they were just around the corner and for us to come and get it. Strange, since when did Wednesday have the bottle to do something like that? At first I told them we weren't interested as we had bigger fish to fry. Then one showed his face alongside two Chelsea so 80 of us left the pub and followed them down the road. They showed straight away and around the same number came towards us, something was wrong, they should be scattering by now. But they ran at us, this was not Wednesday. They looked good; all of their front line was tooled up, distress flares, bats, knives, ammonia and CS gas. They backed us off and caught one of our boys. A big fat Chelsea fan had him face down on the floor and was sat on him. I ran over and kicked the Chelsea fan off him and then beat a hasty retreat into the pub. We were gutted that we had backed off but we saved face by convincing ourselves that we would have done them if they had not been tooled up. Blades never use tools; call us naive but we prefer to use fists and boot.

We did get our revenge, on the way to the match we were on the tube, in the next carriage were around 25 Chelsea, the same ones we had just been involved with. They received as vicious a beating as I have ever seen, some Blades got off and ran round onto the carriage in front so we had them surrounded. The only ones to escape were the ones who cowered under the seats or hid under their unconscious mates. We didn't class this as much of a result because they were well outnumbered but we had to have revenge and they were tooled up.

We came across Chelsea again when we played QPR late in that season. After the match we were heading towards a main road, as we reached the top, the road just filled with boys. We ran straight into each other, it didn't last long – it never does, the police arrived and made a few arrests but we'd showed them we could handle the top firms home and away. During this time we were a force to be reckoned with. Everyone knew each other; we were like a big family, always looking out for one another. If someone didn't have any money, we had a whip round; we would do anything for each other. After this there was a bit of a lull as far as violence was concerned. It was becoming too much of a risk, chasing Wednesday around town, then getting 'dawn raided' by pissed off police. We always have a firm at home but are always well policed. We often have sporadic scuffles but major 'offs' are rare. However, over the last couple of seasons things have picked up.

We don't like Barnsley. They think they are equal to us off the pitch but we're simply too good and too strong for the pit dwellers. A couple of seasons ago we played Barnsley away, as we pulled into the train station the police wouldn't let us out and put us straight on the train back to Sheffield. The following year we decided to get taxis straight into Barnsley town centre and meet up with the rest of the boys in a certain pub. It didn't take them long to find us, we ran straight at them and they were off. By now our location was known to the rest of their boys and a large crowd gathered outside, again the police were with them. We decided to make a move towards the ground. They came down the road, there were only a couple of police horses between us and at last this was our chance to show them who were the top boys in Yorkshire. We ran straight through the police and into them. Most of them scattered all over the place, the ones who stood didn't stand for long. We had taken a risk and a few of our lads had been arrested but at least we had given it to them.

By this time I was 27 and one of the top boys. I remember when I was younger and used to look up to Steve Cowens and hoped that one day I would be as well respected as him. I feel I have achieved this. Steve has always been a cut above a normal thug. He maintains a code of conduct that has always set him off from the rest. Even Wednesday lads respect the way he conducts himself. There's no gamer boy than Steve but he doesn't overstep a certain mark.

The violence doesn't happen as often as it did. I turn out now for the big games, this season 1999/2000 we once again bashed Barnsley and took the best away firm we've had for years down to Fulham, 250 boys on board. Of course Fulham were not our targets, we wanted Chelsea. We searched Kings Cross and all their usual haunts to no avail.

I've got a good job now and I'm married with a young son, so I watch myself. When the police are around I always think twice, as I am a known face. The one thing I do regret is the time we've wasted chasing Wednesday around, a lot of our lads have been arrested when we have bigger and better fish to fry. The trouble has slowed for me now but when it comes along I LOVE IT.

# POLICE IN OUR TIME

## FOOTBALL INTELLIGENCE

## MAY THE FORCE BE WITH YOU

## FLETCH

## DO AS I SAY, NOT AS I DO

## 'KILL, KILL, KILL THE BILL'

## THE PEACE KEEPERS

# FOOTBALL INTELLIGENCE

'Cowens, fuck off now or you're nicked.' Charming words directed my way from one of South Yorkshire's finest. The police are the legal umpires in the game played by two rival firms. It's crew against crew, with the boys in blue refereeing the events.

Filth, plod, bizzies, old bill, coppers: all terminology used to describe the police force. Black bastards (because of the colour of their uniforms) is another, but to me there is no axe to grind. I have played the game knowing the risks. Without the Law, there is no law, and with 95 per cent of police, you know the score. They are just doing their job, albeit sometimes poorly, for example the Hillsborough Disaster. It's the other five per cent that disturb me. Do as I say not as I do might be their motto. I suppose the flipside of the coin if you took 100 of Sheffield United's firm, at least five per cent of them that would be messed up individuals. It's no different, really.

In the ideal football hooligan world, the police would simply let you get on with it, firm against firm, boys against boys, survival of the fittest. No proper boys seek fights with 'normal' football fans. The shirters and flask carriers are left well out of it – at least, by everyone except that mindless five per cent.

The police have a tough job now because crime is at a record level. Poverty, drugs and organised crime have seen them stretched to the limit. Football hooligans shouldn't be priority number one in any of the forces up and down the country. Child molesters, rapists, murderers, hard drug dealers, smacked-up burglars going into people's homes, all make football violence pale into insignificance. A 1999 television documentary, *Mersey Blues*, about the Liverpool police really opened my eyes. I couldn't believe how stretched their force was. Imagine doing unpaid overtime in your present job. Would you? Would you fuck! That's what is happening at forces up and down the country as they try to meet their financial restraints.

In 1999, I was arrested. I say arrested: they came to my house and asked when it would be convenient for me to go to see them. It was a bit like arranging an appointment at the doctors. They took twelve weeks after the alleged offence to come and see me, then it was, 'Give us a ring on this number and we'll see you when it's appropriate.' All very nice and friendly are the CID nowadays.

I have had more than my fair share of run-ins with the plod. On a couple of occasions I have been arrested for nothing, really, but that's the gamble a footie thug takes, it's no good crying about it afterwards. God knows I got away with a lot. Once your face is known, the bizzies are after you and watch your movements intently, so it is more than likely that they'll have you in the long run. I know I've got to be squeaky clean after this book hits the shops. The football violence that goes off today has gone totally away from the days when I was bang at it. Its all bollocks now. Firms have increased the use of weapons and are much more vicious when the chance of a ruck comes along. Almost everything is pre-arranged; the days of the unexpected battle are long gone. Also, the police know too much and this has driven the violence further underground.

Nowadays, rucks are sometimes arranged at England games. Imagine, this is how it goes:

England v Sweden (Wembley Stadium), the Globe public house, Baker Street, London.

'All right mate, who are you?'

'We're Pompey, who you with?'

'I'm Stoke pal.'

Then it's a few beers and a few stories of the rucks they've had lately. A quick exchange of mobile numbers and it's, 'I'll give you a ring a couple of weeks before we play at yours next season, we'll get it on.' A handshake, and the new found friends have arranged a forthcoming off. A similar arrangement can be made over the Internet. Fair enough, that's how violence is sorted nowadays, but it's not my cup of 'cha.'

Sheffield police are more clued in than most. The temptation to follow other forces and 'dawn raid' United's firm in the Eighties must have been strong. The BBC, myself included, were running amok home and away, but the police resisted and the trials against the other football firms collapsed, costing the taxpayer hundreds of thousands of pounds. Those dawn raids saw so-called vicious thugs being led from their houses. On show later for media purposes were various weapons taken from the raided premises. Claw hammers, Stanley knives, baseball bats, a Bosch sander and a Black and Decker workmate. It's hardly an arsenal to go to war with. Items to put up some shelves? Yes (except maybe the baseball bats).

The visit of Manchester City to Bramall Lane in November 1984 saw widespread trouble, with running battles and vans and cars overturned. Thirty-two were arrested and three taken to hospital, one injured in a vehicle turned over by a mob of Blades. All this produced promises by police that the BBC would be sorted out. Under the headline 'ORGANISED TERROR BY SOCCER HOOLIGAN MOB,' the *Sheffield Star* ran a story of how: 'An organised gang of troublemakers are bringing terror to the terraces of Sheffield United. They are to be banned by name from further United matches. Police have identified which pubs they meet in before matches to plan violence and they have detailed information about their tactics.'

Tactics? 'Four, four, two or shall we go with a sweeper system today, Fletch?'

Between 1982 and 1992, 743 people were arrested in and around matches at Bramall Lane. I always worried about a police raid. On 5 November 1990, four scrapbooks of newspaper cuttings, calling cards, photos of brawls and a good few charge sheets were used to start our bonfire. I thought it was for the best, although I've regretted it ever since. The scrappies could have been sound for research purposes for this book. The football intelligence officers that follow the lads know the score. They know hooligans (I hate that word) are not all mindless morons hell bent on destruction. Some even have a bit of pride in the mob they tail. I can imagine them chatting to their colleagues who keep watch over another set of hoodlums: 'My lot went to Birmingham last week, one hundred of 'em, had a bounce around and went straight into Brum's mob.' I bet some of them are chuffed.

There's no doubt that South Yorkshire Police have made some serious mistakes over the years. Some have been genuine errors but others have had very worrying undertones. Just how a troop of night club bouncers and Wednesday's boys acquired photos and personal details of 14 United hooligans, only the police will know. As a result, a few United lads received threatening phone calls and one had a petrol bomb thrown at the wall of his home. I wonder what senior officers would have done if a child or wife had been injured as a result.

Another strange incident occurred before a home game in the mid-Eighties. Outside the South Stand, one of the local police 'conveniently' dropped a colour photo file with three of our boys on it. I say conveniently, as it was dropped just as a few of our crew walked by. The photos consisted of two mug shots and a photo of one of the lads at a game. The description of the boys as dangerous thugs was way over the top. One of the lads, nicknamed by police as 'Jesus,' was highlighted as a 'high-risk' hooligan. It seemed the police were sending a message out to us.

I began to notice police awareness of myself around the same time. After one home game against Leeds, we were mobbed up outside The Cricketers. The police split us up and I ended up at the bottom of Bramall Lane. I noticed two Barbour-clad geezers near to me three times. A roar went up back towards the ground, and as we ran towards it, the two Barbour boys were chatting to two uniformed officers across the road. We ran past them. I heard a shout and glanced behind me. It was the Barbour boys.

'Come on, Sheffield,' one screamed. I turned round and went towards them with my arms spread out in a challenge, then twigged just in time that they were CID. As I turned to walk away, one kicked me up the arse and shouted, 'Shithead.' I kept my temper in check and replied, 'Fishing tomorrow on your day off?' before jogging away. This was alarming. I realised they were prepared to instigate trouble around football so as to achieve an arrest.

The CID became more and more cunning. We had to keep our wits about us. In the following years, we spotted them with their cameras in various places in and around London Road: the chip shop, the amusement arcade, the camera shop, the high-rise flats. Because we had sussed them, any photos taken would have been just as useless as the hundreds of others taken of lads doing nothing more than having a beer and chatting. I often wonder what they did with all the snaps.

Sometimes, however, they were successful in their attempts to gain evidence against the BBC. The filming of a CS gas attack on a nightclub not only led to arrests and convictions but also made local television news. Sheffield police obviously let the TV company have their nightclub video footage as a 'we've got the situation under control' exercise. The pictures did show our lot bang at it. They should have smelled a rat as that night, as none of the bouncers had weapons and they didn't want to know. The tape reminded me of the time that police filmed a pre-arranged off between Man United and Man City. That was also shown on national news as a message to boys up and down the country.

# MAY THE FORCE
# BE WITH YOU

South Yorkshire Police began to get their act together football-wise in the middle to late Eighties. As a result, United's mob began to get paranoid about there being a grass among the firm. Even worse, some thought an undercover bizzy had infiltrated the ranks. Gary Armstrong, a Sheffield-born lad who, for the purposes of writing a book, studied United's crew between 1985 and 1995, became the chief suspect for a while. Gary's research culminated in the book *Football Hooligans*. In writing it, he had to put up with some grief, so it is testimony to the man that he stuck in there and overcame the initial problems.

'He's here, fucking copper,' was a phrase that rang in Gary's ears. He was even threatened on a couple of occasions. I knew he was on the level and stuck by him, telling all and sundry that if he was a copper or a copper's nark, then I was Mahatma Ghandi.

Paranoia continued as police kept popping up at very disconcerting times and places. They even followed a coachload of us all the way down to Southampton. We sussed them as soon as we set off. It was quite funny as we hit a traffic jam ten miles from Southampton. I told the driver to switch lanes so the CID's white Nissan was directly behind us. They hung back 100 yards as we all waved at them. One of the lads put a sign up to the window: If You Get Close Enough To Read This, Fuck Off.

Another time, we had arranged to get into Stoke town centre. I borrowed a removal van. I told the lender I was moving house and, as he owed me a few favours, he gave me the keys. My plan was to get all our main boys to Stoke and earn a few quid in the bargain. Two hours later, 50 of Sheffield's finest were in the back of the van, and two hours and 15 minutes later, the van was impounded by the police. We hadn't even left the centre of Sheffield when two riot vans pulled me in.

'What's the problem?' I asked innocently.

'Do you know you've got fifty of Sheffield's worst in the back of that?' the officer asked, a trifle sarcastically. Worst? I thought they were the finest thugs we had. The back shutters opened and a huge plume of cannabis smoke bellowed out. Muz's face was a picture as he fell out of the back of the van with a reefer on the go. I'm glad the bizzies pulled me in or I'd have been locked up for manslaughter: all the boys were sweating like pigs and we had only been on the move two minutes. I told the sceptical officers that six mates and I had arranged to go to Stoke but the rest had just piled in and threatened me. I was released without charge and managed to get to Stoke in time for the second half.

More fuel was added to 'grass' rumours when one of our lads was arrested weeks after a fight in town. Even I began to feel concerned when I was dragged off a coach en route to Grimsby. We had mashed Wednesday the previous week and someone (and I know who) had given my name to police. Three vanloads of police raided our coach and arrested a few United boys, only two of us for football related matters. I have no doubt that over the years police got information from a few individuals but I also think that those individuals had chosen their information wisely; although sometimes arrests were made, the charges rarely stuck. A couple of United's boys got off very lightly with one or two bad charges. Still, 'he's a grass' was a regular comment. I wasn't sure. I still believe that if it was one of our lot, he chose to give the 'right' kind of information, the Teflon kind. I also believe that someone close to United's mob is still involved with the police.

# FLETCH

'There are around five United followers who revel in the planning and execution of violence against other followers. They have about 30 others who are willing to follow them and do the actual fighting.' This quote came from the head of the National Criminal Intelligence Service's football intelligence unit. The same unit claimed to know the name of each man and who the leader was.

The leadership issue involving United's firm was laughable. Although we had 'top boys,' no one could really say or do anything that would automatically make the rest follow. I was looked on by many as being one of United's main bad lads, but it was never like that. I had my say. If I thought we should do this or that, I voiced an opinion. But leaders or media-instigated 'generals' did not exist in our structure. Plenty of people in and outside our mob thought that a lad called Luey and myself were the leaders of our firm. Luey was a 'boss' boy, someone who had the balls of ten men. But his impulsiveness, plus the fact he liked playing to the crowd, often let him down. I was sure in the early years that he saw me as a threat to his reputation because I sometimes challenged what he wanted to do. Although both top boys, we would often disagree. This led to occasional tension between the two of us. In truth, despite not agreeing with many things he did, I admired Luey. He was a top hooligan and that's all that mattered to me. I couldn't be bothered with the 'I'm top boy' attitude. It was childish. I let my actions do the talking.

Speaking of leaders, the name 'Fletch' led to much amusement among our mob in the mid-Eighties. Information about this fictional character was deliberately fed to police. The bizzies had been far too interested in trying to find out who organised the firm for our liking. Everyone was in on the wind-up that a Cockney called Fletch was our main actor. He was said to be an exiled Arsenal boy, aged 28, who travelled only to big games and sorted things out. Police even found a BBC calling card with Fletch's name on it; it had been conveniently left in the Lansdowne. I'm not sure the police swallowed the wind-up completely but their comments added to everyone's amusement.

'Where's Fletch today?'

'We know who he is and we'll get him.'

They never did.

# DO AS I SAY, NOT AS I DO

Over the years, I have seen plenty of bad policing at football matches. Sunderland, Walsall and Doncaster all tell disturbing stories of poor organisation and brutality by the forces of law and order. Another occasion was in 1988. Renk, Housey and myself had been having a gargle on London Road. As we moved from pub to pub, an unmarked car screeched up alongside us.

'What did you fuckin' say?' a bloke shouted out of the passenger window.

We were just about to give it them, then realised they were CID. We continued walking. One jumped out of the car and pushed Renk from behind saying, 'What, big mouth?'

Renk turned around. 'Leave us alone, we've done fuck all.'

The CID man then tried to trip us up, grabbed Renk and arrested him. Housey and I protested, then the other bizzy arrested

Housey. 'We'll be back for you tosser,' one said as they drove off with the lads in the back.

I am a tosser; I'm good at it after years of practice. I flagged a taxi. It was days like these you could easily lose your liberty. I was dying to hit one but that's what they wanted. We were just faces from football and they gave us a hard time for nothing. Remember this when you read stories of convicted football hooligans.

# 'KILL, KILL, KILL THE BILL'

Attacks on the police by Blades have been extremely rare. In total I've seen a policeman punched about ten times. Three of those assaults were by one Blades boy who avoided arrest every time. There have been plenty of attacks on police vehicles, with cars flipped over or damaged. One Sunday, a few Blades were having after-bird in a pub when the police burst in and demanded everyone leave. This they did, only to turn the unaccompanied transit and vans onto their roofs.

In the 1980s, end-of-season disorder was commonplace. When Wimbledon came to the Lane in 1984, a 2-1 defeat left 23,000 fans frustrated as our promotion push hit the rails. Over 1,000 fans gathered at the bottom of Bramall Lane. This was at the height of the miners' strike, when tensions between South Yorkshire's working class population and 'Maggie Thatcher's Militia' were strained, to say the least. Mining communities and villages surrounded Sheffield. We all had mates who were miners and felt for them and their families as the Tory Government tried to grind them into the ground. Trust in the police was non-existent.

Twelve mounted police charged the crowd to disperse it, supported by 60 colleagues on foot. They were met by a barrage of stones and bricks. Two horses fell to the floor and an officer was pulled off his mount and attacked. The bizzies were chased up Bramall Lane. That sight of galloping horses in retreat, and police vehicles damaged in their wake, will live with me forever. Riot is the only word to describe it. Later in town, more rioting took place and more police vehicles were damaged. Twenty-eight people were arrested.

I thought events like these had been left behind in the riotous Eighties, but the end of the 1998-99 season proved that when boys turn out in force, and are left frustrated through lack of opposition, the police can be targeted as a release. Bristol City have a tidy firm. We'd had a couple of beauts with them over the years, so their visit to Bramall Lane for the final game of the season wasn't going to be taken lightly. They needed a win to stay up. Two hundred and fifty Sheffield boys waited for their Bristol counterparts, but City brought only 400 fans, with no boys to be seen.

Soon attention turned to an old foe, Sheffy Wendy. They had taken a little mob to Forest that day and a welcome home committee awaited their return. Train times were checked and 200 United met in The Globe on Howard Street, overlooking the station. A scout came back with the news.

'The train's pulled in, come on.'

Two hundred Blades poured down to the station, only to be met by around 80 police with truncheons drawn and dogs snarling. More riot vans screeched up. Wednesday could be seen through police lines and a few United tried to get them, only to be arrested. Two Blades began struggling with police. Then it went off. To a huge roar, United's boys went into the police and punches were exchanged with truncheon-wielding coppers. Police were clearly shocked and frightened as bottles and glasses crashed around them. The police backed away, then turned and ran into the railway station. Wednesday fans, who two minutes earlier had been jeering United's attempts to get at them, fled with police. Riot vans were left in the middle of the road, their doors open.

I kept out of it all. There is only one winner when you take on Johnny Law. Plus, CCTV cameras surrounded Sheffield station. The tapes would be analysed and arrests would no doubt follow. Around 20 minutes later I stood outside the Fraternity bar. My plan was to get a taxi, go home early and order an Indian takeaway. I knew the bizzies would be well on top and arrests would be made throughout the night. I've seen it all before with Sheffield's finest: upset them and they upset you, arresting you for nothing more than eating a kebab in a built-up area. And my yellow 'Stoney' coat made me stick out like a beacon.

Just as I was about to ring home on my mobile, ten bizzies bounded up.

'What you organising?' one snarled.

'Chicken madras and mushroom rice,' I replied, trying to hold back my smirk.

They snatched my mobile and gave me a bit of pushing and pulling.

'I'm phoning our lass to order some snap,' I pleaded.

My home was highlighted on the phone display. My mobile was returned with the order that I fucked off out of the town or I'd be nicked.

I ambled off in no particular direction. The police helicopter hovered above. It always seems to follow – or is just paranoia? I headed down to the taxi rank at Sheffield train station. From the Globe pub to the station the scene resembled a street in Beirut. Debris and broken glass were everywhere. The station was still heavily policed, so I nipped into the Howard Hotel for swift one. Three bouncers blocked my way.

'You can't come in here.'

They knew I was United but I was on my jacks and the bizzies were bombing about everywhere. I barged past one bouncer and went straight to the bar. The others followed me, then stopped, having decided it wasn't worth it. Lager in hand, I walked back outside to have a word with them.

'Look mate, I'm sorry about that but the bizzies are on my case. What's gone off?' I feigned ignorance.

'Fuckin' hell, have you missed it? United's lads have just chased a hundred coppers into the station. They shit themselves, never seen owt like it mate,' one bouncer excitedly relayed. I went back inside and sat down in a corner of the pub. A drunken conversation was going on between three lads.

'There must have been four hundred of them.'

'Yeah, but most of them are wankers. Get them one on one and they're nobody.'

'Wednesday couldn't turn a mob out like that though.'

I listened in, catching their eyes occasionally. The conversation went on. I summed them up. An Ellesse tee-shirt, a Wrangler denim, one with bulky Adidas trainers on, the ones with the big tongue sticking up above ill-fitting jeans. Wednesday fans. I pulled the United programme out of my jacket and started to scan through the crap they print for two quid. Then an interruption.

'You a Blade, mate?'

I glanced at the programme in front of me, as if to say, No, I'm Kilmarnock.

'You been t' Lane today then?'

'Yeah.'

'We've just got back from Forest, Wednesday are shit, we're going down next season.' He was right. We had a lengthy chat about football and the rights and wrongs of the game. Then it came.

'BBC have just attacked us as we left the station. They chased coppers in't station an't lot.'

I could still feel the nervousness in his voice. I smiled. Although these lads weren't boys, I couldn't resist it.

'Have Wednesday took a firm today?'

'Yeah, about eighty of 'em.'

'Oh, I didn't think Wednesday had a firm nowadays.'

The three were just football fans who pretended they knew a bit about the bollocks. They dropped the names of a few Wednesday faces. I knew the names but didn't let on.

'I've heard of a few of them but I wouldn't recognise their faces. But I've probably seen the back of their head a few times.' This went straight over the crossbar.

'D'you know Donald?' one asked.

'Yeah, he's got a farm hasn't he?'

'No, he...' The joke was missed again, so I interrupted.

'Yeah, I know him. I work with him.'

'What, for Corkadam? What's your name then?'

'Steve Cowens.'

It went quiet. They looked at each other. 'We've heard you're the BBC's main boy.'

'No, I don't bother that much anymore. It's bollocks.'

They went on about the people they knew who in turn knew me. One asked if I wanted a pint. A couple of drinks later I was on my way home in a Joe Baksi. I told our lass that I'd nearly got nicked for phoning home. She smiled and said she had told me to stay away from town. Of course she was right. She always is. Although I'm a different person from the Steve Cowens of old, I'm still tarred with the same brush. It won't go away and I've got to live with it. Sometimes I get sick of it. I've been in all sorts of mythical trouble over the past couple of years. My reputation goes before me.

But sometimes I love it.

I made the right decision in getting out of town that night. Plenty of United were arrested as they walked from pub to pub. In the following week more arrests were made in raids on Blades' houses. You can't give it the bizzies and expect to get away with it.

# THE PEACE KEEPERS

Over the past two or three years, South Yorkshire Police have used a new tactic to combat the BBC. The alarm bells started to ring after the arrests of most of United's leading hooligans during trouble with the Owls Crime Squad. Hardly any Wednesday have been detained yet over the past two years over 70 United lads have. In two incidents, police let the OCS walk to pubs in which United lads drank. When the inevitable chase started, the officers moved in and arrested several BBC. After the derby at Bramall Lane in December 2000, 33 united followers were detained during a major disturbance in the West Street area of the city; once again, no Wednesday arrested. Around a year earlier, 15 United lads were attacked by 30 Wednesday outside a bar in town. United chased the Wednesday lads and two were knocked out. The events were caught on CCTV and 10 United were arrested in raids on their homes. The police then showed mug shots of three more in the evening newspaper. The police know who are the boys in Sheffield and they are intent on arresting anyone who steps out of line.

An incident in Sheffield city centre in 1989 proved that police were prepared to let it go off in order to try to arrest a few culprits. United had played Wednesday in a midweek Zenith Data Cup fixture. Such is the rivalry in Sheffield that 30,464 fans turned out for this meaningless match. We went looking for the snort beasts' crew all night but couldn't get near them. The police were on our case.

We split into two groups, with most heading back down to London Road. Around 30 of us settled undetected in The Hind pub in town. Me and Adam, a youngster whose dad used to be top boy with the Shoreham Barmy Army in the Seventies, went up town in my car on a scout. At the bottom of West Street I turned a corner and had to drive through 50 Wednesday as they crossed the road. We shadowed their movements. They walked down Carver Street towards the vicinity where half United's crew waited. I sped down to The Hind. Inside I gave the shout.

'Come on, they're here.'

Without a word, our lot stood up and left. We headed up Furnival Gate towards Wednesday's oncoming crew. Sure enough, we bumped into them. Wednesday had mobbed up outside Ki Ki's nightclub. We ran up but two bizzy vans were parked up at the side of Wednesday. We were on one side of the dual carriageway and they on the other. Both sides exchanged the verbals. Then, to everyone's surprise, the two riot vans sped off. We steamed straight across as the roar went up. I hurdled the perimeter rails and ran straight into Wednesday's startled boys. They scattered.

The two riot vans returned: the crafty coppers had driven around the block, let it kick off, then returned for a few arrests. In the 30-second interim, Wednesday had gone. We stood where they had been. The police couldn't really arrest anyone, as there was no fighting.

This event was not unique. For two or three years, police seemed to be letting it go off, then making arrests. This tactic has recently been reintroduced after fights between the BBC and OCS and most of United's main actors have recently been arrested. Detection rather than prevention seems be the policy.

In a May 1992 visit to London, we had an unfortunate experience with PC Jobsworth. I should have known the day would be different when our van broke down on the M1 only ten minutes into our journey. Twelve half-stoned mates sat pondering what to do. A quick call to a builder pal meant we had another van. The problem was how to pick it up. Kav and Bobby tried to hitch a lift on the slip road down to the M1. I couldn't believe it when an old battered Landrover pulled up. The old farmer-type geezer offered a lift to the pair of them. He got out and opened up the horsebox attached to his car. Kav and Bobby jumped in, being careful where they trod, and disappeared up the M1 with their heads just visible out of the back of the box.

An hour later, they returned with a filthy work van. I jumped in the front with Scratch. The rest laid out a white sheet (taken off Bobby's bed) in the back and got in. Scratch had been working in Spain and had brought a load of mini bangers back with him. They made a huge bang for something so small. He also had some bigger ones and we lit one and threw it in the back. It almost blew the doors off and everyone was deaf for 20 minutes. Scratch skinned a spliff up, and I concealed a mini banger in the bottom of his reefer. Scratch and me had a couple of tugs on it to avoid suspicion. Then I leant back and asked.

'Who's on this?'

Fats, directly behind us, reached out and took it. Twenty seconds later, as he had a pull, it exploded in his face. I don't think I have ever laughed so much. Fats sat there wide-eyed with tobacco all over his dial and the remnants of the joint sticking out of his mouth.

Once in the Smoke, we headed for Swiss Cottage to meet the boys. We often met at Swiss Cottage, as it wasn't too from the end of the M1 and the tube was just across the road. It was easier to get around on the tube than driving around that hole of a capital. Cerys Mathews from *Catatonia* is right when she sings:

> *London never sleeps, it just sucks*
> *The life out of me*
> *And the money from my pocket.*

In 1988, a couple of the lads got some jail for a mini-riot at Swiss Cottage when they went in a pub that must have been the meeting place for the Somalian ethnic community. It wasn't a racial thing as we had quite a few blacks with us, but it kicked off and there were running battles around the Cottage.

Anyway, after a couple of beers we set off to Selhurst Park. None of us had a clue where we were heading and everyone in the van was stoned. I told Kav to pull up so I could ask somebody directions.

'He'll know,' said Kav, as he pulled onto the kerb beside a copper. I wound the window down.

'Excuse me, have you got directions to Selhurst Park?'

The copper came over and leant on the van. His eyes trained in on the wrecked Rizla packets strewn about the dashboard. Scratch and a couple of others in the back had joints on the go and the sweet smell of cannabis billowed from the van.

'I'll give you directions all right. Stay here,' said PC Never-had-a-minute's-excitement. He got on the radio.

'Assistance to Regents Park. Could I request some drug squad officers as well.'

Oh dear.

'You – get out.' He pointed at me, as I was next to the door. 'What's your problem?'

'I know what you've got in there, so get out.' He thought he'd found the Crown jewels. Within minutes, 20 of his buddies had arrived and had us face down on the grass. The van was searched and so were we. After a while we were allowed back to our feet. I went and chatted to a dog handler.

'We were only going to a football match. What's the matter with him?'

'It's a bit of excitement for him. He's only the park copper. We know what you've got in the van and as long as there's no weapons on board then there's not a problem,' the dog man said.

I was relieved. There was enough of the green stuff in the van to keep a Rasta stoned for six months. Bobby came over to me. He seemed to be walking all funny.

'Fuckin' hell Steve, I've had to put twenty-five wraps of billy down my bollocks. I've got boxers on and they're falling down my legs.'

I glanced down to his feet to see a wrap fall off his Kickers and onto the grass.

'Fuck off away from me, you bastard,' I told him with a smile on my face.

Everyone had names and addresses taken except me and Bobby. We were just returning to our van when a stern-looking sergeant came over. Bob was still sprinkling wraps of billy out of the bottom of his jeans, like Steve McQueen with the soil in *The Great Escape.*

'You two haven't had your names took,'

We'd had ten minutes to think of something, so I gave my name but a false address: 'Steve Cowens, 74 Pale Valley Road, Charnock, Sheffield.'

He wrote it down and turned to Bobby.

'And you?'

'John Smith, but-but I drink lager.' I had to turn away as I cracked up.

'And your address?'

'76 Pale Valley Road, Charnock.' I couldn't believe it. Bobby had suddenly moved in next door.

'Neighbour of yours, is he?' the copper asked me.

'Looks that way.' Again I turned away to hide my smile.

Bobby was no rocket scientist but he could have had a bit more savvy. We climbed back on board and set off with the words 'Behave yourselves lads' ringing in our ears. Everyone picked up their ganja from where they had left it. A rolled spliff lay on the front seat. The bizzies couldn't be arsed with a bit of smoke. I suppose they wouldn't be able to prove whose lump was whose anyhow.

The game was the final one of the 1991-92 season. A 3-0 defeat didn't stop the usual charge on the pitch at full time for a player's shirt. I was determined to get one to add to my collection of four. On the whistle I grabbed Budge, who had a start on me, and pulled him back over the perimeter fence. I sprinted on but my efforts were in vain as United's players were swamped. Blades fans did the Tartan Army trick by swinging on and breaking both crossbars. As I returned to the seats, I saw Budge and a few of our lot looking in the grass at the side of the pitch.

'What's up?'

'You broke my gold chain and I've lost it.'

In my haste to get on the pitch I had yanked his chain off. Two coppers walked over and asked what we were up too.

'I've lost a block of cannabis. I know it's around here somewhere,' I told him. The bizzies looked at each other, then over their shoulders, then started to help with the search!

'What's it look like?' asked one.

'Brown and a bit like an Oxo cube.'

Then one of the lads shouted up 'Found it' and pulled Budge's gold chain from in between the advertising hoardings. Both bizzies looked at me and laughed. 'Nice one,' said one, then they walked away laughing. Two sides of policing in one day: the complete dick followed by the sensible 'we know the score' brigade. If only more police adopted the latter attitude.

I have got a feeling that police will get together with someone at Bramall Lane and have me banned from matches after this book is published, even though I'm no longer the thug of years gone by. My children now often accompany me to beautiful downtown Bramall Lane. I want them to have the pride and passion for the club that I have, without the violence. But United as a football entity are wrecked. Years of neglect have seen our once great club slip into mediocrity. Big sides like Man City and the giants of the North East have been through the same mill. It was not that long ago that Newcastle, Boro and Sunderland were playing in front of crowds of well below 10,000. They have shown some ambition and are now established Premiership clubs. United need to get a chairman and a few directors that have the club at heart instead of lining already bulging pockets. In fairness the club does seem to be slowly moving in the right direction, although thousands of loyal fans have stopped going and I don't blame any of them. It's heartbreaking to see what a few businessmen have done to the club we love.

So if I am banned from the Lane, I will be upset but so be it. If the people who supposedly run the club put as much fight and passion into it as I have over the years then we won't have a problem. United do seem to be trying to turn the corner and local people have been installed in important areas, the most important being Neil Warnock, a lifelong supporter, as manager, but I'm afraid we've slipped so far behind in recent years that I can't see any prospects for years to come.

# BOUNCERS, BATS AND CS GAS

The BBC has had plenty of set-tos over the years with bouncers. Back in 1982, one nasty incident springs to mind. Myself and ten mates, all aged 16-17, went into town every Friday and Saturday night, visiting the usual six pubs before finishing off in a club called the Bar Rio. We used to have plenty of rucks and the seven Bar Rio bouncers started to get on our case. They started making us take off our United badges in order to get in. The bouncers were all Wednesday fans and one night, things came to a head when I refused to take my badge off.

'You've got a daft parrot on your jumper so why should we take our badges off.'

This was a reference to the bouncer's Owls badge on his acrylic jumper. I was barred for two weeks.

A month later we were having a gargle in a pub across from the Bar Rio. As we played pool, Horsehead came running in.

'Steve, them bouncers have kicked Mark's missus, she's eight months pregnant.'

I looked out of the window. Mark stood gesturing in the middle of the road and his missus was sitting on the pavement, crying. I told everyone to grab pool cues and out we went. I ran across and steamed into the bouncers. Timmy and the rest laid siege to the pub doors. The bullies tried to have a go with two baseball bats but we managed to get in and chased them through the crowd of startled revellers and over the bar. The police came and I was arrested but Timmy blagged to them and they let me go.

Tim and I then hid and ten minutes later the police moved off. Our plan was to attack the bouncers again but they locked the doors. They had seen enough of these diamond-Pringled hooligans for one night. We left it for two weeks then went back to the club. It went off again as ten bouncers tried in vain to do us. We had prepared ourselves well and had planks of wood hidden around the corner. Once again we chased them into the club.

The head bouncer was a big fat git. I could not believe it when two weeks later I was on my dinner hour at work when Horsehead came running into the canteen.

'Steve, that fat Wednesday fan is up the yard loading his lorry,' he said.

We were off, we ran out into the loading bay and sure enough he was loading one of our wagons. He had started work for us two days earlier at a different depot. His face was a picture as we went over.

'Come on fat twat, remember me?'

He dived into his truck and locked the door. With a smirk on his face he tried to get the keys out of his overstretched denims. I ran round the other side of his cab. Bingo, the door wasn't locked. The engine started as I pulled the door open, yanked myself up and leant over, punching him as he drove away. He quit the next day and new bouncers were appointed shortly after at the Bar Rio.

The worst episode, however, involved the BBC in a 'bouncer war' and led to police setting up a surveillance operation outside a Sheffield nightclub. The Palais at the bottom of London Road was one of Yorkshire's premier nightspots in the late Eighties. The rave scene was in full flow and Ecstasy the drug of the moment. Most of United's firm went to the club and, to be honest, they ran the show in there. A couple of BBC lads saw it as ideal opportunity to make a lot of money and started selling E's. Young lads were used as runners. The same scenario was happening up and down the country as football hooligans took over the rave drug scene. The 20 or so local bouncers who worked the Palais knew most of the lads, so there wasn't much trouble. Then in 1991 a new club manager appointed 22 bouncers from the Nottingham area, who began the task of driving the BBC out of the club. It sparked a year-long feud and also led to many injuries and arrests.

Things came to a head early in 1992. In collusion with local police, the bouncers barred anyone they considered to be BBC. I was never stopped from entering the club but once inside the bouncers' tactics became apparent. They would let a few Blades in, then systematically beat them up. After two weeks of being barred, the BBC took matters into their own hands. Most had been barred from a club through no wrongdoing, although a couple of the boys had taken over the selling of Ecstasy in the club.

The first scenario saw 25 Blades attack the bouncers who, knowing this was inevitable, were armed with bats and knuckledusters. In the doorway fracas, several Blades were injured and two were arrested. A plan to storm the Palais a week later was scuppered by a large police presence. Trouble brewed for months. Bouncers would shout abuse at passing Blades boys who in turn would start to fight or give the verbals back.

When 20 steamed the doors one Saturday night, the bouncers for once were not prepared for the scale of the attack. After being sprayed with CS gas and shot at with nautical distress flares, they retreated into the club and fighting broke out in the foyer. Two surveillance cameras captured the incident and this led to the arrest of four Blades. All were charged with serious offences, two under the Firearms Act. The club had to be evacuated due to people suffering the effects of CS gas. The video footage was later shown on Yorkshire Television news and led to condemnation by police and club workers of the despicable BBC.

I never once got involved. Although I could see our boys' point of view, I also felt that two United lads in particular who had been making a nice living out of their E sales in the club were egging the other Blades into the conflict for purely selfish reasons.

It soon became very apparent that the Nottingham bouncers had bitten off more than they could chew. In August, after the first game of the 1993/94 season, around 40 Blades were walking past the club after drinking in town. An argument led to a fight. The bouncers were carrying bats and also threw two bin liners full of bottles. One Blade was knocked unconscious by a rounders bat and several received glass cuts. Once out of ammo, the bouncers were chased back into the club. Two were captured and only saved from a bad beating by three police vans screeching to the scene. Once again the bizzies took it out on United's lads. The club surveillance camera had (not surprisingly) been switched off when police asked for a copy. Innocent bystanders however informed police of the bouncers' attack. Three were arrested but later had charges dropped.

An attack on the minibuses that ferried the legalised thugs to Sheffield saw a van burned out and signalled an end to a war started by doormen but finished by Bladesmen. Not long after, the Nottingham firm quit the scene. The original local club bouncers were re-employed and everyone was allowed back into the club. The war that should never have started was over.

Another long running dispute between bouncers and the BBC started in 1991. A well-known local United player, who had plenty of friends in the wrong circles, started the hostilities through no fault of his own. Berlins was a popular pre-club bar. It was huge inside and an ideal stop-off before going on to the Europa or Capital nightspots. The United player in question – who shall remain anonymous – was assaulted by the bouncers. The fact that he was on crutches at the time made it worse. A month later, 50 Blades marched up to the club to have a quiet word. The bouncers ran inside and closed the doors. The club had two CCTV cameras overlooking the entrance, therefore verbal exchanges were the extent of the hostilities. But the seeds had been sown. This went on for months. We heard that the bouncers in Berlins were increasing in numbers and tooling themselves up. They gave out plenty of verbals and even threatened Blades that they would visit their houses.

In 1992 the balloon finally went up as 80 Blades simultaneously attacked Berlins from the front and the rear entrances. Bouncers fought back with bats. I watched the whole event unfold from across the street. Two Aussies had come over to Sheffield to visit their cousin, a lad from round our way. I had taken them out of the way and the pair of them stood there, gobsmacked, as events unfolded.

'Strewth!'

Our boys pushed the surveillance cameras skywards so no evidence could be obtained but police were never far from the club and blocked off both ends of the street. Eight Blades were nicked and charged with affray.

One month later, 70 Blades went down to the club again. This time the large police presence prevented any attack. Around five non-hooligan Blades waved to our lot who were walking by; the bouncers promptly attacked them and sprayed Mace in their faces. Events went from bad to worse when the bouncers sought the help of Sheffield Wednesday's mob. Worst of all, the doorman were somehow supplied with police files on individual BBC members. Mugshots, names, ages plus the districts in which they lived were all furnished, culminating in six Blades receiving threatening phone calls and one having a petrol bomb thrown at his house. An older, retired Wednesday boy passed on the photocopied details to us.

As if to prove a point, the other bouncers in Sheffield (who all worked for one of two agencies) started acting up. Another Blade was assaulted in a club by the bouncers. Enough was enough. A week, later 30 Blades entered the club just before opening. Bouncers were attacked and the bar area damaged. After that more and more bouncers became involved, some of whom had previously got on well with Blades. Unexpectedly one Saturday a certain pub frequented by Blades had almost 30 doormen on patrol. They threatened ten Blades with bats. Some ten minutes and a few mobile phone calls later, 80 Blades attacked the bouncers. They made the mistake of coming outside. The Blades hooligans went about their work, the bouncers were chased back inside and two were captured and given a severe beating. A week later one of our boys bumped into one of the bouncers, who he knew, and sought an explanation for their over-zealous behaviour. None was forthcoming. He left the bouncer with the warning that the BBC could turn out 150 boys if necessary. Needless to say hostilities were dropped and the city returned to the relative peace.

In Sheffield now the bouncers know the score. They know that acting the Big-time Charlie leads to trouble. There are still plenty of 'Check me out, I'm a bouncer, I'm hard' types around but generally it's quiet.

# A TO Z OF VIOLENCE

Here, for what it is worth and in no particular order, are the top hooligan firms that I have encountered over the years.

**6.57 (PORTSMOUTH)**

**ICF (WEST HAM)**

**LTE (LINCOLN)**

**BUSHWHACKERS (MILLWALL)**

**SERVICE CREW (LEEDS)**

**NAUGHTY FORTY (STOKE)**

**MAYNE LINE/COOL CATS (MAN CITY)**

**FRONTLINE (MIDDLESBROUGH)**

**SOUL CREW (CARDIFF)**

**HEADHUNTERS (CHELSEA)**

**ZULU WARRIORS (BIRMINGHAM)**

**SNORTY FORTY (EVERTON)**

# ALTRINCHAM

November 1981. I didn't see too much of the game as I was thrown into the street after five minutes for giving the verbals to a few Manc trendies through the fencing. I could remember little, due to a couple of bottles of cider and some magic mushrooms that one of the older lads insisted I try. After the match I punched a boy with a snidey one, but there you go.

# ARSENAL

In October 1981 Arsenal visited Bramall Lane for a League Cup fixture. Their Gooner firm drank in the Pump Tavern on a quiet back road close to Bramall Lane. Seventy of us went to confront them. They poured out led by two tall blacks, their trenchcoats flapping around like Batman's cape in the wind. But the Gooners were sloppy. They had enough time to get their crew into the street but for some reason didn't get everyone out. We went at them, one was punched to the ground and in a panic they turned and ran into the pub. They could not all get in at once and the back lads took a bit of a beating. One was pulled to the floor and kicked around. To add insult to injury he had his trainers nicked and his pockets rifled. United were in the fourth division at this time and pulled off a shock 1-0 win (Bob Hatton).

United took that slender lead to Highbury two weeks later for the second leg. They also took a following of over 3,000 fans. Fighting broke out before, during and after the match, which United lost 2-0. The worst of the trouble was after the game near the away coaches. A full-scale battle was only broken up when dozens of police on horseback charged into the ruck in which fencing had been ripped up and used as weapons.

The Gooners never showed in Sheffield during the four years we were in the Premiership. In 1992 and 1993 we took a tidy mob down to North London. The latter of the two games saw around 80 BBC show off around Highbury. When Arsenal did finally got some boys together they were chased.

February 13, 1999. This game will be remembered not for the trouble but for the cheating of the Arsenal internationals Kanu and Overmars. The now infamous incident has been well documented and the FA Cup 2-1 defeat was nullified. United took a huge following of over 6,000. We met 200-strong in the World's End pub in Camden, the place where we had come unstuck against Chelsea. At Arsenal we were escorted from the tube station by 50 coppers, eight on horseback, but 30 of us broke off and headed up a side street.

As we headed past the North Bank, I could see around 80 boys hanging around. It was five minutes before kick-off and the streets were pretty crowded. Arsenal sussed a few of our lot at the front and moved toward them, not knowing there were more of us behind. We ran in and startled them. Arsenal had the numbers but couldn't shift us. Two of our lads were nicked and the police restored order. I was 'largeing it' and saw a Stone Island-clad Arsenal boy giving it the big 'un. He had a huge nose and I couldn't resist an insult.

'Oy, Yiddo, shouldn't you be at Tottenham?'

I gestured at his nose and he went mad. It was a comment which nearly cost me. I had a bright yellow Stoney coat on, so I was hardly inconspicuous. After the game, with United's fans going mental over the Overmars 'goal', I arranged a lift home with Phil, a retired United boy. I didn't fancy a night in London supping piss-poor lager at extortionate prices. The trouble was that Phil's car was parked at the other side of the ground. We walked up towards the main road that runs adjacent to Highbury. As I turned the corner I bumped straight into Arsenal's firm, with the guy from Nose City right at the front.

'He's one,' screamed big nose.

I turned and ran like the wind. Arsenal's boys gave chase but I already had a head start, so I slowed and kept turning clapping my hands like I was going to steam them (as if). The trouble was that there were quite a few Arsenal walking up and I nearly got captured for acting the goat. When I got to the bottom of the road and to the sanctuary of United's coaches, I leant on a wall to get my breath back. Wasser and John (two United boys) came over and I told them what had happened. I arranged a lift on their coach, as I didn't hold much hope out for finding Phil again. The coach was parked near the front of the convoy. The police had formed a cordon at the front of the coaches to block off the road.

Arsenal's firm of about 100 came down another street and bounced around shouting at the other side of the bizzies. United's fans tried to attack them but were beaten back by police. I saw a gap between the police and a white van. I was still pissed off at being chased so I went for it. I managed to get through and went at Arsenal's firm. Just what I aimed to achieve on my jacks was anybody's guess. I bounced around 'football style' and Arsenal came at me. One bizzy tried to grab me and another tried to whack me with a spring-loaded truncheon. I took off my jacket and dived onto the coach.

I'm supposed to be done with all this shit, I thought, as the coaches pulled away. The radio reported on the journey home that Arsenal's manager Arsene Wenger had offered to replay the game and the FA had agreed. We got to travel back down ten days later. Eighteen Sheffield had been arrested at the first game. The second passed off reasonably peacefully. Arsenal again won 2-1.

# BARNSLEY

Generally it's been one-way traffic in these Yorkshire derby rucks. I'm sure Barnsley's firm, the Five-O, adopted its name from the fact that whenever we played them at Bramall Lane they always came in five minutes after kick off. I will, however, give them ten out of ten for a class effort four years ago. After we had played at Oakwell their firm caught a train to Sheffield an hour later to seek our boys out. That's a first in my book.

But the Five-O Crew never really had a result against us. I could write about the time we ran them out of Barnsley bus station, the time we took their town centre before and after a game, or the occasion when they attacked the Outpost pub and our lot later went into them through the police lines and scattered them to the winds. I have chosen to write about a night in 1987 when they did have a good go.

An evening game at Oakwell produced a turnout of 150 BBC, heavily monitored by police. Sixty broke away and found a small pub near the ground. The scouts went out and came back with news that the bulk of our lot had been escorted to the ground. They also told us at least 100 Barnsley were following behind.

We immediately went out along the dark side streets towards the hill that led up then back down to Barnsley's ground. I walked ahead with Buzzer, who knew a lot of Barnsley's lads. We bumped straight into their crew. I punched one, causing him to fall. Our lot ran up and a roar went up from both factions. Barnsley came into us and we stood. Police on horseback tried to keep the rivals apart but to no avail. Everyone was bang at it, dodging police then wading in. More police arrived and most of our lot got rounded up. Ten of us split and went back down the road we had just come up. We again bumped into their lads, who charged in numbers. It was backs to the wall stuff but we stuck together and stood firm.

In the ground, the atmosphere was tense. Barnsley were on one side of the terrace, us on the other, with only the tunnel and police separating us. United fans twice tried to invade the pitch and police drew truncheons and made numerous arrests. I knew it was going to go off after the game. We got our crew together and tried to leave just before the end, but the police were having none of it.

As the crowds poured out, we managed to keep around 100 of our lot together and slipped off up a side street. We then doubled back and came out near the main road. Barnsley came from nowhere. A huge 'off' began in the dimly lit street. Aston was hit by a plant pot. Barnsley had it sussed and bricks rained down on us. We couldn't see them coming in the darkness and quite a number received head injuries. Neither side gave an inch.

Then I was hit from behind by what felt like a runaway train. A snidey horseback copper had ridden down the grass verge so I didn't hear him coming. It's not pleasant being hit by a horse. I was totally winded. As I gasped for air, two Barnsley copped me and I fell over a garden fence under a flurry of blows. A roar went up and our lot managed to back Barnsley off. I got my breath back, but I'd had the stuffing knocked out of me. As police gained control and herded us up, we heard the sound of more trouble going off. The rest of our lot were going at it with Barnsley nearer the train station. I'll take my Lacoste hat off to Barnsley that day, they went for it big time and it's perhaps the best they've managed in numerous games between the two Yorkshire rivals.

# BIRMINGHAM

We have engaged in some major rucks with the Zulu Warriors over the past two decades, as I have already described. None of them surpassed the confrontation between the BBC and the Zulus in 1997. It has been described by many of those present as the best set-to between two rival mobs ever witnessed.

On 1 January 1985, they were our guests at 'beautiful downtown' Bramall Lane. We were meeting at the Blue Bell on High Street in Sheffield centre at twelve bells (midday). I was a little late but my timing appeared to be perfect: as I walked up an alley that led onto High Street, I heard the roar of boys 'at it'. Running around the corner, I saw 50 Birmingham steaming the doors of the Bell. Our lot were trying to get out and a furious fistfight was going off. Then, BANG.

I thought a Brummie had a gun at first, but the plume of smoke told me otherwise. It was a flare. Our lot had a surge just as I approached, so I steamed in from the side. More of our lot came around the corner; they had run round from the Blue Bell's back doors. We got Birmingham moving.

'Run, you fucks,' someone bawled.

Then this geezer stopped and held his hands like he had a gun.

BANG.

The red nautical distress flare flew over our heads. The sniper was almost captured as he turned and ran with the rest of them. We chased Birmingham right through town and all the way down to Bramall Lane. With it being New Year's Day, town was empty; just as well, as Quick Draw McGraw was firing flare bullets like they were going out of fashion. It was the first time we had seen them. They even fired one from the away end into the John Street Stand seats, where we had a firm of around 500 boys.

This was nothing, however, compared to what was probably the most vicious and highly-charged battle the BBC ever had, when the Zulu Army came to Sheffield in September 1997. Over 300 United boys patrolled London Road prior to the game. The two teams had a long history of conflict and this confrontation would be a yardstick of supremacy.

Birmingham arrived late, just before kick-off. Around 100 police kept the two factions apart but the verbals were in full flow. The Zulu firm looked impressive, loads of blacks and boys who really looked up for it. With five minutes to go before the end of the match, they left the ground and headed for London Road. This foxed us completely; they obviously had their own 'game plan'. They attacked a pub called the Pheasant, were 20 Blades were drinking. In the ensuing brawl, two Blades were slashed.

Mobile phones suddenly beeped into life with news of the intrusion and we ran towards London Road in dribs and drabs. The most ferocious battle kicked off, with boys steaming in like this was going to be their last ever brawl. A Pakistani youth from Brum was waving a knife around like a madman. Lads were getting dropped, jumping back up and steaming in again. A huge roar went up.

'BBC, BBC.'

Birmingham wobbled. A lad ran through to their front line brandishing a Stanley knife. He was downed and finally Brum broke ranks and ran down London Road. The Stanley man was caught and beaten to a pulp. This was a fight for only the brave or the insane. The police helicopter hung overhead, with the command to 'stop fighting' coming from a megaphone.

The Zulu, who took the worst hiding I've ever seen, was in hospital for four days. Someone very kindly sent him a card saying, 'Get well soon, the BBC.' We give them a lot of credit for their gameness and the way they have held a steady mob together for over 20 years now. The major difference between us and them is that we don't need knives.

After the big row at Sheffield, the return game in February 1998 was eagerly awaited. The game had been switched to a Sunday and was to be screened on Sky TV, which often meant a lot of lads watching it in the pub, but we still managed a turnout of 100 Sheffield United on the train. On the journey, two plain clothes police tried to mingle with our mob by pretending to be Spurs fans returning from their game at Wednesday the day before. Our lot sussed they were bizzies (after all, who travels from Sheffield to London via Birmingham?) but one or two Blades passed small talk. The police captured our lot as the train arrived and escorted them to the ground.

After the game, a large group of Birmingham waiting outside. Everyone went into them and they scattered. Birmingham's firm must have spent a grand on mobile phone calls as they got themselves together and tailed our movements.

Finally they charged at the escort, chanting: 'Zulu, Zulu.'

Everybody started laughing and ran through the police towards them. The cops struggled to contain the situation until more officers arrived. Although the police won the day, United had taken took 100 boss boys to Brum with no mugs. It would have been a brilliant off but for the Old Bill.

Birmingham came mob-handed again in August 1998, stopping off at the Travellers Rest on City Road. A few of our lot had the mobile phone numbers of Birmingham's top boys. They tried in vain to arrange a meet. Birmingham had split up into two groups. We saw 50 boys queuing outside the turnstiles and thought that was their mob, so we headed off for the game. Around 15 of us headed up to the South Stand. We were just about to go in when around 50 boys came around the corner of Cherry Street and onto Bramall Lane. They saw us, then the roar went up. Their mob was mostly blacks and surprisingly had no police with them. We spread and went towards them. Mally ran into them but the CID screeched up and jumped out with spring-loaded truncheons. More police arrived. I grabbed hold of a black guy and dragged him away from their mob.

'You come with me.'

Me and Tiler laughed as he screamed 'Help, help' to the police. I let him go and he fell to the floor in his haste to get away.

Before the game finished, I went out of the ground to see if Birmingham were going to try leaving early again. Our mob had already left in the hope that Birmingham would use the same tactic as the previous season. As I sat on a wall, I noticed a black guy speaking on a mobile. I recognised him as one of Brum's main actors. I headed over and listened in. He was onto their firm and then he noticed me.

'Ouright mayte,' he said in that Brummie drawl.

I had just begun to ask him where their mob would be later when Keith popped up, tried to hit him and chased him down Bramall Lane as the police looked on. Ten of us bumped into him again later near Sheffield station. He and some of his mates were chased into the train station.

# BOLTON

My second visit to Fred Dibnah land was in October 1988. Once again the season ended in promotion, and once again it went off. I was in one of two cars containing nine of our boys. We had no plan for the day and arrived at the ground 30 minutes before kick-off. As we walked towards the car park, I noticed a large group attack four lads who fled towards us. I recognised one of the retreaters as a non-hooligan Blade who I had played football against.

We ran to their aid. Bolton came at us so Holder steamed into them. It was all hands to the pump and I got trapped between two cars in the melee. Swinging out wildly, I kept them at bay and when a copper tried to arrest me I still had enough wits about me to give him the slip. In the fracas my Burberry scarf had gone from my neck and a Chicago Bears hat, which I had borrowed from Sam, had also disappeared. Bolton's mob were in the football club car park 20 yards further up the road. Sam pointed down the road where a Boltonian was ripping up his Bears hat, laughing as he did so. I then spotted another boy laughing with his mates. He had my Burberry scarf in his hand. I went on one, slipping past police into the car park and running through a dozen Bolton to land a beaut on the thieving sod's chin. He dropped like a stone. I grabbed my scarf and then waded in as the steeplejacks attacked me. I must have looked like a mad Bay City Roller fan, waving my scarf around furiously with my clenched fist still holding it. Once again the bizzies moved in and I escaped unscathed.

In March 1993, United had an FA Cup quarter-final at Blackburn's Ewood Park. United managed to get a goalless draw. Outside the ground the lads chased 100 Blackburn off an embankment which, due to the construction of a new stand, overlooked the pitch. On the way home everyone disembarked at Bolton. This was a spontaneous decision. Once in Bolton's pubs, the opposition was sought out. We were told by a local where we could find our equivalents and set off to a nearby boozer. Bolton came steaming out of the bar and it kicked off briefly before they did one. The pub windows were totalled.

# BRADFORD

It always went off at Bradford in the 1980s. Their firm, the Ointment, always had a pop and even brought a tidy team to ours once. A bit of a rivalry developed when 30 of our lot bumped into a coachload of Bradford in a late night stop at Leicester Forest service station on the M1 in 1986. One lad (a Villa Youth boy travelling with United) was badly injured and the Bradford coach had windows smashed in return. Police arrested three and charged them with affray, culminating in one Bradford lad receiving a nine-month prison sentence.

Later in 1986, United's away game at Bradford's Odsal Stadium was given the name Denim Day. All our lads wore denim shirts. Our three hooligan coaches were taken straight to the ground and at 1.45 pm we were the only people in the ground. United's players brought out cups of tea for us after their pre-match warm-up. Photocopies from the *Leicester Mercury* were found scattered on the away end seats, detailing the Leicester Forest incident and the Ointment were to chant the name of this service station throughout the game.

After the match, ten Rotherham Blades were attacked by Bradford's boys. In the ensuing fight they managed to chase off their attackers, only for one 17-year-old Bradford lad to run into the path of a car. He died instantly. Five Blades were arrested for the incident but released without charge.

In the return fixture in March 1987, 80 Bradford arrived in a fleet of cars and vans. Myself and the two other United hooligans bumped into them, then led them down to London Road. One of our lot saw the situation and ran ahead of us, returning with 40 boys. We went into Bradford, who did the off. We were surprised at the numbers they turned out but agreed it was a show for their deceased friend. We also had sympathy. Although we were all hooligans, no one wanted a rival dead or maimed, that just wasn't what it was all about.

# CARLISLE

The ten lads who travelled up to Carlisle with me in 1986 got a bit of a shock when after the game we were attacked by around 30 young dressers. We held our own and perhaps even got the better of things. Later on we cruised around the streets and ended up jumping out and having a go at the same Carlisle lads that we had fought at the ground. Carlisle's Border City Firm are more famous for their notorious hooligan Paul Dodds than anything else. Dodds is a face with England and loves the publicity he gains through his misdemeanours.

# CHELSEA

The last home game of the 1994-95 season saw the visit of Chelsea. It was a chance to put one over the infamous Chelsea crew and Blades turned out in force. Around 250 BBC met in town, then later moved on to London Road. Rumours circulated that Chelsea were again meeting up with Wednesday. Quinny, a top face with Wednesday, had strong links with Chelsea but this didn't excuse the meet of two mobs. We have never teamed up with anyone else.

The game passed without incident. Afterwards, 200 United met at the Cross Guns at the top of London Road. It was a pub we never used but we knew that Wednesday/Chelsea would head for the Nursery Tavern on Ecclesall Road. We could work our way down through nearby flats and avoid police. The plan worked well enough as we ducked and dived our way to Ecclesall Road and the 200 of us eventually surfaced only 250 yards from our target. However, the police saw us as we closed in and around 100 officers blocked our path.

We wanted Chelsea so badly that loads of Blades tried to break through the police line. In response, they attacked us with long staffs. A number of our lads were nicked and our group was split. I went in the Devonshire Arms at the bottom of Ecclesall Road. Around 40 Blades sat around, pissed off. I had a swift half and informed our boys that I was going to the Nursery on my own. I'd had enough. In frustration more than anything else, I walked up. Around 200 yards later, I heard a familiar voice

'Steve, what are you doing?' It was Raggy, a close mate.

'Rag, I've had enough of this shit, I'm going up.'

'What for? Gonna steam in on yer own eh?'

'I don't know but I'm going up.'

'Then I am.'

The two of us walked through the Nursery doors. We immediately saw Quinny and a few other Wednesday lads. He looked at me and shook his head. Raggy went and got two lagers.

'What's happening, Quinny?' I asked.

'Steve, these lads don't fuck around. They're nasty bastards.'

'Quinny, you might think this lot are the dog's bollocks but to me they're just another set of boys.'

A few Chelsea sussed us out and came over.

'Where's your fackin' firm mate?'

'Our fackin' firm's just tried to get up here and have been fighting with police.'

More Chelsea came around us. Some of them were sound, others not. This bulldog-chewing-a-wasp-type geezer, big scar down his face, came over.

'Go and fetch your fackin' boys, we're Chelsea, we'll kill you.'

'What, forty of you?'

'Yeah, forty. You're shit, Sheffield.' He couldn't talk without growling.

A tall Chelsea lad butted in, 'Steve, go get your boys and we'll have it away.'

I was getting well pissed off now. I noticed that a sea of unfriendly faces were hemming us in. 'Look, I've told you we can't get up here, the bizzies are everywhere. Get taxis into town and we'll come, don't worry about that.'

I told a few Wednesday to take them into town but they didn't look impressed. Raggy and I supped up and left. I think we had outstayed our visit. Bulldog and a few of his cronies were getting a bit too aggressive for my liking.

The rest of our mob was at the bottom of London Road and we all met up. Around an hour later, a scout on patrol in a car came back with the exaggerated news that 100 Chelsea were on the move and walking down Ecclesall Road to town. Around 200 of us ran up to cut them off. We came out at the back of a large supermarket and ran across towards Chelsea. The bizzies had them in an escort as we ran towards them. Six police on horseback rode around the supermarket car park chasing us like demented Frankie Dettoris.

Later, news came through the hooli-vine that Chelsea and a few Wednesday were in Berlins in the city centre. This was a chance to kill three birds with one stone: there had been trouble between Berlin's bouncers and Blades in previous weeks. Later that night 100 BBC headed straight off and attacked the pub. Bouncers used bats and CS gas to repel repeated attacks. Wednesday and Chelsea were inside. Police came from everywhere and blocked both ends of the road off. They nicked and clubbed everything that moved. Eight Blades were arrested and charged with affray. What pissed us off even more that night was a so-called main Wednesday face was sat in a bizzy van pointing Blades out to police. Eyes was nicked but said nothing and was eventually released without charge. It was a very frustrating day. We had turned out all our main boys and would have gone through anyone, but all we had to show was a load nicked and a few club windows smashed.

Chelsea are without doubt a high profile firm. They have strong links with far-Right groups such as Combat 18 and have a large following at England matches. Some of their main boys are proper thugs who take their violence very seriously. One of a series of TV investigations called *MacIntyre Undercover* featured Chelsea's Headhunter firm. As a result of the programme, in December 2000 two Chelsea lads, Andrew Frain and Jason Marriner, received jail terms of seven and six years respectively. There was hardly any evidence against the two of them other than letting their mouths run away with them. In the same week as their trial a convicted drink-driver was before the courts on a charge of taking the lives of a family of three whilst drunk at the wheel of his car. He received a four-year jail term. You can see how football violence is over-hyped and how the courts look upon people seen as 'generals' who organise the violence.

## CHESTERFIELD

Whenever we travelled the short distance to Chezzer, all and sundry used to turn out to fight for the woollybacks. If you could stand up straight and had a donkey jacket, you were in Chesterfield's crew. They tended to disappear up their arses before and after the game but when we went on their kop (which was standard procedure for us) they used to come at you from all sides. They would put on a decent show to protect their precious end (sorry, shed) from their big city rivals. Over the past couple of years the so-called Chesterfield Bastard Squad has built up a tidy little mob and been involved in quite a few incidents.

## COLCHESTER

Colchester away in 1981 saw a pitched battle behind one goal. We lost 5-2 in a game on *Match of the Day*. You could see on TV that everyone was bang at it as United attacked the goal at one end. The game was also remembered because of a Rotherham Blade called Drip. On a side terrace it was going to go off when a couple of their lads put biker helmets on and pulled the visors down. Drip, cool as you like, walked over, chatted to one, then flicked his visor up and finger-jabbed him in the eye. Drip died in a car crash not long after, but he was one game lad that will always be remembered.

# COVENTRY

Coventry's firm are a joke. I don't know why this is, as it has the reputation of being a tough city, full of car workers. We went to Highfield Road at the end of 1990/91 season, sat in the home seats, went onto the pitch at the end, then chased their boys out of the ground.

In 1997, United visited Coventry for an FA Cup quarter-final. According to the experts, we hadn't a prayer. United sold their 5,000 ticket allocation within two hours. None of us had a ticket, thanks to Raggy being so laid back and not realising the demand. Bally then played a blinder by driving all the way over to Highfield Road, spinning a yarn to the ticket clerk and returning with four tickets for Coventry's seats. A van was hired and off we set. Loads of our boys travelled ticketless, including five in our van. At Coventry we went to a pub near the train station. We met up with Keith and Ian, two Everton boys. A Blade in our van called Skinner had met a Coventry fan whilst on holiday in the Canary Isles, and he showed up along with his very chesty girlfriend. As the 15 or so of us had a drink, 30 Coventry came in. Keith was sure it was going to go off and was on edge.

'Simmer down. Five of us would go through this lot,' I assured him.

As kick-off neared we made our way to the van, still clutching plastic glasses filled with plastic lager. We had got down the side of the pub when a few Coventry started acting up.

'Stop,' shouted Jake.

Everyone jumped out – except me. I just stood laughing as our lot chased Coventry away. Keith had by now got over his nerves and was running around like a head-the-ball. I had to laugh at Bally as he tried to glass one (sorry, plastic one) but instead covered his white Stone Island jumper with beer, then nearly fell flat on his arse as he tried to kick a Sky Blue in retreat. It was a thin air shot I've seen a thousand times: you try to kick someone you are chasing but as you pull your leg back, they're gone, and your leg swings around in mid-air like Nick Faldo's seven iron.

Skinner's non-violent mate and his bird had jumped in the van for a lift and by this time both were looking a tad nervous. I apologised for everyone's behaviour and tried to explain it away by saying that the FA Cup had got everyone over-excited.

In the ground we took our seats. By chance, we were right in front of Skinner's Coventry couple. The guy looked very uneasy but made us as welcome as a man trying to make someone welcome who's not really welcome can! Me, Jake (who was on crutches), Raggy and Bally sat together. We all knew each other inside out and no matter what came our way, no one would leave the others' side. One-nil to Coventry, then Marcello scored.

'Gooaal.' We jumped up.

'Yeah. Get in.'

We hugged and kissed like you do, then realised half the stand was staring at us.

'Sit down, you wankers,' a geezer ten rows back shouted.

'Fuck off, dickhead,' I returned fire.

Then he started giving it the 'after the match your gonna die' shit. That was it. I was up the seats to him. Bally and Jake pulled me back, but gobby got the drift.

We drew 1-1. Outside the ground, United's firm gathered at a pub on a corner. Marvin dropped a Coventry lad with a vicious punch which landed the lad at my feet. I looked down and as police rushed over, then walked away with that 'it wasn't me, guv' look on me dial. And that was that.

# DERBY

The Derby Lunatic Fringe had some strange ideas of when and where to turn up in Sheffield. In 1984 and 85, they turned up three times, much to our annoyance. On the first occasion, they walked down West Street on a Friday night, an area where Wednesday drank at the time. Some four weeks later, around 100 Derby stopped off in the city centre en route to Rotherham. They attacked the Blue Bell pub in High Street. The 20 Blades inside were powerless and pissed off that Derby had shown up when we had an insignificant fixture. Later in the day 70 Blades waited for Derby's return, which was thwarted by police who stopped them from leaving the train station. The third time was again on a Friday night, which is bizarre.

In January 1986, United were drawn at home to Derby. We expected them to come in numbers and our turnout touched 300 but they never showed, much to our frustration. Derby's relegation the following season gave us the chance to put the record straight and our away game on the November 22 saw a crew of 250. The police thought they had it sussed and escorted the five hoolie coaches directly to the ground from the motorway. Despite this, when in traffic five miles from the ground around 100 of us jumped off and walked. A large police presence prevented our rendezvous with the DLF.

Our home game against them that season gave an indication of the BBC's often rudderless leadership. In the week before the match, arguments took place about where to meet. Some said Derby would come by cars and vans, therefore a pub on their route would be best. Others argued that the DLF would arrive by train and a meet in town would be more attractive. So our firm was all over the place on match day. I played football against Derby for the supporters' club that morning (I scored a hat-trick by the way) and when me and three other boys tried to locate our mob, we found chaos, with 30 here, 40 there and 20 somewhere else. Derby didn't show and it was a good job really. It went off after the game but police were close by and nipped it on in the bud. So BBC v DLF – nil-nil, I reckon.

# EVERTON

The scouse scallies are well-known disciples of the blade, as we found when we encountered them on 26 September 1984. Everton visited Sheffield in the then-League Cup and it went off at the bottom of Bramall Lane, 150 yards from the ground. Forty of us bumped into a similar group of Everton. As we jumped over the pedestrian railings, Everton came at us. To a man they had one hand in their jackets, the old 'I've got a knife ploy.' We had none of it and just went into them. The result was ours and a few of the Everton lads I have since met were there that day and acknowledge the fact.

# NOTTINGHAM FOREST

There is no doubt in my mind that Forest have got some good boys and a fairly large crew but for some reason or another we have never had trouble moving them along. One of Forest's main actors over the years was a lad called Boatsy. He became good friends with a couple of United boys, having met them through England games. I met Boatsy around 1987 when he and another Forest lad came to Sheffield on a Saturday night. They tagged along with United's firm, who were on the lookout for Wednesday up West Street. Twenty-five of us went into the Limit nightclub, which Wednesday used every Saturday night. We got in early so we would be able to get stuck in before they knew what was happening.

After around half an hour it became obvious that a few United had blinked and our 25 had become 15, including our two Forest mercenaries. The OCS used to have around 50 lads in the Limit, plus 20 more who called themselves the Stocksbridge Owls. As they began to gather in the packed club, we had a conflab: should we steam them now while we had enough numbers, or should we wait until most of their firm was in? All of Wednesday's boys had made their way in and were standing in their usual spot at the back of the club, near the toilets.

One of our boys came over. 'Steve, I think we should fuck off, it's well on top in here.'

He was right. Even the bouncers had Wednesday links, so they wouldn't be very helpful to our cause.

'This is the buzz, well outnumbered on their patch,' I said. 'It's what it's all about.'

I studied our little crew. There was Tiler, 18 years old and strutting around like a peacock. Howie, another lad, game as anything. The rest looked at ease. We'd be all right.

I headed off to the khazi, always a dangerous spot for an ambush in a situation like this. A lot of Wednesday clocked me and although I knew many of them, I expected a few to try and jump me. I stood at the urinal tensed for a sudden attack, but nothing happened. Then, 'Steve, you'd better get out here quick.'

A Wednesday lad called Flem had come into the toilet. He said Wednesday had surrounded our lot at the bar. I ran out and went through the crowds, then turned to face 40 Wednesday.

Chirpy, Quinny and Steve, all from Wednesday's old school, started the ball rolling.

'Steve, get these cunts out of here man, it's taking the piss.'

I told them there had been 25 of us at first but a lot had bottled it and that if we were going to go we would have, you know, gone. In the tense atmosphere, I glanced at Boatsy and his Forest mate. It was then I realised that he was the business as a boy. He was leaning on the bar, his heavy-buckled belt hanging loosely from one hand, a can of Red Stripe in the other.

A Wednesday lad leaned through and tried to grab Tiler. 'He was there last week when I got battered,' he explained to Wednesday.

'Right then,' I said, grabbing both of them by the arm. 'You two go and sort it out.'

Tiler was up for this but the Wednesday lad was not.

'Er no, it's er...'

I cut him short. 'Shut it then, all mouth and no bollocks.'

I had a quick chat with the old school and to be fair to them I reckon they could have done us but we had a bit of mutual respect. Our lot had another drink and we left. Through it all, Boatsy was completely unconcerned.

I bumped into him again in Lille during France 98. As we swapped small talk, he suddenly dropped his baseball-capped head. I thought he was eyeing up my footwear. He looked up again.

'That was Derby, they don't like me,' he said as 40 boys walked by.

Their walk turned into a sprint later, as 70 Brum chased the DLF. I'm surprised our lot didn't bump into the Zulu firm, as United had 60 lads hanging around for the Colombia game. The *Daily Mail* had a front-page photo of three heavily-tattooed Blades boys sat around before the Colombia game. 'Tat-hooligan,' was the headline, and the article went on about the three being part of a large group of Sheffield United followers called the BBC, who had gone over to France for trouble. Another United boy was interviewed on French radio. Borny was out of his skull on drink when asked by a local reporter, microphone in hand, 'Are you are football hooligan?'

To laughter from other United boys, he replied, 'Yeah, I'm with the BBC from Sheffield.'

'What will you do if England lose today?'

'We'll smash the fuckin' lot up.'

Back to Forest. There was one occasion when I reckon they would have pushed United's mob all the way. The final game of the 1992-3 season saw 5,000 Sheffielders travel to Trent Bridge in what was also Brian Clough's last game in charge of Forest. He was a legend there for the success and trophies he had brought to the city. Our boys were split that day among different modes of transport. Ten of us travelled in a van and parked near a pub at the side of the River Trent. As we walked towards the ground, a huge firm of around 200 lads appeared from a side street. We held back and just stood looking at a very tidy crew. United pissed on old Cloughie's bonfire by winning 2-0 but he came out and waved at the Blades contingent, who sang his name in respect. That didn't stop Forest's boys whacking anything from Sheffield outside; their unmerry men were even giving it to shirters.

# GILLINGHAM

A Tuesday evening game on 15 March 1983 at Gillingham saw a United following of no more than 500. None of our boys travelled except me, Kizzer, Eyes, Chilly and Mash. As we sat in traffic after the match, around 15 Gilly boys spotted us and moved towards our car. We jumped out on the orders of Eyes and I struck one in the face with a full can of coke. They did the off but came back and things looked bad.

Then I remembered something one of the older lads showed me. I fumbled for a 50p piece, then held it between my thumb and forefinger.

'Come on, who wants slicing.' I waved it about in front of me. It worked. The Gillingham thought I had a blade and we chased them again. We laughed later at their feeble attempt at soccer violence.

Speaking of Chilly, I became really good friends with him. Although he became a professional footballer he also stayed a mate. He had a brother who ran with Wednesday's mob but he was a Blades thug. He signed professional terms with Rotherham and George Kerr, the club's manager, once had to go to court as a character witness after Chilly was arrested for a misdemeanour at a United match. As far as I know he now lives in New Zealand.

# GRIMSBY TOWN

Grimsby Town's firm, the Cleethorpes Beach Patrol, are the most frustrating crew around. I have been to Blundell Park eight times – it would have been nine except for a police raid on our coach en route in which I was arrested – and each time they seem to turn a decent-sized crew out but never want to know.

In 1985 we took 200 boys there and ran them all over the place. It was the same scenario the following season when 60 of us had Grimsby off. Later we got split up and eight of us bumped into their main firm. The 40 or so of them were manoeuvring for an attack when we launched one of our own. Howie, Nobby, Paul, Nudger, Renkie and myself steamed in like madmen. Police rushed over and Grimsby had missed their chance.

A couple of years ago two of our lads did the business in their seats. We looked on from the away end as Harry and his mate got stuck into 20 Grimsby. It was quite amusing; Harry is a game lad but quite mad, on this occasion he was into the Grimsby mob, his arms going 60 to the dozen and Grimsby's lads flying all over the place. Then the stewards and the police ran down and got a hold of Harry. He shrugged off a steward, took off his baseball cap and bowed to the cheering away end.

In January 2000 we visited their place. Our new manager Neil Warnock had lifted the gloom which had hung over Bramall Lane for years and we were on a wave of optimism. So many went to the game that 500 Blades were locked out. Earlier, 40 United boys had gathered in O'Neil's Bar in Cleethorpes. Fifty Grimsby came to the pub; as usual they were half-hearted in what they were doing. The police rounded up our lot and escorted them to the match.

We were going to have another drink but decided to head off for the game, time was getting on and it was a fair walk from Cleethorpes. Four of us walked to the match, Pricey (who can do a bit), Nipper (who's last fight was at junior school so he still maintains that he's unbeaten) and Bally (who will do a bit if he has too but would rather not, thank you very much). On the route we bumped into some Grimsby.

'Your gonna get it,' one screamed as they fanned out.

Pricey and I both looked at each other.

'No, your gonna get it.'

They were off. Then they followed us, throwing bricks from 50 yards away. We walked onto the main road that leads to the ground and bumped into eight more of their boys. We were on one side of the road, they were on the other. No bizzies around. They crossed towards us. I intercepted the first one.

'Come on then,'

They didn't want to know really and started with the verbals. A car stopped and two coppers jumped out and suddenly Grimsby started showing off. Pricey twatted one and I slapped another. The police were soft and ask for assistance.

The big lad Pricey had hit was giving it the old chestnut: 'Is that your best shot?'

Police on horseback arrive and escorted Grimsby up to the ground with us still walking parallel to them. The big lad started rubbing his face.

'Don't rub it mate, it wasn't his best shot,' I shouted.

He went mad and started bitching to the police. 'That twat over there has just chinned me.'

We all cracked up.

# HUDDERSFIELD

Over the years, United's visits to Huddersfield have produced outbreaks of large-scale disorder. They have never visited the Lane mobbed up but have turned out in numbers at home. Their main pub is in Huddersfield town centre, not far from the train station. My first visit was in January 1983 and we went 150-handed on the train. We had it away as soon as we hit Huddersfield. The Terrier boys couldn't cope and we ransacked them all over town. Down at the ground it went off again outside a pub as 50 of us stormed the doors. Then after the drab 0-0 draw 30 of us split from the police escort. We bumped into Huddersfield not too far from the station. This time they had a huge crew together and went into us toe-to-toe in the darkness. Fortunately the rest of our lot who were being shepherded into the train station heard it go off and came out behind Huddersfield. It was murder. No one knew who was who, including the police, who charged in on horseback.

When order was restored we went onto the platform and waited for our train. Everyone was on one and in the boredom of waiting we split into two large groups. Both sides then began chanting at the other then we steamed into each other. Our lot did this a lot and to an outsider it must have looked like a proper brawl. The bizzies certainly did and waded in truncheons drawn. Two or three Blades were arrested. We were only having a laugh!

My next visit was again in January this time in 1986. A coachload of us made our way from the town centre to the ground. A similar number of Huddersfield came down at us from the Crescent pub. I don't know why but they were up for it more than us. Although we didn't back off, it was their boys that took the initiative and steamed in. It could have been naughty but for police intervention. Mally was arrested and I was going shitpot with everyone.

'What's up wi' you lot? That was shit. Sort yourselves out for fuck's sake.'

We got our act together down at the ground and ran Huddersfield at the back of the main stand.

For the final game of the 87/88-season, United again visited Huddersfield. We were staring relegation in the face and only three points would be enough, depending on other results. We took a large firm and Huddersfield even had trouble keeping their kop as 100 Blades fought battles during the game. Around 250 of us sat in the main stand and, on the final whistle, invaded the pitch. I got a United player's shirt then joined in the charge towards the Huddersfield mob, who wisely did one after a brief scuffle near the corner flag. United won the game but were still relegated after a play off with Bristol City.

In the following season, United were drawn at Huddersfield in the FA Cup third round. I travelled with the boys but wanted to keep out of trouble as I had two court appearances coming up. We travelled by train and after a 1-0 win headed back to the station. Around 20 of us had held back from the escort and found ourselves left to our own devices. As we approached the town centre, Huddersfield came from nowhere. We were on one side of the road, Huddersfield on the other. Taz was bouncing around in the middle of the road. Annoyed at our hesitation, he turned towards us and shouted, 'What's going off? Umming and arring with Huddersfield?'

Kav ran towards a big bearded bloke fronting for their crew. Kav planted him right on his chin. The guy was out on his feet. Then Kav banged another who dropped like a stone. It was all too much for me and I ran in with the rest. Huddersfield backed into the road but did not run. I steamed in, tripped and fell to the floor. Police officers came running from all directions and one went for me. I was off and managed to get away. Five minutes later we walked past where it had just kicked off. There sat on a bench with a couple of mates trying to bring him round was Grizzly Adams, who Kav had kayoed.

I have since met a few of the Huddersfield lads and have not travelled to their ground with our mob over recent years. I bumped into them at the back of the stand at the McAlpine in 1998. One or two shook my hand and asked if our lot had travelled. Later, 15 of our boys had a great brawl with 25 Huddersfield.

# MANCHESTER CITY

An evening League Cup tie at City on 2 November 1988 produced a turnout numbering 50 in 12 cars. We met at Glossop and convoyed in. After parking in one of the most dodgy areas I have seen around a football ground, we marched to the match. A few black and mixed-race lads saw us so we expected hell on our return to the cars. After a scuffle outside the ground, a few of our lot informed some City of our whereabouts.

After the match, we got ourselves together and walked away from the main crowds into the darkened streets. Bodies seemed to appear and disappear in the darkness. I thought we would be ambushed, so told our lot to pick up bricks and planks. Once we got to the road we had parked on, it went off. I was surprised that City did one. They didn't seem organised at all, even though they had had plenty of time to get themselves together. A couple of Blades were arrested as we went for it.

Our lot jumped into the cars and edged away from Maine Road in slow-moving traffic. I was driving and my car was near the front of the convoy. Around 100 yards up the road I could see activity and told the lads in my car to get ready; this was going to be difficult as my car was a two-door affair. There was a pub on the left and a lot of lads outside it. The two cars in front of me got past and I was bang level with the pub when glasses came flying. We jumped out and Pete went straight into them with a large plank. Pecker was hit with a brick that bounced off his head. It was one of the best headers I've seen, as the brick was destined for my car and he deflected it away. City backed into the pub and we ran back to the cars and went up the wrong side of the street. We were sitting ducks and knew the last few cars would cop it. All of us managed to get way unscathed.

# MANCHESTER UNITED

I'm not sure why, but the Reds have never turned out a firm of any note on any of their many visits to Bramall Lane. Of the times we played them, all we had to show was a small ruck with 20 dressers. I did once go to Hillsborough with an avid Man Utd fan from Worksop. We went on a coach with 50 Worksop Reds, 30 of whom looked the part, and they steamed a few Wednesday outside The Gate pub at Hillsborough. I suppose if they got all the different firms together – the Cockney Reds, the Salford crew, and so on – they would have a huge army that would take some shifting.

In November 1990, we took a good firm to Old Trafford. The three coaches of boys that day were left disappointed as the Mancunian fuzz had it well sussed. Our three coaches were singled out. We were pulled in for an hour, photographed and videoed as we alighted, then escorted to the game. It's a frustrating place to visit if you're on the look out for an off.

The following season, I travelled ticketless to the so-called Theatre of Dreams. There were always plenty of touts about, so I asked one for a ticket as near to the away fans as possible.

'This one's bang at the side of your fans,' the lying Manc told me.

I was actually near the half way line. All my mates took to their seats in the away end. Well, it's a decent seat, I thought. I wasn't in it long, though. As my beloved Blades took to the field, I jumped up shouting, 'Come on Blades.'

Bad mistake. Some Manc threw one at me. I ducked and went for him. All around me people spat and tried to nail one on me. Stewards tried to rescue me. I was throwing punches like they were going out of fashion. It was quite scary but it got the old blood pumping. I have always had a low opinion of all the aeroplane gestures and Munich air disaster abuse that away fans adopt at Old Trafford, but after being spat on it crossed my mind to give them some. I know it's stupid, but how else can you abuse the most successful team in the country? Anyway, I thought better of it. I managed to get out and the kind stewards lobbed me into the streets for my trouble.

Over the last couple of years, I've heard that Man United has been bouncing a tidy firm around. If they can't get a good mob out with the success they've had, no one can.

# MIDDLESBROUGH

Boro have a nice tricky crew but it hasn't always been like that with the Frontline. In the mid-Eighites we went to theirs and did the business. In March 1985 our crew landed in their town centre at midday. We ran Boro, then at the ground invaded their seats. A few Boro were clipped, leading to a charge across the pitch by a load of their boys. Scuffles broke out but we were too big and too strong for them.

A year later we headed back up to Ayrsome Park for an evening game. Forty of us got involved in a battle in a car park before the game. Paul and Terry led us into them. Again we got the better of things. The crowds at these games, unbelievably, were 5,177 and 5,678 respectively. Middlesbrough as a club have made terrific strides. It is the same with the Geordies and the Mackems and just goes to show how a bit of ambition and enterprise can bring the fans flooding back. Sheff United have stood still for years.

Twenty of our lads bumped into Middlesbrough a few seasons ago. We'd played Stockport away and Boro had been at Manchester for a FA Cup semi against Chesterfield. The 100 Boro boys chatted to our lads without any trouble. The Boro lads looked like they'd been in the wars. The night before, they had had a running battle with Hibs Casuals in Blackpool. According to the Middlesbrough lads it was a 'mad one' with distress flares and other weapons used. To make matters worse, or better, depending on your viewpoint, they had then been at it all day with Man City. A lot of Boro boys had black eyes, blood all over them and ripped clothes. That proved they had had a good go. I rate Boro.

# MILLWALL

I have already mentioned how the 1977 documentary about Millwall was a TV landmark for football hooliganism. Another came in March 1985 when footage of the Lions' travelling army ripping up seats and then chasing police in an FA Cup-tie against Luton were beamed around the world. Despite having a team that through the years has been even worse than ours, Millwall have a hardcore firm who could mix it with the best. Chelsea and West Ham lads will reluctantly testify that theirs are the fixtures that Millwall's Bushwhackers most looked forward to and relish. In one famous late Eighties battle, a 700-a-side kick off between Millwall and West Ham saw police openly admit they could not control the situation. Like West Ham, Millwall have a mob drawn mostly from a tight-knit community, coming from in and around Deptford in south east London. The only thing that lets them down is they have had far too many years in the lower divisions. Brentford, Orient and Charlton aren't the London opposition they want.

Two years after the Luton riot, we headed down in a coach to watch United play Millwall. It wasn't a 'thug bus' but 30 of us jumped on one of a few coaches that a local entrepreneur ran to all games. Most of our lads were aged 22-23 and were close mates. Quite a few hadn't been to Millwall before so I took great delight in telling tales of my visits. I exaggerated events and enjoyed looking at one or two uneasy faces. One lad produced a distress flare, saying he would 'shoot the first fucker' he saw, and to my surprise around eight of our lot were carrying. Weapons in Sheffield United's firm were very rare but such was Millwall's reputation that our lot had taken their respect a little too far.

The journey down was highlighted by the arrest of Gregory for the sinister crime of nicking a packet of chocolate Munchies at a service station. He was let off as the evidence had been eaten, but did he get some ribbing that day. I could just see the headlines, 'Football thug in mystery chocolate theft.' At Millwall, police made us get off the coach and walked us along with two other coaches to the ground. It was a good pose as 150 of us passed some of their lads. In the ground it was the usual verbals through the fence as United's and Millwall's boys traded insults. I was not involved in the slanging match but stood near to the fence, where a black geezer was shouting and taking the piss out of my checked jacket.

'Aquascutum mate. Heard of it?' I enquired.

The flat-nosed black guy carried on, so I let him have it. 'Oy, pancake nose, shut up, you've already had one too many seconds.'

Even a few Millwall lads laughed as he threw a seven and went demented, saying he would cut me up outside. After the match we tried to get to the other side of the ground but police forced us back. We jumped in the coach and, after 15 minutes of travelling, everyone started to relax, so I warned them about the ambush a few years earlier.

'Fuck off, we're miles from the ground,' said Shots.

Our coach was being followed by two supporters' coaches with no police escort. In the distance I could make out a few boys up to no good.

'Get ready, it's going to go,' I yelled.

Our lot jumped from their seats as Millwall poured around the corner. A mob of around 120 lads belted the buses with bricks and other debris. Like a fool, our driver panicked in the slow-moving traffic and bolted the coach down a side road. Millwall pursued us. A few of our lot were loading distress flares and leather coshes came out of leather coats. The street looked like a dead end and Millwall had us. I opened the fire exit at the back of the coach. We kept Millwall at bay with ashtrays, bottles, cans and anything to hand. They swarmed around the coach. I saw pancake nose trying to smash a window with a plank. A distress flare kept them at bay as three of our lot aimed at Millwall through the open door. Our driver swung the coach around the tightest of corners and we headed away at speed. The mixture of relief and disappointment was immense. It would have been on top big time if we had been stuck at the bottom of that road with 120 Bushwhackers wanting to do the moonstomp on us, although getting off the coach was out of the question.

Only nine months earlier, 50 of the Londoners had stopped off in Sheffield after a game at Leeds. After a city centre battle, one Millwall lad was taken to hospital and died five days later. Local press had it down as a Sheffield United-Millwall conflict, when in fact no United hooligans were involved. The lad's head injuries were caused by a misplaced drop kick aimed by himself at one of the Sheffield 'townies' they fought with. This, however, added tension to any SUFC v Millwall fixture, as did an intrusion just three months later by 12 Millwall boys whose van had stopped off after a game in the Midlands. Trouble flared in an outlying district of Sheffield after a Millwall lad tried to mug a local youth. A major fight saw 17 arrested, of which 11 were jailed for three months on a charge of threatening behaviour. Another Londoner was jailed for two years for attempted robbery. The local papers again whipped it up as a United v Millwall vendetta, so our journeys to London were filled with rumours of revenge and ambushes, all whipped up by a media who did not care about the truth.

# NEWCASTLE

Is it just me, or do Geordies seem to be everywhere? No matter where you go, there are hundreds of them. When 20 of us went to Blackpool for Raggy's stag night, we bumped into 50 of the brown ale boys. The day went well enough and we swapped stories over a few bevvies. They were proper boys, not the shirt and scarfer types.

At around 10.15 pm, we found a little boozer on a side street just off the promenade. We were all wrecked, due to the 'Leo Sayer' we had drunk ourselves through. The lads stood on chairs singing United songs. Jason and I were at the pub doors pretending to be bouncers.

'No white socks mate.'

'Sorry mate, not tonight, no centre partings.'

'How old are you mate?'

'Twenty-seven.'

'Sorry, over twenty-eights today.'

We had a laugh as people walked away with bemused expressions.

Then a large group of men came running round the corner and with a shout ran at the pub. They slowed when they recognised us from earlier. It was our North East pals. Too late. I planted one on a tall Geordie, and he stumbled back. Our lot ran to the door and the Geordies piled into us. A top ruck kicked in. We managed to get into the street and, for the next five minutes engaged in hand-to-hand combat in the alleyway. Lads were getting dropped, jumping back up and steaming in again. A huge metal industrial bin lid was thrown back and forth.

Loads were injured, including myself. One of ours needed 22 stitches in his chin. Police came but the brawl just carried on. We were still rucking on the seafront 60 yards from the pub. A bizzy grabbed me and I was going to the nick until a Geordie ran up and planted his size nines in my bollocks. The officer let go of me and Raggy chinned the Newcastle lad. We chased them up the seafront and Kev picked up a huge stick of rock from a stall and smashed it over one's head. He then stabbed him in the head with the jagged edge that was still left in his hand. Our van was like Emergency Ward Ten on the way home, with black eyes, stitches and enough bruises to fill a three-week old fruit bowl

We had a few other ding-dongs with them over the years, especially at an FA Cup semi-final at Old Trafford in 1998. I didn't get involved but fighting occurred before during and after the game. Several arrests were made and one Sheffield lad received a jail sentence of two years. What was extraordinary that day was the policing. The Manchester riot police adopted a new tactic. Instead of arresting culprits they systematically beat the shit out of people, guilty and innocent. Several of our lads also had their Stone Island badges ripped from their jackets. One off-duty police inspector from Newcastle was hurt as the riot squad steamed into a pub full of Blades. They were accountable to no one, with no visible numbers and their faces covered with crash helmets.

# NORTHAMPTON NOVEMBER 1981

Our boys travelled by coach to the evening game. I went in a car due to work commitments. The plan was to go on their kop. So after drinking in the pub that was in the corner of the ground, around 15 young trendies, myself included, made our way onto their end. We stood at the front behind the goal. Although we had been sussed before the kick-off, we weren't too bothered because the coachload would be in soon, or so we thought. However, the criminal masterminds had been thieving at a motorway service station and had all been locked up. We were on our own and when Mike Trusson equalised for us with only two minutes remaining, it came on top.

Backs to the fence, we lashed out and did our bit. The police ragged us out of the gate and we had just started our walk to the away end when Trusson scored again. We went mad. The full time whistle went as we got to the halfway line. One-nil down with two minutes left and we had come out winners. We lost our minds and ran from our escort onto the pitch to congratulate the team. I got a bollocking next day from my boss who had travelled to the game and had seen me acting up.

# NORWICH

When the fixtures for the 1991-92 season were published, we saw we had Norwich away in August, which meant one thing: Great Yarmouth for the weekend. Forty of our boys travelled to the coast on the Friday before the game. We arrived in good time and by six o'clock were all shaved and shampooed. There were plenty of other 'normal' Blades around and the night was pretty peaceful apart from a vociferous singsong in a seafront bar. Around 30 of us headed off to a club. We had a great night and when Jeff Beck's 1970 classic *Hi Ho Silver Lining* came on the music system I thought the roof would lift off:

> 'And it's hi, ho Sheff United,
> Everywhere we go there's aggro.'

The locals became restless and as we made our way out of the club, it went off. It was a bit chaotic at first. Bouncers, locals, clubbers and our lot all mingled together and little fights and scuffles broke out. When we got together outside, the lot went. The bouncers and local hoodlums were attacked in the doorway. Howie stuck a dart straight in one's arm and he fled screaming. Luey ran in with two milk crates swinging wildly. It was too much for them as 30 soccer thugs went to work. As the Old Bill arrived, we just crossed the road and headed away. None of our lot was apprehended.

The next day saw the usual glorious sunshine that always seems to be around on the opening day of the English season. Norwich are a weird mob. You never see them until you get to the ground. Then they seem to spring up out of rivers. When it goes off, they disappear as quickly as they surface. The match itself was very entertaining and two late Norwich goals gave them a 2-2 draw. We had seen a few boys before the game but they didn't want to know, so we didn't expect much afterwards. Fifty of us walked into the town centre and settled in a pub in the market square.

We had been drinking for around an hour when 50 Norwich screamed around the corner. They didn't last long and were straight on their toes. Housey captured one and relieved him of the sweatshirt tied around his waist. Another Norwich lad was beaten and had his top ripped off. One was from Marks and Sparks, the other from Burtons. There are some very nice clothes shops in Norwich but they're obviously not used by the Canaries crew.

The following year, we visited Carrow Road again. As 60 BBC drank in a pub nearby, me, Kav and Dom went to look around a few clothes shops. We were just heading down a precinct when we saw a commotion. I ran down and saw 25 Norwich attacking three non-hooligan Blades in a shop doorway. I knew one of them and the three of us steamed in. Norwich split to allow the Blades to run free. Then it was our turn. They came at us with a huge bloke at the front. I ran into him and he copped me one. The lads we had saved just left us to it – cheers, boys. Then Kav saved the day with a bullet of a punch that seemed to cave the big man's face in. He was out cold before he even hit the deck. Two of their lads had motorbike helmets and were trying to club us with them. Kav picked up a huge paving slab and held it above his head as he walked towards them. The familiar sound of sirens broke up the hostilities. I had to laugh at Kav and his Hercules impression, even though it hurt my split lip.

# OLDHAM

For some reason, Oldham was a place that didn't agree with me or the United team. Every time the Blades play there, something bad happens: either United get two players sent off or I end up in trouble. I have seen the Blades at Boundary Park eight times, but two games stick out from the rest. The first was in November 1985. I played for United's supporters' club in those days; we would regularly have a match against the supporters of the team United were playing that day. I really enjoyed it. It has always been my dream to play for the Blades but this was as near as I got. The lads in our side weren't exactly angels and these pre-match games, intended to facilitate fan friendship, ended after our lot chased the Bradford team all the way back to the changing rooms after a bad foul.

On this particular day we had beaten Oldham Supporters 1-0, then had a few drinks at a social club. Me and Richie, who was also a young United hooligan, were going out in Sheffield city centre when we got back. I had got a pricey Hugo Boss blazer and a United tie on. As we got to the ground, we bumped into a couple of BBC lads. They told us that 20 of our lot had been bang at it in Oldham town centre. As we chatted outside their main stand, it kicked off further down the road. We ran towards the trouble and I could see around eight of our lads at it. Raggy got dropped with a snidey one that relieved him of a tooth. I chinned the geezer that had done the dirty. As we fought, police arrived and I was apprehended. Richie protested my innocence and, being as baby-faced as baby-faced gets, I told the officers that Richie was my younger brother and he had been attacked. I also pulled out a cracker:

'Please don't nick me. I play for the club and I'll be in big trouble.'

The bizzies let me go with a stern warning. 'You should know better. Go on, get in the ground.'

My blazer had come in useful. I wasn't exactly lying when I said I played for the club; supporters' club, not football club though.

Another time, eight of us travelled in a work van from our local. Kav drove. I sat in the front with Scratch as it was filthy in the van and my clothes are important to me. The game itself was the usual Oldham affair, losing 2-0 and down to nine men and that was before half-time. A spirited second half saw us pull a goal back, but at the final whistle it was still a defeat.

Outside the ground it kicked off on the road leading to town, but we merely looked on as a few of our boys chased Oldham down the main drag. Everyone had arranged to meet on London Road once back in Sheffield. We usually went to town, but one of Wednesday's main actors was having his stag night, so knowing they would be mob-handed, an intrusion onto our sacred ground was expected. We knew Wednesday would be in the Nursery Tavern at the bottom of Ecclesall Road less than a mile from London Road.

Once our van got back to Sheffield, we were at the right side of town to head down Ecclesall Road to assess the Wednesday mob. I then had the bright idea of hanging out of the front passenger window holding onto an eight-foot scaffold pole while Scratch held onto my legs.

'I'll shit them up. Drive past slowly,' I told Kav.

As we approached the Nursery, Kav slowed. Wednesday had a good mob outside. Then as we got level, Kav just stopped. I was hanging out of the van, scaffold pole in hand, with 50 Wednesday looking on in bewilderment.

'Want some of this?' I enquired. Then I realised a bizzy van was parked at the side of the pub with the bizzies looking at me. I slowly pulled the pole back into the van. To my relief, Bender, a well known ex-Wednesday hooligan but now a businessman, walked over.

'Steve, hell man, have you lost it or what?'

I shrugged. 'Are these coming down London Road later, coz we're ready for them Bender?'

I talked to Bender but my eyes trained on Wednesday's uneasy firm.

'Yeah, I think so, but I'm not. It's all bollocks. There's a good mob out though, touching ninety.'

'They'll need them,' I said as we drove off.

I thought the bizzies would pull us, but they didn't. Nice one Bender. When we eventually got to London Road, around 40 of our lot stood drinking outside the Pheasant. I told them what had happened and that Wednesday had a good crew out. Our boys were pretty laid back about it. They had seen it all before.

Around 8.30 pm they came as expected, a good mob with some big lads I had never seen before. The next was deja vu. As our boys ran towards them, a few started to disappear causing the 'double six' (domino effect). They weren't up for it and all bar two ran. Those two were pounded before police moved in. I stood smiling at a Wednesday lad I knew well.

'Same result again, just not good enough,' I shouted to him. He shrugged his shoulders and mooched off.

# PORTSMOUTH

In the 1980s and 1990s, Portsmouth's 6.57 Crew were one of the top five firms in the country. They derived their name from the time of the morning train they would catch to away matches, travelled to big games in numbers and always seemed up for it.

My first experience with them was the opening game of the 1982/
83 season. Fifty of our boys travelled in six cars and a van. It went
off before the game at the back of their stand. The toe-to-toe
ruck was even and police moved in quickly. There was more
fighting after the match near the coaches. Then we got our firm
in a convoy and took Pompey by surprise. A mob came near our
van, the doors flew open and we were out. The cars also emptied;
a few of our lot had wooden rounders bats. A lot of Pompey lads
got a beating until police came and made us wait for two people
to come and identify us. After half an hour they let us go.

I don't know whether the police set it up to split our van
away from the cars, but it came on top as we drove, through a
shopping area in crawling traffic. Ten Pompey came and we
jumped out at them. Then we realised the car behind us also
contained some of their lads and they were on CB radios (no
mobiles then). Within a minute our van was surrounded. Smithy
tried to get out but we pulled him back. He had a bat but everyone
else was unarmed. They smashed a few windows before Eyes drove
up the wrong side of the road to get away.

In 1984, Pompey were due to visit Bramall Lane and pulled
a flanker on us. Around 60 of us had settled for a midday drink in
the Penny Black when a scout came in and informed us that
Pompey were in the Rutland, about a mile away. Ant, the scout,
said they had a massive mob, but we took his estimate of 300 with
a pinch of salt. Ant couldn't rest in a pub and was always on the
scout for the opposition. He'd had us on some proper wild goose
chases over the years but we still listened to him.

We drank up and moved off. We figured that even if Pompey
had only 150 we would still struggle with our numbers, so decided
to head up town and come down at the pub, instead of along the
long flat road where they had plenty of time to see us. Still, they
spotted us straight away. We ran at them throwing bricks but wave
after wave of boys poured out of the pub. Ant was right; there
were loads of them.

Rowls and I steamed in. The air filled with glasses and bottles,
which crashed around us at an alarming rate. I knew that if I
didn't start backing away I would be history. My hiking boots made
escape even more precarious. As I turned and ran for my life, a
bottle crashed into the middle of my back. Rowls stood to make

sure I got away and threw a brick, which smashed into a Pompey face. Was I glad to get away unscathed.

I turned when the danger had passed and looked at Pompey's crew walking back through the broken glass to the pub. What a mob they had. I'll take my hat off to them, 250 miles and for every mile travelled they must have had a boy.

Before our home game against Portsmouth in 1986, it kicked off at the back of the South Stand. Around 50 Pompey had decided to take a walk around the ground. A similar number of our boys met them head on. We were coming down the grass banking and the 6.57 saw us and fronted up. They ran at us, then stopped. A few of ours laid in to them. Holder ended up on his arse as he ran in and slipped. I didn't get involved really, as too many police were present and I had a bad charge hanging over me, the result of a town centre brawl. Insults and sly punches were thrown as the bizzies took the 6.57 Crew to the away end.

After the match, a minibus pulled into Sheffield bus station, full of Pompey's boys. These were all good lads and a 15-a-side brawl ensued. This was the bollocks; bang at it for four minutes, toe-to-toe, fist-to-fist, no weapons. Lads were going down like skittles, pulling themselves back up and pitching in again, until the police intervened. Ten minutes later the van drove past the Penny Black pub as we stood outside.

'Top ruck lads. Cheers. See you at ours,' one shouted.

Our lot smiled at each other. We had nothing but praise for the Pompey lads' front.

# PRESTON NORTH END

Three young Blades and myself travelled to Preston for the evening game on 31 January 1984. Near the ground we bumped into Eyes and five older Blades. As we stood talking, around 20 boys bounced out of the darkness and came at us. The older lads started to twitch, but Eyes was a well-respected boy. The older lads knew that despite the numbers they had to have a go, and we were up for it. Before anyone could speak we went at them. Preston were shocked at our sudden attack and were soon off like gazelles. I remember Scaifer, an old Barmy Army boy, later asking other United boys who I was. He was well impressed and told everyone. 'He's fuckin' crackers, that lad.' I took it as a compliment.

We had actually played there nine months previously, again an evening game, in what was one of the most ludicrous trips I ever made. Me, Waz and Doyley had taken the day off work to go. We missed the train and later on missed the coaches, so we were stuck for transport. Waz suggested we went to the Kelvin flats in Sheffield and ask his Scottish neighbour if we could borrow his car. In desperation we caught a taxi to the flats. When we knocked on his door, the jock was pissed as a newt. We asked him if we could borrow the car 'to nip to Rotherham' and offered him a fiver for his troubles.

'We'll put some petrol in as well,' Waz offered.

Jocko nodded and passed me a small screwdriver. This was the key to get in the car and also to start it. The dark blue Ford Cortina was a heap of junk but off we set to see our beloved Blades. The car drank petrol like Oliver Reed (God rest his liver) drank pints. We eventually stuttered to Deepdale with 25 minutes of the game left.

The turnstiles were shut so we decided to climb a wall onto Preston's end. I ripped my Sergio coat on some barbed wire (I never had any luck with coats). To add insult to injury, as we weaved our way through the crowd to a decent vantage point, I asked a Prestoner. 'What's the score, mate?'

As I spoke, Stewart Houston volleyed the ball into his own net. Everyone was jumping about around us.

'One nil to Preston,' he gleefully replied.

It was the only goal of the game. We had a bit of a ruck outside and I got a fat lip. Then on the way home our mobile scrapyard broke down. Waz and me nearly kicked off with each other as tempers frayed. This was turning into a nightmare.

After an hour an AA van pulled into a petrol station. We rushed over. The AA geezer had a look.

'Alternator's fucked, amongst other things.'

We had hardly any money left after spending around £30 each on feeding the car's drink problem. He repaired the engine but only after I left my gold sovereign ring and Waz left his gold belcher chain on the understanding that we would return on the forthcoming Saturday with the £85 we owed. I eventually got home at 5.30 am and had to be up for work two hours later. On top of that we had to return to Lancashire on Saturday to get our gold back. A stop off in Manchester shopping on the way home cost me £140 on some designer clothing. All part and parcel of following the Blades.

# PORT VALE

Sixty Blades went on Port Vale's kop when we visited them in the Fourth Division in 1981. Running skirmishes erupted along the terracing. The game was filmed by Yorkshire TV and the next day the highlights showed Paul Richardson (probably the worst player to grace the red and white of SUFC) with hands on his hips about to take a corner. Behind him all our lot were bang at it with the Vale boys. What was funny looking back was plenty of our lot had duffle coats on. It looked like a load of thug Paddington Bears.

In 1988 we visited Vale Park and Vale turned out a big crew. We had a right set-to in the car park prior to the game, then a fine ruck outside the seats after the game. I got booted in the mush as I ran up steps and tried to steam into them. There's only one winner with that sketch. One notable thing about Vale's mob was that they had no dressers at all. They looked like German thugs, i.e. scruffy.

# QPR

I don't think Queens Park Rangers have a firm worth talking about, though they do have strong links with the headbangers from Stamford Bridge. That's why I call them Little Chelsea. The first time I noticed the connection was in March 1991. We had beaten Chelsea 1-0 at home and I got involved in a quick ruck with our London counterparts. Police had split our mob as we hung around after the game, so we headed towards Sheffield station in dribs and drabs. I walked along with Jack, who was and still is a 'boss' boy. On the other side of the dual carriageway walked eight more United boys. I saw Jason point up the road and they set off jogging. Around 15 Chelsea had walked out of a side street and it was game on.

As the two groups squared up, Jack and I ran up towards a roundabout, as we couldn't get across to help. I noticed our boys were beginning to twitch as combat commenced. Chelsea then ran the eight Blades. We got to the roundabout and I ran across and hurdled the steel barriers with Jack not far behind. Chelsea turned on us.

'Come on boys, we're going nowhere,' I challenged.

They came at us and a black guy squirted ammonia from a Jif lemon bottle all over my Stoney top. We still stood firm. It was about to come on top when police screeched up.

A month later we travelled down to Loftus Road for a game that was crucial for our top-flight survival. A 2-1 victory saw the Sheffield hordes leave the ground in good spirits. As we headed down a street to the main road that led to the tube station, QPR came at us from nowhere. I then saw a few of the faces I had seen only a month earlier, notably the black guy who had ruined my Stone Island jumper. We were straggled out and it came on top at first. I picked up a large traffic cone and stood firm. Slim was at my side along with around ten others. We held out until the rest of our boys caught up and steamed in. Police charged in on horseback as we had them on the move. I spotted one Londoner shoot up a house alleyway so I followed. The gate was locked at the end and I punched him to the ground.

Seven years later, we played them on 21 December 1998 at Loftus Road. My pop star mate Paul Heaton, generous soul that he is, laid on a coach for the boys. On the way down to London, cans of Stella and bottles of vodka were passed up and down the coach. We stopped at some traffic lights in London; six alcoholic down and outs were sitting on the pavement outside a bank. I stuck my head out of the driver's window and beckoned one over with half a bottle of vodka. He tottered over and grabbed the bottle then blessed himself as if it was heaven-sent. We were all pissing ourselves as he danced around a Burberry-attired lady who had just been to the cash dispenser.

Once in Shepherds Bush, we headed for the Fringe and Firkin. Before long, 150 Blades had gathered. Although football violence was no longer number one on the list of my priorities, I also knew that if it came my way I wouldn't turn my back on it. Nothing happened before the game: the local dibble were on our case and Sheffield's FIU watched on. At 2.40 pm we walked *en masse* to the ground with an over-the-top police escort. Paul Heaton had zipped up his coat, concealing most of his face. He was also totally shit-faced. Me, Raggy and Kav were in hysterics at what followed. We had hung back behind the escort (I never was one of the 'surrounded by bizzies' types) where Sheffield's football intelligence officers were following United's crew from behind. The three of us in turn were just behind our plod.

'Pop star' turns around, looks back and walks unsteadily over to the Sheffield police.

'Right fuckin' firm us mate,' says pop star.

'Yeah?'

'We'd batter any cunt with this lot.'

'Where have you been? I haven't seen you at a game for ages,' says the copper.

Pop star has still not tumbled that it's the Sheffield plod he's talking to, nor the fact that the bizzie knows him.

'Sheffield United me, mate.'

'Yeah, I know.'

Pop star, looking baffled and befuddled by drink, shrugs his shoulders and stumbles off. Me and Raggy giggled like two schoolgirls who had just seen their first picture of a naked man. Shippo (as we call our copper) smiled at his mate before turning to Rag and me.

'You got enough out for Chelsea?' he teased.

'I think so, don't you?'

At the ground, United had taken a lot more than QPR had expected. This led to huge queues. Luckily Nipper had acquired three complimentary tickets from a Rangers player. So me, Kav and Nipper took up our seats in the South Africa Stand. I noticed a few Rangers lads sitting behind us: I had seen them mouthing off with a few of our lot outside. I glanced back. They had clocked us and were giving it the usual 'you're dead' bollocks. Kav and I had both been there before so it didn't really bother us, but Nipper, who had got us the tickets, wasn't too happy. Nipper is a good mate but trouble is not his *forte*: he jokes that he would sooner have a leg off than get in a fight. He had two pet sayings when trouble was brewing: 'You, outside. I'll make a right mess of your knuckles,' and 'You, outside, if I'm not out in five minutes start without me.'

One Rangers lad, a Stone Island-wearing dwarf, was mouthing off until around 60 of our boys piled into the stand. He suddenly went quiet, until the coppers came in.

'These are Sheffield, get 'em out, it's another Portsmouth this.' He was all mouth but it worked. We were led out to the away end.

Another 2-1 win saw us in good spirits. Afterwards, around 200 of us headed back for the Firkin. En route, we got split up. Kav and I bumped into the QPR dwarf and his cronies. There was only a handful of our lot around and the verbals went off.

'You're shit. Chelsea would do you,' one said after doing a hop, skip and jump when I went towards him.

'It's a cert you mugs couldn't do it. Rotherham would have got you on your toes,' came my reply.

'Get down to Victoria later, we're meeting Chelsea.'

'It's Chelsea we've come for, not you mugs, we're staying around here until last orders so you come to us.'

I saw the sawn-off hooligan again and went into the middle of their lot and patted him on the head for a good 20 seconds.

'A bit small for a hooligan aren't you?' I quizzed.

One hundred yards further up the road, it went off. Kav and I ran towards the trouble. Once again we ended up in the middle of the QPR firm. I copped for a snidey one from a black lad, which split my lip. I grabbed the offender's leather jacket by the collar and scraped my nails down his face, girlie-style. It was all I could do as the police were swarming everywhere. The police arrested quite a few QPR, including the dwarf, and a couple of our lot.

We went to The Globe in Baker Street then back to Shepherds Bush until closing time. A couple of Chelsea boys came in the Firkin late on, had a look and went straight to the phone booth, but their firm never showed. I was thankful really, as the 40 of us left were rolling drunk. The 40-year-old dwarf, by the way, was called Gregory. I later found out that Greg is a bit of a face with the Cockney crews but, Jesus, he made a twat of himself that day.

# SCUNTHORPE

For a Fourth Division game, United visited sunny Scunny in 1981. We had a fair old ruck before the game. What was unreal was that Scunthorpe's top lad was in fact a lass! She was a huge fat girl with a white cricket jumper on which must have needed the wool from

25 sheep to make. She was well into it though and in the brawl she twatted one of ours, who said he couldn't hit her back because she was a woman. During the game, sporadic fights broke out on their kop, which was frustrating for the 50 of us sat in the side stand. We could see Blunder Woman going for it big time. Eventually we had enough of watching and spilled down and across the corner of the pitch into Scunny's kop. In the melee that followed, one Scunthorpe lad broke his arm and leg when he dropped over a 15-foot wall.

I'm no sexist but there's no way I would run around with a mob that had Jo Brand leading it.

# STOKE

Stoke's Naughty Forty have been involved in trouble all over the country. They have a strong England following and this led to a 15-a-side brawl between Blades and Stoke in Leicester Square prior to one international in 1985.

The first trouble I encountered with them was in 1983 at an FA Cup third round match at Bramall Lane before a crowd of 23,329. It kicked off before the game near to the ground, when 80 Stoke lads were attacked in a pub. Glasses, stools and anything else that came to hand were used in the combat. Half an hour after the match, a 0-0 draw, myself and 25 United lads bumped into two vans and two car loads of Stoke boys who were filling up in the petrol station bang outside Bramall Lane. In the vicious brawl, bats, bars and a hammer caused injuries to two of our lads and a Stoke lad was beaten unconscious. It shocked me how the Stoke lads had gone to a football game with an arsenal of weapons that a small army would have been pleased with.

The replay saw another running battle close to Stoke's Victoria Ground. It was a horrible place to visit and the natives were far from friendly. Their new ground, the Britannia Stadium, is also a shithole: built on a hill, miles from anywhere, no parking and made from Lego. Whoever chose the location and design want their bumps feeling.

We played at the Britannia in 1997 and the whole thing was a farce. John and I arrived at the turnstiles at 2.15 pm but didn't get into the ground until 3.30, as thousands queued to get through one of only two turnstiles open. Some of United's 5,000 strong following had enough of the wait and went into other areas of the stadium. Policing was a joke and when United scored there were scuffles all around the ground. If ever trouble could be blamed on the authorities then this day was it.

After the match it went off in the car parks around the ground and major trouble led to many arrests. The pisspoor organisation led to an apology to United fans from the Stoke board of directors. No wonder their last match of the 1997/8 season against Man City produced so much trouble.

Another personal confrontation with them had come a few years earlier, in March 1996. Around ten of my close mates met up in a pub close to Bramall Lane. I had a couple of 'comps' for the match, so half an hour before the kick-off I walked up to collect the tickets from the back of the South Stand. I had just come out of plaster having spent the previous six months on crutches due to a snapped Achilles tendon from playing football. I picked up the comps and was heading back when I came across 30-40 boys. As I limped past, one was giving me, 'Where's your fuckin' boys, you're shit Sheffield.'

'Go up London Road, dickhead, but saying that, our boys only turn out for good firms.'

This didn't go down well. One took a swing at me. I dodged it and threw one back. The police rushed over and grabbed me.

'For fuck's sake, I'm on me jacks, these fuckers don't know the score,' I pleaded.

The bizzy promptly sent me on my way. When I got to the Sportsman pub, the story of what had happened was just about finished when I glanced out of the pub doors. Around 25 of Stoke's boys were at the doorway.

'Fuck me. That's them.'

I rushed towards Stoke and my mates followed. Stoke backed away from the door, then they had a go. The twelve of us had a right go and did well. I copped a beaut on the nose but as the blood poured, I carried on steaming in. The police arrived and nicked two of my mates. This did my head in. The football intelligence officers that followed both teams had seen Stoke showing off on Bramall Lane, then for some unknown reason they had left them to walk to a pub and cause some more bollocks. No Stoke were arrested and two of my close friends, who hadn't gone for the trouble, were apprehended. I felt it was my fault, though the bizzies should have had their act together. They redeemed themselves later by releasing the Sportsman Two without charge.

# SUNDERLAND

Roker Park used to be a nasty place to visit. There are nasty bastards on the terraces, nasty bastards stewarding and nasty bastards policing. I travelled up to Roker twice and then twice to the brilliant (but stupidly-named) Stadium of Light.

In 1989 we took a few boys and had a mad one in a boozer near the ground. Around 25 of us had just about necked our second pint when the roof caved in. I knew it was going to go, the atmosphere could be cut with a knife as the Mackems took exception to us drinking in their boozer. More boys came and the lot went. Many were injured.

Out in the streets, we got ourselves together. Sunderland's mob must have touched 80 but we launched into them. They were startled and we got the better of the off. The police had us surrounded in no time, so we looked forward to resuming hostilities after the game. We got a few more boys together during the game then went out with a couple of minutes to go. After hanging around for a bit, Sunderland came with a huge mob. Forty of us did well. They must have been impressed by our bottle. I loved it when the chips were down.

Two years later, we took 60 boys up to Roker. Glyn Hodges, our Welsh international, headbutted Sunderland's Gordon Armstrong as he left the field, having just been substituted. The Sunderland Echo blamed the major fighting on the streets surrounding the ground on Hodges but in truth it was going to go off anyhow. Nine people were arrested and locals described the atmosphere as ugly and intimidating. Speaking of Hodgy, I liked him. Not only was he a very talented footballer – when he could be bothered – but he would mix it as well. John Harkes copped for one in a Sheffield derby and although the referee and his assistants missed the knockout blow, 20,000 Wednesday fans screamed, 'It's him, it's him,' and persuaded the ref to give Hodgy his marching orders.

When Sunderland visited the Lane in 1998, they brought a firm of around 60 boys. After the match they got away from the police and we had a quick set-to on the cobbled back street adjacent to Bramall Lane. I remember a tall, well-dressed Mackem boy totally unaware of police charging up behind him.

'Cum on, we're Sunerlan,' he shouted.

I sort of nodded towards him, trying to let him know that the bizzies had arrived. I never liked those who tried to get rival boys locked up. We're all in it for the same reason so why add to police statistics? I have seen some fine acts of chivalry amongst hooligans: once at Blackpool I got a rival freed by saying he was my cousin and we were just arguing. Anyhow, one of South Yorkshire's finest clubbed the Mackem and he was on his way to the cells.

A perturbing story, which involved people from Sunderland more than their lads, happened when we visited the Stadium of Light in January 1998. It involved ex-footballer Billy Whitehurst, a legend who played for both clubs in his career. Never mind your Roy Keanes or David Battys, Billy would have them for breakfast. Alan Hansen calls him the hardest man he ever played against. He and a group of United players were once abused by 40 Wednesday hooligans in a Sheffield bar. A bottle was thrown, hitting David Barnes, United's left-back. Billy stood up and asked who was top boy. A Wednesday lad I know made the mistake of his life and went outside with him. One punch later, Billy was back having a drink and the Wednesday lad was on his way to casualty, unconscious with a broken jaw.

Billy and his Sunderland mate Eric ran the Cricketers pub bang outside the Lane. A lot of our boys would drink in there and Billy was a very popular landlord. Billy and Eric had arranged to go up to Sunderland on the Friday before United's game. Around ten locals from the pub, all avid Blades fans and no strangers to the odd bit of trouble, travelled with them. In Sunderland they sorted their digs out and Eric took them to a pub which one of the lads described to me as follows:

'I've been in some rough shitholes before, but that place took the biscuit.'

The evening had passed without incident. Although the locals were as rough as monkeys, our lot got on with them and a few lines of charlie were snorted in the closets. Billy and the other lads went into town to a club, leaving Mick and Kev behind. The idea was for them to come to the club later with some of their newfound friends. A few taxis were ordered and they went to one of the Sunderland lad's houses so he could change. The duo were invited in and, after taking their shoes off, sat on the sofa. A Mackem lad passed them both a tinny.

It was at that point that things turned strange. As soon as the ring pull on Kev's can was opened, they were both jumped. In a frightening scenario, both were stabbed twice. They managed to scramble out of the house, minus shoes, ran a couple of streets away and with blood pouring from them, rang an ambulance. Kev had been stabbed in the arm and back, Mick just below the eye and in the lower back. At the match, I bumped into them at the back of the stand. We all wanted to go back to the house to turn the cowardly tossers over but Kev and Mick had been so charlie'd up that they couldn't remember where it was.

At the same game, police and stewards nearly started a riot. The stewards had been throwing United followers out by the dozen for nothing; I think a couple went out for having dodgy haircuts. Ten police also waded into a row of seats not far from where we were sat and dragged a young lad over the seats. He was 15 if a day. A grey-haired gent stood up and remonstrated with one officer, who promptly put him in a headlock and started to drag him out. It was unbelievable. To make matters worse, the old man's son tried to calm the copper. He had one arm holding up his three-year-old daughter and one trying to pull the officer's arm from his dad's neck. More police rushed in and tugged at him, nearly causing him to drop his daughter.

Everyone went crackers and Blades started fighting both the police and the stewards. Brawls broke out all over the away end. Some of the bizzies started to panic. I have never felt more like steaming a copper than that day. Generally the police are fair with hooligans: if you take a liberty, they take one, no problem, but that day they were legalised thugs and the stewards were the same, hiding behind their luminous jackets. I'll never forget big bad Billy Whitehurst's face as he jabbed a copper in the chest with his finger, demanding to see the officer in charge. When the head dibble appeared, Billy told him baldly, 'I used to play for both these clubs and you coppers are a fucking disgrace.'

The local radio station was bombarded with complaints from fans and United received hundreds of letters regarding that day's events. But as usual naff all gets done; after all it's only football fans.

# SWINDON

As far as I'm concerned the best thing to come out of Swindon is Mel Messenger's tits and only half of them are real. For the game at Swindon on 4 December 1993 we hired a minibus and went down with 17 boys. Scuffles drove. He is a great character, is Scuffs. Last year was his 50th and he is still doing a bit with the boys. I think he's kidding about his age as he only looks about 38. His mother must have pampered his bollocks off.

We had a few beers in a pub outside the ground. Quite a few Blades were in and the home fans weren't pleased we had occupied their boozer. One mouthpiece was chinned, just to let them know the score. They may be able to take liberties with shirters but we were seasoned soccer thugs. We headed off to the match without any more trouble. The plan was to go back to the pub after the match and have a couple of beers, then stop off for the night on the way home.

The drab 0-0 draw was predictable. Me and Scratch left early and went back to the pub. It was pretty obvious that the locals had formed a reception committee. We made our way to the bar, although Scratch wasn't too impressed by the situation. Raggy then came in and, having a shrewd head on his shoulders, knew trouble was a brewing. He had just gone to the bar when Swindon's finest rushed the main doors. Our lot were outside trying to get in. I barged over, knocking people flying in the crush. A couple of Swindon had bolted the doors.

'Let 'em in, we'll kill 'em,' I shouted, pretending to be a Swindon fan. I unbolted the door, opened it then turned and chinned a big dozy skinhead. I got covered in beer but no one touched me. Raggy came rushing through the crowds, yanking people behind him. Our lot outside tried to get at Swindon, but the police and Sheffield's football intelligence lads kept them at bay. One Sheffield officer's face was a picture as me and Raggy came out of the main doors at our lot. We all cracked up as Swindon's police ran over to us thinking we were going to steam in, then stopped as we shook hands with some of our lads. We were escorted back to our minibus.

On the way home, we stopped at Lichfield. Everything went fine, though we had a few groups of lads giving us the 'they're not from round here' look. At the end of the night we were all trolleyed. Then it happened, something I hate. Tiler ran over to a lad eating chips and banged him one for nothing. He was out cold. That set the tone and while I walked back to the van, a few of our lot went on an 'anybody will do' mission. I was disgusted. I loved a ruck but you have to have willing participants.

Scuffles was waiting in the driver's seat and I explained that too much beer had turned our lot into dickheads. Ten minutes later, as we drove away, blue flashing lights lit up the darkness. Twenty police surrounded the van and the lead officer explained that two people were coming to identify their assailants. I was in the front with Scratch. He was fumbling in his pockets. Then he jumped out onto the pavement next to a few bobbies and started turning out his pockets.

'I've lost me ganja, Stevie. Have you got my gear? I've lost it.'

He was too drunk to know what he was saying. I ignored him. Meanwhile Scuffles, our driver, was shovelling Polo mints in his mouth. He had consumed enough beer and powder to see off Shaun Ryder. Luckily, he wasn't breathalysed; I don't know what good the Polos would have done.

The police brought two lads up. One had his nose where his eye should be. They picked out Linny and Anston. Neither had been responsible, apparently, but both ended up in court and just escaped jail terms. That was perhaps the only night I wasn't proud to be a Sheffield United boy.

# TRANMERE ROVERS

With 13 games of the 1982 season to go, United had virtually secured promotion when we visited Tranmere Rovers in March 1982. Kevin Sampson's novel *Awaydays* is based on their crew, which he dubs The Pack. I named them the Stanley Family after our visit. Fighting broke out throughout the match in their main stand. We were bang at it yet the police seemed reluctant to make any arrests, so it went off again and again. The tense game ended 2-2 only after United's keeper, Keith Waugh, saved a last-minute penalty. We were chuffed and around 100 of us poured onto the pitch at the final whistle. Tranmere steamed on and it went off, with the United players getting involved as they left the pitch. Police escorted us to the away end. In the streets it was going off with pockets of Blades scuffling with small groups of Tranmere. We bumped into 15 scallies. The seven of us didn't last long as the little corduroy posse produced sharp Sheffield steel from their Patrick cagoules. See you later. Titch was nearly slashed as he was chased down someone's garden. We all escaped unscathed but two Blades were cut up that day.

# WALSALL

October 9, 1982. Another game where the police went completely OTT. We had settled in a boozer in the centre of Walsall and were quietly playing cards and pool. Then officer Dibble and his hired thugs in uniform arrived. Two police dogs were let loose in the pub and police formed a tunnel at the entrance doors. One dog was hit over the head with a pint pot as it savaged Sharkey's arm. As more police piled through the back door and hit out at random, we made a beeline for the exit doors. Police systematically coshed everyone as we ran through their tunnel of love. I got two minging weals across my back and a few lads had gaping head wounds.

Further up at the ground a fight broke out between rival fans. I threw a long plank at the Walsall boys and was spotted by police. I was wearing a reversible golf jacket which was navy blue on one side and sky blue on the other. I quickly switched my coat round behind a hedge. Unluckily for Gaz, he had got the same jacket on and was nicked. He was later relieved of £180 by the courts, which I helped him pay. It was the least I could do.

# WEST BROM

West Brom's firm are strictly a home-only mob. They're a bit like Richard Branson's hot air balloons; they don't travel well. I have only seen them in Sheffield once and that was only a stop-off visit on their way home from a game. We attacked them outside the Old Queens Head near Sheffield station. It was a brief affair: as quick as Ted Rodgers could say '3-2-1', they had gone, leaving one poor stooge behind to take a bit of a battering.

In 1998 an early season game at the Hawthornes convinced me that I had been involved in football violence at the right time.

In the Eighties and Nineties it was great fun roaming another town centre not knowing what was round the next corner. That was the whole point: it was a journey into the unknown. Would their crew have 50 boys out or 300? The game at the Hawthornes demonstrated how much the violence that surrounds game has moved on.

United's top boys had been on to West Brom's boys with the idea of arranging a meet away from the ground and the town centre. A village was suggested by West Brom but the idea of getting 50 lads to an area no one knew proved to much of a stumbling block, so the 'off' was off. In the ground, West Brom's lads gathered in the seats near the away end. Our lot sat in the bottom corner of the away end. The two groups were 25 yards apart. The football intelligence officers looked on as both sides rang each other's mobiles and exchanged insults. As I sat behind our lot, I couldn't help thinking how different it all was. It's a whole different game, one I don't like. All this Internet-arranged violence. I know that better policing has forced violence away from the grounds but if boys can arrange an off on a computer, do they think for one minute that police aren't going to get onto the Net themselves and monitor these conferences? I would be paranoid, going to a pre-arranged battle: caught on camera mate, two years prison, see you later, much later.

As West Brom's and United's hooligans slagged each other off, I had to laugh at one of our lads who was on the phone to a very excitable Pakistani Brom boy.

'Oy, Starni. Tell that lad just in front of you I want a word.'

I gazed over as the Brom boy handed his mobile phone to a fat, Henry Lloyd-clad character.

'Put that pie down you fat bastard, Henry Lloyd don't make jackets bigger than that XXL you've got on.'

Fat man jumped up, pie still in hand, giving the two-fingered salute toward us.

The police down there are either backward or not very quick on the uptake. As the crowds left the ground we made our way to the main road. West Brom casually waited for us, the roar went up and the tightest, most claustrophobic ruck you'll ever see went off. There was hardly room to move in the packed crowds. It looked like the protagonists were dancing with each other rather than fighting. I bet this scenario happens at every West Brom home game as their dopey plod look on.

## WOLVES

January 17, 1998. Wolves brought a mob of around 60 and chased some BBC2 after the match. The BBC2 are United's younger hooligan element. The youngsters had built an impressive little firm together around this time and although they lacked experience, the 40 of them stuck together. They have all but disbanded now. Forest, one of our main actors, stood on his jacks and had his baseball cap nicked. He gave the United youngsters a right bollocking.

April 5, 1999. I was working on the door of a pub close to Bramall Lane for this fixture. I work most big games. It keeps me out of trouble and earns me a few quid. United had turned out a big mob and knew that Wolves had arrived. They had settled in the Howard but were surrounded by police, so an attack was out of the question. At 2.55 pm the Wolves lads looked more like sheep than football fans as they were escorted past around 100 United boys outside the Cricketers pub. Forest saw a tall black guy wearing the hat he had lost the previous year. He went mad.

'I'll give anyone a hundred pounds if they get that hat back.'

After the match, 150 BBC went for it. Wolves were attacked as they left the ground and ran back into the stadium. It was one of those games when everyone seemed to lose it. The police struggled to regain control and several United boys were arrested. The coaches were attacked. Then a mass charge caused panic amongst the Wolves fans. I don't know why the Sheffield police do it but they let both sets of fans out at the same time and they have to walk through each other, a recipe for disaster. Wolves lost their bottle completely and offered no resistance, a good job really with the mood our mob were in that day.

No-one did get Forest's hat back, or claim the £100.

# THE ENGLISH DISEASE — WHY?

## ENGLISH CULTURE

## THE PRESS

## UEFA-FIFA

I had intended to stay away from the England scene while writing this book. But in the light of events surrounding Euro 2000 and the murders of two Leeds fans in Istanbul, I feel the subject of the English abroad needs to be addressed.

# ENGLISH CULTURE

It is very difficult to explain to the outsider what actually makes a hooligan do the things he does. The thrill and excitement of the violent encounters provide lads with a natural high, the adrenaline pumps and the buzz is immense. All our nation sees from the comfort of their own living room is endless TV footage and press reports of English football fans in trouble again. No one sits down and thinks for a minute why our country breeds lads who love to fight. We English are viewed as a nation of fighters. The point is when English lads go abroad they feel that they are actually representing their country. Those lads will fight for what they see as national pride being at stake.

Songs that are often heard at international games include 'No Surrender to the IRA' and 'If it Wasn't for the English, You'd be Krauts'. These have nothing to do with football but have everything to do with national pride. How many times have you seen an English football fan, pint in one hand, the other clenched in a one-fist salute, singing *God save our gracious Queen*? Even the 'normal' English fans belt out the theme tunes of old World War II movies such as *The Great Escape* and *The Dambusters*. Again we subconsciously link our national game to war. We are a war-liking country, of that there is no doubt. Society has failed to find new uses for the aggressive streak in the English male. Our pathetically weak and under-funded education system has suffered from years of neglect and this in my view is one of the main causes of our problems. The lack of discipline in our youngsters is our education system bearing its fruit.

As the youth of today grows older I can only see things getting worse. In less than 20 years, our youngsters have moved on from boredom pastimes of nicking apples and the odd game of knock and run. Now you see 13-year-olds hanging around shopping precincts drinking alcohol and smoking drugs. Vandalism is at epidemic levels as youngsters relieve their boredom. Even Tony Blair has had the problem of his 16-year-old son being found shitfaced in Leicester Square. To the youth of today it's the done thing, English culture shining through. Maybe military service is the only answer for a return to discipline amongst our youth.

Our culture will never change. Banning suspected hooligans from travelling abroad, tougher prison sentences and taking away civil liberties would not address the problem; it lies much, much deeper. Our society needs looking at closely; if we get these initial areas addressed then you may start to see results. Football violence in this country is blown out of all proportion. At the end of the day it involves one group of lads wanting to fight with another group who are of the same mind. It's not rape or murder but plenty of people get themselves into a right lather about it. The problem is nowhere near as bad as it once was. Nowadays football firms pick three or four games a season were they turn up for aggro. Not so long ago these firms turned out week in, week out.

# THE PRESS

Recently I was lucky enough to be asked by Paul Heaton to accompany him to Italy. His knowledge of the Italian game is second to none and so Channel Four had asked him to summarize the Lazio-Inter Milan game from the Olympic Stadium in Rome. During the game, Inter and Lazio fans pelted each other with bottles and other missiles right under the noses of the police. I sat watching the events thinking that if this were an English game, those fans would be arrested left, right and centre, then CCTV would be studied and culprits banned from football matches. Over there no one batted an eyelid. The next day's papers reported nothing of the incident (according to Paul who can read Italian).

Something else I couldn't believe was the volume of racism. Every time Milan's Clarence Seedorf touched the ball, it seemed as if every one of the 80,000 spectators started with the monkey chants. Black players over there are subjected to this every week. The racism in the English game is virtually non-existent now, yet the English press have a field day if any sort of race issue is raised at a ground. Emmanuel Petit was called a French so-and-so while playing for Arsenal and that was newsworthy over here. It is simply media hype, the same way that football violence is reported. One small incident will lead to front-page news. What the newspapers seem to misunderstand is that hooligans love the publicity they gain through the press. If violence has gone off and it has been reported, the hooligans think they have done a good job.

The press follows English fans abroad for one reason: they want to report on English fans in trouble again. I know a lot of English football fans are no angels. Games abroad also attract plenty of what we call dickheads, the sort that smash shop windows, abuse passers-by and get pissed on four pints. They aren't boys (hooligans) and are looked on with disdain in the English fan infrastructure. Yet these same lads are the ones the press always latches onto. The press actually want to see trouble, it makes great news and sells newspapers. That's the reason why you see hundreds of freelance photographers at English games. Sometimes there are more cameras than fans. It's a well-known fact that some photographers offer English lads money to misbehave so that they can get a great photo: a nazi salute, throw a bottle, there's £100 for you mate.

During Euro 2000, England's first game against Portugal passed without incident; in fact the English fans played football with the Portuguese prior to the game, but that wasn't reported. It's not the news they want to print. Football violence sells papers and you could almost sense the disappointment from our media. Then came the Germany game, at which trouble was inevitable. Two hundred English attacked the Germans with a few plastic chairs. The result was total hysteria by our press and a threat of expulsion by UEFA. The pictures of the English involved in trouble were played over and over again. I guess at the end of the day people love to watch the violence, even if they are disgusted by it. I have been abroad to see England play and I know what goes on. During the 1998 World Cup in France I saw 100 riot police attack a couple of hundred English for absolutely nothing. The press was there in numbers but nothing was reported of the incident. Imagine if our police had treated another country's fans this way during Euro 96, there would have been hell on. If proof was ever needed as to how hyped up and sensationalized the subject of the English abroad is, then here it is. Of the 933 arrested or deported at Euro 2000, only 23 had soccer-related convictions. No one utters a word as hundreds of English are arrested *en masse.* Those lads were systematically rounded up and deported for nothing more sinister than being an Englishman in a bar.

At the same finals, 2,000 Dutch went on the rampage after their expulsion at the hands of the Italians. The Turks caused trouble at every game they played, culminating in thousands rioting after their knockout defeat by Portugal. The Turks then smashed up shop windows, assaulted local people and tried to attack a few English fans sat drinking in bars. What happens? Nothing. Brussels mayor Franciou-Xavier de Donnea swept the Turkish riots to one side (nothing to do with the large Turkish community in Brussels) saying that it was a party that turned sour, adding for good measure that the English had instigated these problems. I'm not trying to say that English fans are blameless but most of our lads that go abroad feel victimized and persecuted and as a result some react to this anti-English attitude.

The double standards that exist within the press and media were evident when England fan Mark Forrester was arrested with 34 others in Brussels during Euro 2000. Mark has always protested his innocence but has been charged and has to keep travelling back and forth to Belgium for court appearances. An appeal to the BBC to view footage taken during the trouble – that might exonerate him – was greeted with this statement: 'The BBC can't take sides with the police or general public due to the safety issues for our camera and broadcasting crew.' Yet the same station was only too happy to let police use footage taken from *MacIntyre Undercover* as evidence. This led to two Chelsea lads, Andy Frain and Jason Marriner, getting jail terms of six and seven years respectively. Quite simply double standards – footage can be used to convict yet not to try to prove innocence.

# UEFA-FIFA

England's attempt to bring the 2006 World Cup to our green and pastured land was a non-starter. Everyone knew this but we still hurtled headlong into a FIFA-induced bid. We can be a very arrogant nation. This arrogance was embarrassingly evident when we broke our promise with the Germans that we would back their bid for 2006 in return for their support in our bid for Euro 96. We then backtracked on this agreement and stood against the krauts. Imagine if they had done the same to us, there would have been a national outrage. FIFA used us and England never had a chance with our bid. UEFA also showed their double standards during Euro 2000: 'England will be expelled if there is any more trouble from there fans.' Yet the Germans, Dutch and most of all the Turks don't even get a slapped wrist.

If UEFA wanted to be seen as intolerant to violence then they should have acted years ago in Turkey. Two Leeds lads might still be alive today if the footballing powers had stamped down on the 'welcome to hell' brigade. English clubs have been subjected to appalling treatment when visiting Turkey. Their police look on smugly as the locals bay for blood at the arrival of an English team at the airport. Bags of piss are thrown and threatening slogans are used as a welcoming to visitors. Nice. If two Turks had been killed at Elland Road then not only Leeds but all English clubs would have been banned from European competition as quick as you could say English Disease. Those Leeds lads bore the brunt of UEFA's lack of action. The knock on effect was that the trouble in Istanbul brought English fans closer together. All the bullshit about the Leeds fans provoking the trouble by abusing local women and burning Turkish flags was not swallowed. Trouble at the Arsenal-Galatasaray UEFA Cup Final was inevitable. Arsenal's boys wanted to show the Turks that the English are not easily intimidated. No matter how much you like or dislike your domestic rivals, we are all English and the sense of the injustice for English fans was then carried over to Euro 2000.

One of the major problems surrounding English fans abroad is that they feel hated and persecuted by everyone from the local people to police and even our own government and press. The English lads feel isolated and the response is they stick together. A lot of English fans that travel abroad don't actually want any trouble but find themselves in a situation of fight or flight and 99 per cent of the time it's the fight option we English take. If the English are challenged, then the 'these colours don't run' mentality kicks in. The only way to stop the English getting in trouble abroad is to stop them travelling completely, which then takes away people's civil liberties. There is a fine balance with our club and national team games abroad; this balance often tips over into trouble.

# CONCLUSION:
# LOOKING BACK

## WILL THE TROUBLE EVER STOP?

## HOW TO STOP FOOTBALL VIOLENCE

Has it all been worth it? Well I doubt it very much, but then what in life actually is? You work a third of your life just to get by and have enough in your pension to eat and keep warm during retirement. Another third is spent asleep, so the third that is left you have to enjoy. This life isn't a dress rehearsal and most people's lives are crap. With the boys, life takes on a new meaning, with a reason for being. To belong to a bunch of bad-asses is as exciting as life gets. The kick lads get out of football violence is immense, immeasurable. It's a natural high which nothing can come close to. To live life on the edge, you or them, do or die and any other clichéd expression you can think of. Fighting for your club, city, country and your mates is what it's all about.

I couldn't believe that during the rioting in Marseilles at France 98, some idiot pundit said, 'Look at their faces, they're actually enjoying it.'

Get outta town. Does anybody actually think that boys don't enjoy fighting? For fuck's sake, man, they wouldn't do it otherwise.

I said in the introduction that I had no regrets, well that's not exactly true. I'm not proud of putting my wife and family through the ordeal of my misdemeanours. She has read this book and is shocked at the level of violence I was involved in. But it has happened and there is no going back. Before the birth of my first child, I didn't care about anything really. I lived for Saturday afternoons with the boys and the rucks that went with it. My children have definitely changed my outlook. Plus as the years roll by you get older and wiser. I know the urge still lurks around, as my recent lapse back to the good old, bad old days proved. People stop fighting at football when they're ready. It's as simple as that.

Not one boy will have said, Well, old Tony Blair wants us to stop battling, so I guess that's me done then. Yeah right. My reasons were a combination of family, work, policing and, to be frank, I had gone as far as I could. I had reached the top and looked over and there was nothing else to prove. When you're a top boy, you are expected to do the business week in, week out: people rely on you and I got sick of it. It is in my blood forever, I know that.

I'm not going to suddenly say it's wrong for boys to fight at football. It's up to them. I would be a complete hypocrite to do that. I have fought for Sheffield United and the BBC for most of my life. I have read all the books on football violence, from the never-ending Chelsea books to Kevin Sampson's *Awaydays* and Mickey Francis's great book *Guvnors*. What really does my nut in are those Brimson brothers. They have written numerous books, supposedly with the aid of lads' stories from all over the country. The two of them have made a very nice living, thank you, out of football violence with books, videos and TV appearances. They claim to have been boys, yet they haven't got the balls to stick their necks on the line. They now say that it's all wrong and they have seen the light. As Watford hooligans they saw nothing anyway! One of them took a bit of a beating and it's, 'Fuck that for a game of soldiers.' Boys don't suddenly turn into angels overnight. It's in you right from the bottom of your trainers.

While writing this book, all the memories came flooding back, I look back and think, Jesus, I really did that? But deep down I know it's still in me locked away. It is a part of my life that has happened and there is no going back to change things. I have travelled to places like Torquay, Newport, Chester, Brentford and Exeter, places where you would be lucky to get a black look, never mind a fight. This shows that my first love was football. Hooligans, it has been said, don't care about the game. Why then do I now see retired United hooligans in the stand with their kids watching the Blades? The violence has gone for them but still their love of the game and United remains. My wife and I are bringing up a son and daughter; they both know right from wrong, how to respect their elders and have good manners. The last thing I want is for my son to get into trouble at football. My upbringing taught me all the aforementioned values but it just happened that as a teenager I got into something which only a year earlier had been as far from my mind as becoming an astronaut. Many boys had good upbringings and now hold down good, well paid jobs. The image of some tattooed skinhead signing on at the dole office then going off to football to kick lumps out of someone is a myth.

# WILL THE TROUBLE EVER STOP?

The answer to that is no, not completely. When you get a game with the passion football creates, there's bound to be the odd problem. But the sight of 200 boys walking around a rival's town centre looking for their fellow protagonists is rare these days. When I was in my early twenties, everywhere you went you saw hundreds of lads bang at it. The youngsters coming through now will be lucky to see two rucks a year. United's younger boys, the self-named BBC2, haven't a clue; they have missed the boat. It is not their fault but they simply haven't got the experience we had at their age.

Over the past ten years we have seen a decline in football violence within our shores. I've noticed over the last three or four years that when I've seen a crew of boys, there does not seem to be as many younger lads as there used to be. Therefore, as older boys slip into retirement, the violence associated with football is bound to decline. That's not saying it will disappear completely. The rivalry and hatred will always be there. The police probably feel that, relatively speaking, football violence is at an acceptable level. It is nowhere near as bad as it was in the previous three decades.

In the Seventies, scarfers and 20-inch flare boys battled it out on each other's kops. Innocent fans were fair game and going to places such as Man United, Chelsea, Millwall and Leeds required one to be well insured. Now it's not a tenth of the problem it was then. The bizzies, though, will not rest on their laurels. Now it's all camera in your face, helicopters, courts, prison sentences, dawn raids, grasses, bans from grounds, taped mobile phone conversations and football intelligence officers. The result of all this has been that violence has been forced away from grounds and has become more organised. It is nothing now for firms to phone each other up and organise a ruck away from a ground or a city centre because of CCTV.

A hooligan can get three years for being a part of a major 'off' while a dirty smackhead burgling bastard who has frightened an old woman into a heart attack would get much, much less. Sentences for football violence have been blown out of all proportion. Boys fight with others of a like mind. Innocent fans aren't brought into it. Everyone knows the score, except of course the people who make up the rules. Take the word football away from hooligan. You've still got a hooligan, someone who will fight for what he sees as his. People say that boys (hooligans) don't care about football, well think again. Boys have as much pride and passion about the game as anyone else. The lads I've grown up with have a passion for Sheffield United Football Club, just as much if not more than any other Blade. They have put their lives on the line for what they see as furthering the club's name. As Paul Heaton rightly said in an interview for a magazine, 'In the Fourth Division, the only cunts following United were the hooligans.'

Fighting between lads at football is not football's problem, it's societies. Ask any landlord or bouncer in Blackpool: it goes off there every weekend because groups of lads are out on the piss. It is just as likely to be lads from Leamington Spa or Kings Lynn that kick off as it is for lads from Sheffield or Leeds. They don't have a football team but groups of lads + seaside + drink + rivalry = trouble. They all go together, it's the English way. We've been brought up in a society which says we are English, nobody messes with us, were a nation of fighters. Football is our national game. We gave it to the world. It's all pride and passion. So when you get large groups of males travelling to different grounds, there's bound to be the odd ruck.

Football has been and still is an excuse for that release of aggression. If it was not football it would be something else. The English male is brought up to fight for what he sees as his, whether it be territory or pride, that's the way it is and it's going to be that way for a long time to come. Society breeds these lads to stick up for themselves and then faceless people try to portray them as mindless animals. These people want to take a look at the real reasons why this country breeds such passionate and patriotic subjects – because that's what they are in their own eyes. They think they are fighting for their country, just like they do for the clubs they support all season long.

The media, politicians and academics haven't got a clue, sat in their ivory towers passing comments and judgements to only half a nation. The other half aren't stupid, they know the score. Walk through Moss Side, Brixton, St Paul's, Birkenhead or any tough council estate in any city. People there have to look after themselves, it's a 'dog eat dog' culture in Britain today. These areas and the people living in them have been created by the very same people who then look on through rose-coloured spectacles and see football hooligans as some form of alien monster. This monster is one our society and culture has created.

# HOW TO STOP
# FOOTBALL VIOLENCE

The answer is far from easy. Until our past as the ultimate fighting force and our country's politicians end the arrogance which they have to everyday people's lives, then nothing will change. The people who run our country have lost touch with ordinary folk but it has been the same for years. Our present political situation should bring up the issue of changing the actual reality of people's lives. Yet the only thing the Government want to do is claim headlines with tough talk and build more prisons. Once again this is a short-term philosophy that does nothing to tackle the initial problem.

Greed has completely taken over professional football now. Players get paid vast amounts of money for doing something which they enjoy. It takes a working man a year or so to earn what an average player can earn in a week. Until there is a mass Sky dish destruction, fans will continue to get poorer while the players and their cronies get richer. There is no loyalty amongst players and managers: it's, *How much? I'm off*. Most chairman have lost touch (if they ever had it) with the fans, it is all business, 'market product' and 'revenue streams'. I still love the game and I will follow United to the end of the world but it does leave a bitter taste in the mouth. I take my kids as much as possible now. I have brought them up like I was, with red and white blood running through their veins. I want them to love Sheffield United Football Club as much as I have. I hope you have enjoyed reading my book.

# UP THE BLADES!

## WWW.BLADESBCREW.CO.UK

# GUVNORS

## THE BEST-SELLING AUTOBIOGRAPHY OF A SOCCER HOOLIGAN GANG LEADER

## BY MICKEY FRANCIS WITH PETER WALSH

**F**OR FIFTEEN YEARS, Mickey Francis and his brothers led a violent gang following one of Britain's biggest football clubs: Manchester City. They fought scores of battles with rival 'firms' until their bloody reign was brought to an end by the police Omega Squad in the most successful undercover operation of its kind.

*'I have had hundreds of fights, on the terraces and in shopping centres, in pubs and night clubs, in motorway cafes and train stations. I have been stabbed, hit with iron bars and beer glasses, kicked unconscious, punched and butted. I have been threatened with death by people who meant it. I have been chased alone through dark alleys, hunted like a dog, and suffered cracked ribs and broken hands and black eyes. I have dodged bricks, coins, rocks, cans, distress flares, planks of wood and bottles filled with piss. I have been beaten by policemen, arrested, fined and thrown in jail. And I have dished it out. In spades.'*

**GUVNORS** tells it like it was in the heyday of the soccer hooligan culture.

**'Compulsive reading... riveting stuff.'** – *INSIDE SPORT*

**'The most explosive book about soccer violence... EVER!'** – *SUNDAY SPORT*

Available at all major bookstores priced £6.99

# COCKY

## THE RISE AND FALL OF CURTIS WARREN BRITAIN'S BIGGEST DRUG BARON

## BY TONY BARNES, RICHARD ELIAS AND PETER WALSH

CURTIS WARREN is an underworld legend, the Liverpool scally who took the methods of the street dope dealer and elevated then to an art form. He forged direct links with the cocaine cartels of Colombia, the heroin godfathers of Turkey, the cannabis cultivators of Morocco and the ecstasy labs of Holland and Eastern Europe. He has been called 'the richest and most successful British criminal who has ever been caught.' This is his explosive story.

*'Curtis Warren gunned his £30,000 silver Honda Legend down the motorway back to Liverpool. He was dressed cool and loose in designer-label sports top, tracksuit bottoms and clean new trainers. A cellphone lay on the passenger seat. He steered smoothly, the automatic gear stick in Drive, his right hand on the wheel, no haste in his movements. Only the regular flicker of his gaze towards the rear view mirror betrayed any tension...'*

**COCKY** is a shocking insight into organised crime and an important and revealing investigation of a contemporary drug baron.

**Shortlisted for The Macallan Gold Dagger for Non-Fiction 2000**

**'Compelling'** – *The Observer*

Available at all major bookstores priced £6.99